(2000-01) Gordon Foxall is the author
of numerous titles on marketing
planning/strategy and consumer
behaviour/psychology. This particular
1997 title has been published only
in the U.K., only in hardcover,
at £40.00, or 80⁰⁰ new in Canada.

Warfare
Luce
20⁰ᶜ

D1290110

MARKETING PSYCHOLOGY

Also by Gordon Foxall

STRATEGIC MARKETING MANAGEMENT

CONSUMER CHOICE

CONSUMER PSYCHOLOGY IN BEHAVIOURAL PERSPECTIVE

CONSUMERS IN CONTEXT: The BPM Research Program

CONSUMER PSYCHOLOGY FOR MARKETING (with Ron Goldsmith)

Marketing Psychology

The Paradigm in the Wings

Gordon Foxall

MACMILLAN
Business

First published 1997 by
MACMILLAN PRESS LTD
Houndmills, Basingstoke, Hampshire RG21 6XS
and London
Companies and representatives
throughout the world

ISBN 0–333–66277–6

A catalogue record for this book is available
from the British Library.

This book is printed on paper suitable for recycling and
made from fully managed and sustained forest sources.

10 9 8 7 6 5 4 3 2 1
06 05 04 03 02 01 00 99 98 97

Printed in Great Britain by
Antony Rowe Ltd
Chippenham, Wiltshire

Contents

List of Tables and Figures   vii

Acknowledgements   ix

Proem   xi

PART I   INTRODUCTORY

1   Only Diverge   3

Disagree, Diverge, Digress, Differ!; Progress in Consumer
Research; Beyond Social-Cognitive Consumer Research;
The Placeless Consumer; A Way Ahead; Plan of the Book

**PART II   THE BEHAVIOUR OF CONSUMERS'
            ATTITUDES**

2   Marketing's Attitude Problem   17

The Social-Cognitive Consumer; Prior Behaviour

3   Why Not Try Behaviour?   35

The Theory of Trying; Synthesis of Attitude–Behaviour
Relationships; The Import of Prior Behaviour; Behaviour
and Attitudes; Looking Ahead

PART III   BEHAVIOURAL SCIENCE IN MARKETING

4   A Science of Behaviour   55

Radical Behaviourism; Verbal Behaviour; Looking Ahead

5   A Theory of Consumer Situation   77

Operant Interpretation of Consumer Behaviour; Operant
Classification; Contingency Category Analysis; The
Consumer Situation; The Interpretation of Consumer
Decision-Making; Consumer Decision-Making as
Rule Formulation; Summing Up

PART IV   WHAT MARKETING DOES

6 The Marketing Firm   **115**

Marketing Functions; The Marketing Firm; Marketing as
Behaviour; Management of Consumer Behaviour-Setting
Scope; Management of Reinforcement

7 Case Studies of Marketing Behaviour   **136**

Operant Analyses of Marketing Behaviour; Accomplishment:
Large-Group Awareness Training; Hedonism: The Managed
Restaurant Experience; Accumulation: Frequent-Flyer
Programmes; Maintenance: The Design of Airport
Waiting; Summing Up

8 Marketing Relationships   **151**

The Nature of the Marketing Firm; Summing Up

References   168
Index   195

List of Tables and Figures

Tables

4.1 Proximate and ultimate causation in natural
    selection and operant learning   65

5.1 Sources of reinforcement   86

5.2 Operant classification of consumer behaviour   89

5.3 Behavioural and cognitive approaches to decision-making   104

6.1 Typology of marketing mix management   135

Figures

5.1 Outline BPM   78

5.2 Summative behavioural perspective model   79

5.3 Operant classification   90

5.4 The BPM contingency matrix   95

5.5 Consumer behaviour-setting scope   99

5.6 Consumer situation 1   100

5.7 Consumer situation 2   101

5.8 Consumer situation 3   103

Acknowledgements

I am sincerely grateful for the critical comments of Rick Bagozzi, Derek Blackman, John Burton, Tony Dnes, Robert East, Geraldine Fennell, Jean Foxall, Gordon Greenley, Fergus Lowe, Leonard Minkes, Ed Morris, John O'Shaughnessy, Joel Saegert and Richard Shepherd. The usual disclaimer applies.

Some material has been reproduced with permission from my 'Explaining consumer behaviour: from social cognition to environmental control', in the *International Review of Industrial and Organizational Psychology*, vol. 13, edited by C. L. Cooper and I. Robertson, John Wiley & Sons, Limited. Reproduced with permission.

GORDON FOXALL

Proem

The 'Hawthorne effect' denotes a classic source of experimental confound: that in which changes in performance stem not from the manipulation of the independent variables at the heart of the planned investigation but from the unanticipated consequences of intervention. The experiments in industrial social psychology conducted in the Chicago plant of the Western Electric Company between 1924 and 1932 have been classically interpreted as showing that the increased productivity of the participants could be explained by changes in the individual attitudes and collective morale of these assembly workers.

The workers' new levels of attitude and morale were in turn explained by the extra autonomy and control they had gained over their workplace, by the additional emphasis on teamwork, group cohesiveness and shared decision-making, and by the enhanced quality of their interpersonal relationships. The catharsis produced by their consciousness of being experimental participants whose contribution had at last been recognised has also been adduced. The findings of the Hawthorne research have been reinterpreted over the decades, but their import has generally been construed in terms of the motivating effects of cognitive and affective influences such as these.

While there were critiques of the methodology employed at Hawthorne and of some aspects of the standard interpretation, not for thirty years after the initial reports of the research was a fundamentally different explanation proposed for what had happened at Hawthorne. It was based on a reassessment of the primary data and secondary sources and led to a reinterpretation founded on operant theory (Parsons 1974; see also Homans 1950). As a result, an alternative perspective on what occurred in the famous Bank Wiring Observation Room and other experimental settings emerged. Its novel understanding not only of industrial behaviour but of the nature of the managerial practices that shaped and maintained it stemmed from a distinctly different ontology and methodology from that previously taken for granted. The several studies that comprised the Hawthorne experiments were concerned with productivity – or rate of responding, the fundamental datum of operant research (Skinner 1950).

Parsons explained the changes in behaviour in terms of a variable largely neglected in the original investigations and the subsequent interpretations of the findings: *the consequences of behaviour*. The consequences in question were of two kinds: financial rewards and informational feedback, both of which were manipulated in the research, though they did not enter decisively into the investigators' frame of reference, and both of which were related by Parsons to changes in productivity. He showed, for instance, that the structure of piecework rates was modified over time to allow smaller groups of workers to determine their output and thus their pay; this continued until the situation approximated one in which individuals were reinforced for their personal level of output. In addition, workers were frequently informed of their output rates, which were in direct proportion to their remuneration. The original researchers and early interpreters apparently overlooked both sources of explanation for the behaviour observed at Hawthorne.

This is not to offer fresh criticism with the benefit of more than half a century's hindsight, but only to highlight the commonplace observation that research is inevitably constrained by the relevance structures of those who undertake it. The frame of reference of the Hawthorne researchers ruled individual financial rewards out of explanatory consideration because of the new emphases they had adopted on workplace social relationships and group determination of work rates and pay. For similar reasons, the investigators accorded scant explanatory significance to the informational reinforcement provided by the output performance data that were made available to workers at least once a day and, in some instances, half-hourly. Yet the reanalysis of the original data undertaken by Parsons clearly indicates that changes in productivity, both increments and decrements, can be systematically related to changes in these variables. Parsons's reanalysis has not supplanted the orthodox view of what happened at Hawthorne, but social science would be the poorer in the absence of the diversity it has supplied.

This book portrays the behaviour of consumers as influenced by its environmental consequences. It extends this analysis to marketing management and proposes a novel understanding of the marketing firm. Advances in operant psychology make possible a theoretical perspective on marketing psychology that transcends the current social-cognitive orthodoxy. In *Consumer Choice* (Foxall 1983), I expressed surprise at the advances there had been in the behavioural analysis of marketing phenomena during the preceding few years. The progress made since that book appeared is similarly gratifying: from a few basic notions of how marketing managers might rely upon operant conditioning techniques, especially in retailing and promotions, to a comprehensive model of consumer behaviour interpreted in operant terms and its applications to consumption and management.

Consumer Choice could do little more than speculate what the epistemological and practical implications of a behaviour analysis of consumer choice might be. It showed that the attitude–intention–behaviour sequence, so beloved of consumer researchers who interpreted it in terms of the determinative action of consumers' cognitive processes on their overt behaviour, could be accounted for equally well by a behaviouristic framework.

Beyond drawing out the ramifications of that observation for further research, the book could offer no systematic analysis of consumer behaviour in operant terms. In the present work, the critique of the social-cognitive approach to consumer behaviour, which remains the predominant force in consumer research despite the advent of non-cognitive approaches, can be undertaken much more effectively as a result of theoretical and empirical advances in the analysis of consumers' attitudes, intentions and behaviours, and the development by behaviour analysts of theories and methods for the more detailed understanding of human behaviour.

The critique of social-cognitive consumer research now leads far more plausibly to an alternative approach in which consumer choice is influenced by its environmental consequences rather than its alleged mental precursors.

Part I
Introductory

He who knows only his own side of the case knows little of that.

(John Stuart Mill 1859)

1 Only Diverge

DISAGREE, DIVERGE, DIGRESS, DIFFER!

The fascination of consumer research lies in its capacity to open doors on human experience, to help us understand fully its nature and ramifications. This cannot be achieved by the adoption of just one paradigm, nor by the attempted production of some vast synthesis of available viewpoints, nor yet by the accumulation of empirical research results that will eventually learn to speak for themselves. It can be more closely approached by means of methodological pluralism, the intermingling of viewpoints that are tenaciously held by individuals within the scholarly community but prevented from becoming restrictively dominant by the proliferation of alternatives. This research perspective has been forcefully described by Paul Feyerabend:

> Knowledge so conceived is not a series of self-consistent theories that converge towards an ideal view; it is not a gradual approach to truth. It is rather an ever-increasing ocean of mutually incompatible (and perhaps even incommensurable) alternatives, each single theory, each fairy tale, each myth that is part of the collection forcing the others into greater articulation and all of them contributing, via this process of competition, to the development of our consciousness. (Feyerabend 1975: 47)

We cannot rely on the research community as a whole to embrace and appreciate the contributions of diverse viewpoints. Communities are easily swayed by the apparent certainty of collective beliefs that lead them to crucify one day, deify the next. The intellectual vision required must be that of individuals who are willing and able to manage diversity within their own consciousness. The more we 'become' cognitivists, that is, the more we should seek to understand the behaviourist – not superficially or partially or in terms of the post-mortem results with which we were presented as undergraduates but, in depth, as someone else trying to unravel the very problems we are working on. The more we 'become' behaviourists, the greater the urgency of listening to post-modernists, and so on.

We do not actually become any of these persons any more than we were born as them. None of these viewpoints, nor any other, represents final truth. They are not religions but lenses. Intellectual inquiry is democratic:

all lenses are equal. The point at which our exploration no longer wants the greater articulation that calls its antithesis into play is the point at which we close doors and thereby end our search. Apparently, there is nothing quite as intoxicating to the scholar as the self-assurance generated by slamming doors; nothing else so effectively fosters the certainty that we should confine our enquiries to the compartment in which we have ensconced ourselves.

Marketing's attitude problem is not its inability to predict behaviour from prior measures of cognitive variables. It is that it tries so hard to do this that it misses the demonstrable conclusions of its own mentalistic research programme: *(i)* attitudes and other organocentric processes and events are failing to predict behaviour except under the most rigorous conditions of situational correspondence; *(ii)* behaviour is emerging as the significant predictor of behaviour; *(iii)* the next stage in its research programme should be, therefore, an investigation of the situational factors (a) that can be shown to control the initial behaviour from which subsequent responding is predictable and (b) under whose influence the predicted behaviour will fall.

Behaviour analysis is an obvious port of call for researchers interested in taking the next step. Behaviour analysts have been involved in the environment control of human responses for decades and possess the theoretical and methodological insights required by consumer researchers engaged in studying further situational influences on consumer choice. That does not imply showing an uncritical acceptance of radical behaviourism. It does require a reformulation of our ideas about the nature of operant behaviourism. Even textbooks sympathetic to a behaviour-analytical account of consumer choice misrepresent behaviourism as concerned with a view of mankind as automata that cannot think or whose public behaviour bears no resemblance to their thinking, reasoning and decision-making. This gross misreading of contemporary behaviourism closes a door on consumer research. Behaviour analysis cannot only handle so-called cognitive phenomena: it is currently immersed in a number of research programmes that clarify theoretically and through empirical investigation the nature of verbal behaviour and its import for the interpretation of consumer choice *in situ*.

Closer to home for consumer researchers is the fact that the radical behaviourist framework, approached critically, presents an alternative slant on consumer behaviour. It complements current perspectives by drawing attention to the importance of behaviour-setting scope and learning history as explicators of consumer choice and of utilitarian and informational reinforcement as factors permitting clarification of the situational interpretation of consumption. It provides a means of viewing consumers' verbal behaviour – including but far from confined to their decision-making, problem-solving, styles of creativity – and, therefore, of gaining a broader access to the meaning of their actions. It also elucidates the nature and function of marketing management and in the process portrays the marketing system as a whole in a new light. In seeing the marketing intersection as patterns of mutual reinforcement, we clarify what marketing is (as well as what it is not), the origins of the marketing firm, and the behaviouristic standpoint of marketing practice.

The challenge is to overcome what Zaltman and Bonoma (1984) call 'the lack of heresy in marketing'. Though there has been appreciable change since they wrote, it remains the case that 'There is an insufficient volume of heresy in marketing thought, an insufficient number of deviant practices, thoughts and beliefs' (p. 329). Fortunately, as the account of the Hawthorne experiments shows, ours is not the only branch of psychology to major in certainty and minor in understanding.

PROGRESS IN CONSUMER RESEARCH

Since the work of Kuhn (1962/1970, 1963), the restrictive influence of scientific paradigms needs no elaboration. It is in the nature of paradigms to preclude multiple explanations, to pre-empt alternative theories, and this is precisely what the assumption that cognitive structures determine behaviour achieves for the field of social cognition that has come to dominate consumer psychology. As one of the field's leading proponents puts it, answering his own question with cool authority: 'Is social cognition sovereign? Of course it is' (Ostrom 1994: xi).

The social sciences do not follow Kuhn's sequence of paradigmatic supersession, however. (Nor, according to Feyerabend 1970, 1975, do the physical sciences, on which Kuhn's work is based.) More probable is it that paradigms are not replaced so much as eclipsed; one may provide the 'normal science component' of a discipline, that which characterises its current mode of approaching the world with which it is concerned, but not at the ultimate expense of others. Its competitors remain, often supported by intellectually thriving communities of scholars, whose time may come. Even if their fifteen minutes does arrive, they will not have vanquished alternative viewpoints. Intellectual inquiry is not for long dominated by *'femmes savantes'* who determine what thoughts are acceptable knowledge: alternative perspectives have a habit of returning to centre stage. (It is a matter of simple observation that not all of the quasi-intellectual thought police are women any more than they were in Molière's play, despite its title.) This relationship between the orthodox school and its opponents is 'one of simultaneity and interaction', for true scholarship is 'not a temporal succession of normal periods and periods of proliferation; it is their juxtaposition' (Feyerabend 1970: 209).

Cognitivism now constitutes the normal science component of psychology, the dominant (though not the sole) working paradigm. Its influence is pervasive, not least in the social psychology of information processing: time and again, the grounds and implications of behaviour are explicated as though only cognitive constructs were available to account for them. Applied psychology inevitably embodies the paradigmatic preoccupations of its parent. When consumer psychology entered its growth phase in the 1960s, cognitive science was the ascendant paradigm within psychology as a whole (Kassarjian 1982), and the resulting models of consumer behaviour were inescapably cognitive in orientation (e.g. Nicosia 1966; Howard and Sheth 1969). But there is danger in such inevitability, for paradigms other than that which provides the normal science component of the discipline (Feyerabend 1970) may be overlooked despite their potential to illumine the subject matter under review by engendering debate and synthesis, as well as novel problems, hypotheses and methods.

There are, however, two broad lines of explanation in social science, that which generally alludes to unobservable mental structures such as attitudes in order to explain observed behaviour and that which largely confines its explanations to the realm of observation. The former is the more common in the behavioural sciences and, especially, in consumer research. The work of Freud exemplifies this approach in which mental entities are invented to give coherence to the range of observations made by the clinician and to interpret new ones (Webster 1995). Id, ego, superego are inferences drawn from the evidence (reported behaviour of the patient). They summarise, elucidate, organise (at least for the trained exponent of clinical practice) the verbalizations of the client. Whether these entities have an independent ontology is largely irrelevant: they serve the required purpose within the scientific and clinical community in which they have relevance.

No science can get away entirely from entities of this kind. Even radical behaviourism relies on inferred events such as the private verbal behaviour of the humans whose behaviour it interprets. But explanatory systems of this kind lie at the far end of a continuum from that occupied by Freudian and other structuralist theories. Behaviourism has always sought to confine its observations and explanations to the same realm, that of the observable. Individual behaviour is thus explained, on the whole, in terms of its equally visible and objectively available environment rather than through events and processes of more dubious ontology, the contents of the mind. Without denying the existence of private events such as thoughts and feelings, radical behaviourism interprets them as behaviours that are themselves to be explained by reference to the environmental history of the individual rather then as inner causes of public behaviour.

Somewhere between the two comes cognitivism, which certainly embraces experimental science, as does behaviourism, but is freer in its inferences of an intrapersonal realm of activity that explains overt behaviour. Some versions of cognitivism are concerned predominantly with the assertion of human autonomy. But the information-processing variant that is the descendant of stimulus–response psychology (Leahey 1987; Lee 1988) is what permeates current consumer research.

BEYOND SOCIAL-COGNITIVE CONSUMER RESEARCH

An important function of cognitive consumer research has been to establish links between statistical descriptions of buyer behaviour and marketing response. Thus, although it is well documented that consumers consider only a small proportion of the extensively advertised brands and products available to them (Kardes 1994), the import of this fact for marketing management is not immediately apparent. Similar information about the empirical regularities of consumer choice stand in need of interpretation. Ehrenberg (1972) shows that the proportion of buyers of Brand X in one period who buy it again in a second period is $1.23w$ where w is the mean number of times these buyers of brand X purchase it in the period. Again, the consumers who buy brand X in one period but not the next buy it in the period in question with an average frequency of 1.4 units. The interpretation has usually been in terms of consumers' decision processes, inviting answers to such questions as: 'What information is considered when consumers judge products and services? How is product information stored and organized in memory? How is information used to make product-related judgments and decisions?' (Kardes 1994: 400).

The main difficulty with cognitive consumer research has been the inability of the models in question to predict consumer choice. Perhaps the most sophisticated attempt to do so, the Howard–Sheth model (Howard and Sheth 1969; see also Howard, 1989; cf. Bettman 1979), derived from the choice models of the Carnegie–Mellon School, has been extensively tested. But only under the most gruelling conditions of situational consistency can the required correlational correspondence between measures of intention and measures of behaviour be demonstrated, and the results of attitude–intentions–behaviour research are as consistent with a behaviourist model of choice as with a cognitive. Behaviour, not attitude, predicts behaviour.

For all their new-found eclecticism in the use of constructs and methods developed elsewhere, consumer researchers have tended to avoid serious, involved critical analysis of the perspectives within which those borrowed tools originated. They have thus curtailed their search for alternative perspectives. When the shortcomings of a given concept become apparent, the tendency is to attempt to make it more useful by refining analytical techniques (today quantitative, tomorrow qualitative) rather than by seeking a more fruitful concept.

This is clearest in the case of this central concept, 'attitude', perhaps the most widely used explicator of human behaviour. The assumptions on which its use is based may be stated as follows: 'Behaviour is prefigured and largely determined by factors that exist (or can be hypothesised as existing) within the individual. Of all these intrapersonal elements, attitudes that consists of cognitions (beliefs), affect (emotion or feeling) and conation (action tendencies) are of pre-eminent importance in shaping behaviour to particular objects. The prediction of behaviour therefore depends upon obtaining accurate measurements of attitudes, because behaviour will be consistent with the individual's underlying mental dispositions. Although attitudes are dynamic and may be modified as a result of behaviour, the key to changing behaviour consists in the modification of one or more components of attitudes, predominantly through the presentation of informative (or persuasive) messages.'

Any description of a complex perspective that is only four sentences long is naturally a simplification, but most consumer behaviour specialists would agree that the above description contains the major assumptions that underlie most uses of the concept of attitude in marketing.

The problem with this approach is that empirical research on attitude–behaviour (A–B) relationships shows them to be unacceptably weak unless the situational correspondence between them is exceptionally high. Moreover, behaviour is predicted better by behaviour than by attitudes. Yet the response of attitude researchers in consumer research is not to seek understanding of situational influences on consumer choice: it is to refine further the modelling of attitude–behaviour relationships. Mostyn (1978: 83) wrote, on the basis of her wide-ranging review, 'Instead of trying to improve the *A–B* relationship with existing techniques or even trying to improve upon the techniques, it would be more meaningful if researchers could rethink the entire assumptive philosophy underlying the *A–B* relationship.' This book examines the proposition that an appropriate alternative might be akin to the following: 'Behaviour is the result, not of intrapersonal events, but of the consequences of previous behaviour in similar situations. The reward or reinforcement of that behaviour shapes and sustains present and future behaviour of the same or similar kind. Behaviour can thus be most effectively predicted from the pattern of rein- forcements previously received by the individual and changing behaviour depends upon modifying the situation in which it occurs in such a way as to make the reward or reinforcement dependent on new responses.'

THE PLACELESS CONSUMER

Consumer psychology is a burgeoning field (Kassarjian 1982; Bettman 1986; Cohen and Chakravarti 1990; Tybout and Artz 1994). It prospers, nevertheless, within severe intellectual limitations, for it generally reflects the current social-cognitive orientation that dominates consumer research to the exclusion of other developments in psychology. Consumer psycho- logy has become a subject area generally divorced from non-cognitive ex- planations and from consideration of the context within which purchase and consumption occur. Since consumer research has no coherent theoretical framework to classify the situations in which consumer behaviour takes place, it is unable to explain or otherwise account systematically for patterns of consumer behaviour in various situations. A satisfactory framework must incorporate both the spatial and temporal components of the consumer situ- ation as well as its social and regulatory influences and its outcomes.

Hence, the legacy of consumer research's reliance on social-cognitive psychology is that we still lack a systematic framework of conceptuali- sation and analysis for the explanation of situational influences on con- sumer choice. Consumer research contains no paradigm that allows the situational influences on consumer choice to be identified and investi- gated in an organised way, or that promotes theoretical understanding of how the environment shapes consumer behaviour over time. Advances in ecological psychology over the last quarter-century have drawn attention to the ways in which behaviour in specific settings retains a remarkable consistency irrespective of who is performing it, their attitudes, inten- tions, dispositional traits and motives (Barker 1968, 1987; Wicker 1979, 1987). The implication is that these behaviour-settings deserve serious analysis based on the finding that the objective environment is responsible for the shape and content of our ultimate explanandum, behaviour itself (cf. Belk 1975, 1991).

But, apart from a few *ad hoc* studies of consumers' subjective reactions to hypothetical situations described by researchers, there has been no such investigation of situational influences on consumer choice, no appreciation of how the meaning of consumer behaviour is systematically related to the

circumstances in which it takes place. We do not know, that is we can neither understand nor explain, where consumer behaviour is: we are unable
to trace its occurrence, form and persistence in familiar locations. At the
same time, consumer researchers are failing to come to terms with the
most complete explanatory and interpretive framework in behavioural science, one which is thoroughly, indeed exclusively, concerned with the influence of context on behaviour, namely radical behaviourism (Hillner
1984; Leahey 1987; Marx and Hillix 1979; Valentine 1992).

A WAY AHEAD

Impressive as the social-cognitive explanation of consumer behaviour is,
its facts and concepts can be construed equally plausibly but with wholly
different implications by behaviour analysis. This is not simply a case of re-
describing cognitive events in behaviouristic terminology: the research
programme concerned with verbal behaviour analysis parallels that of social cognition in providing an empirical basis for an explanation of cognitive events and processes that stresses their environmental origin and the
contextual causation of all behaviour, verbal and non-verbal.

Research within the social cognition research programme actually points
the way to a more behaviour-based understanding of consumer choice
through the emerging emphasis on prior behaviour as an explanatory and
predictive variable for current behaviour. Studies of attitudinal–behavioural relationships have identified the importance of two central ingredi-
ents of the behaviour-analytical approach. These are the preceding verbal
instructions that guide current behaviour, and contingency-shaped prior
behaviour as a major predictor of current and future responding. But the
prevailing social cognition paradigm has (naturally, within its own confines) interpreted these influences as reducible to cognitive phenomena.

Contemporaneously with the social-cognitive research on attitudes and
behaviour over the last decade or so, a separate research programme has
investigated instructed behaviour within an operant psychological framework of conceptualisation and analysis. What is surprising perhaps is that
the empirical results and theoretical conclusions of the two paradigms are
largely compatible, though the implications of the behaviour-analytical approach present distinct alternatives paradigmatically, practically and as a
signpost to future research. They support the view that behaviour may be
construed as a function of environmental rather than intrapersonal variables; they suggest that the response to consumer behaviour in the marketing organisation operates quite differently from its description in the

marketing literature; and they require a research programme founded on a dissimilar ontological and methodological basis to that which currently predominates.

This book argues, then, that only by incorporating research orientations and findings from non-cognitive psychology can consumer researchers account for these situational influences on consumer choice. But the purpose is by no means the simplistic one of trying to encourage a paradigm shift. In the context of industrial psychology, Parsons (1974) argued that there was no evidence of a credible relationship between any of the affective and cognitive confounds and the increases in productivity for which they have traditionally been held responsible. His advocacy of a renewed concern with 'response– consequence contingencies' as a source of explanation of industrial behaviour invites an exclusive reliance on operant psychology. While Kuhn's (1962) account of paradigmatic succession is a useful metaphor for a study concerned with the interaction of alternative explanations, it presents an unsophisticated view of the growth of knowledge in the social sciences.

The methodological spirit of the consumer research programme with which this book is fundamentally concerned does not judge between alternative social science perspectives in so final a manner as Kuhn proposes occurs in the physical sciences. (The social sciences are not, as he claims, pre-paradigmatic. On his understanding of a paradigm as one of a succession of all-controlling mindsets, they are non-paradigmatic; in the looser terminology used here, in which a paradigm is an orientating metatheory, they are multi-paradigmatic; cf. Feyerabend 1970, Foxall 1990.) Rather, the principal intention is to underline that a complete view can never result from a single paradigm, that scientific progress relies on contrast and comparative evaluation (Feyerabend 1975; Laudan 1984), by proposing an alternative perspective on consumer behaviour derived from a critical reading of operant theory (Foxall 1990; cf. O'Shaughnessy 1992). The aim is to balance a strong emphasis on cognitive interpretation in consumer research, which, like the industrial psychology of the human relations era, remains largely context-free. For, despite the recent emergence of anthropological, hermeneutical and postmodern methodologies in consumer research, the prevailing normal science component of consumer research remains staunchly cognitivist. Just as the Hawthorne conclusions were criticised for failing to comprehend the macroeconomic context in which the research had been undertaken, so consumer research for the most part avoids contact with the environment on which the behaviour it studies is contingent.

The invitation extended by this book is not to a dehumanising, scientistic behaviourism that sees selfhood as no more than a complex of stimulus–

response relations. The stimulus–response psychology founded on Pavlov, philosophised by Watson and theorised by Hull gave rise to modern information processing psychology, though not to the behaviourism advocated here (Lee 1988). Operant behaviourism is 'the very field of purpose and intention' (Skinner 1974: 55). Its contemporary concerns are exactly those appropriated for so long by cognitive psychology. Its promise for us is to contextualise what for so long has been an account of consumer behaviour that is striking above all for the placelessness of its subject matter.

PLAN OF THE BOOK

It is time to put consumer behaviour in its place. Doing so figuratively requires first doing so rather more literally. Understanding the role of consumer behaviour research in the context of marketing analysis presupposes that we comprehend consumer behaviour in the contexts in which it occurs. Only when this has been accomplished, and the overwhelming emphasis on what is going on 'inside consumers' heads' is held in check, can we focus on the behaviour of consumer-orientated firms. Understanding the nature and behaviour of firms, that is, requires that we have an adequate understanding of consumer choice. We will grasp what firms do when we appreciate what consumers do. We may then be in a position to define academic marketing more precisely.

Parts I and II are concerned predominantly with two research programmes. The first is the recent work on the central outcomes of social cognition: attitudes and behaviour and the consistency required of them by cognitive models of consumer behaviour. The cognitive modelling of consumer choice, especially at the level of the brand, depends for its validity and credibility upon there being sufficient correspondence between prebehavioural measures, such as attitudes and intentions, and behaviour itself for the latter to be predictable from the former. The use of Fishbein and Ajzen's (1975) theory of reasoned action and its derivatives have been warmly welcomed by consumer researchers who have attempted to demonstrate this relationship.

Part II is concerned with the derivation and refinement of the behavioural perspective model (BPM) and its application to the interpretation of consumption behaviours. The second research programme is, therefore, that of contemporary behaviour analysis, especially as it relates to verbal responding and private events. The alternative paradigm from which this literature is derived is compatible with a great deal of evidence and thought on the prediction of behaviour gained through cognitive reasoning and method, but it avoids the problem of having to demonstrate consistency across situations. This is a smaller literature than that of cognitive consumer research, one which presents an alternative approach to understanding consumer choice in its social and marketing context. That alternative approach, which has been developed over the last fifteen years or so (Foxall 1996a), begins with an analysis of consumer behaviour that relates it to its environmental determinants. The neo-Skinnerian perspective adopted is particularly apposite, given the need to understand both consumer and business behaviour in contingent relationship with one another. It is argued that a model of consumer choice based on a behaviour-analytical framework can account for the phenomena of consumer choice as well as the more familiar cognitive models.

In summary, this understanding suggests the following which is the central argument of the book. The BPM interprets consumer behaviour as determined by environmental influences, the learning history of the individual consumer and the stimulus control exercised by the current consumer behaviour-setting. The learning history is derived from the sequence of approach, avoidance and escape behaviours that have produced positive and aversive utilitarian and informational consequences in the course of the individual's prior purchase and consumption. And setting stimuli signal the likelihood of these reinforcements and punishments contingent upon current approach, avoidance or escape responses. The model is consistent with the empirical evidence generated by both attitudinal researchers and operant investigations of verbal behaviour, and has received further support from empirical work designed to test its predictive validity in a variety of consumer situations (Foxall 1997b, 1997c).

Part III examines the implications of the BPM for the behaviour of marketing organisations. By presenting a view of the nature of organisational response to consumer behaviour under environmental control, it looks forward to the development of a broader economic psychology which embraces the intra-organisational behaviour of the marketing firm and so contextualises consumer choice.

Consumer psychology is not a sufficient disciplinary base on which to build an understanding of marketing. Such a theory must be founded upon *economic* psychology, of which there are two broad definitions, both of which are represented in this book. One definition is 'the psychology of economic behaviour' (van Raaij 1988). This is exemplified in Parts I and II, which focus on consumer psychology. Another definition of economic psychology is the intersection of economics and psychology, both being essential to the discipline of economic psychology (Lea *et al.* 1987). This is exemplified in Part III, which is concerned with marketing relationships.

Not only can the two disciplines throw light upon marketer behaviour, but each enhances the account provided by the other. A full understanding of marketing relationships requires both disciplinary inputs.

The understanding of marketing management revealed by this analysis differs extensively from that current in the marketing literature. The options open to firms that influence consumer choice are broadly twofold (Foxall 1992b): the manipulation of consumer behaviour-setting scope, and the management of reinforcers (and, less frequently, punishers) to shape and maintain managerially beneficial patterns of purchase and consumption. Marketing management, as generally understood, consists in attempts to change consumers' behaviour by changing their minds. The understanding yielded by the present approach is, however, antithetical to this commonplace view. Marketing management can as well be construed as relying upon a behaviouristic understanding of consumer choice and its own intersection with it to form the marketing system.

Part II
The Behaviour of Consumers' Attitudes

Even if by providing adequate information we change people's attitudes . . . but not their risk behaviors, we will have failed, because information and attitudes do not transmit the [AIDS] virus – behaviors do.

(Bayés 1990: 250)

2 Marketing's Attitude Problem

THE SOCIAL-COGNITIVE CONSUMER

Consumer behaviour embodies all of the activities of buyers, ex-buyers and potential buyers from prepurchase to postpurchase, consumption to discontinuance. It extends from the awareness of a want, through the search and evaluation of possible means of satisfying it, and the act of purchase itself, to the evaluation of the purchased item in use, which directly impacts upon the probability of repurchase (Alba *et al.* 1991).

The models of consumer behaviour that emerged in the mid to late 1960s, on which the central paradigm for academic consumer research has since relied almost exclusively, provided a distinctive meld of cognitive and social psychologies (Andreasen 1965; Nicosia 1966; Engel *et al.* 1968; Howard and Sheth 1969). Fundamental components of this paradigm include the goal-oriented reception, encoding, representation and processes of information, but equally determining was the way in which this cognitive procedure was linked to behaviour in the sequence of belief, attitude- and intention-formation. The initial emphasis was upon high-involvement processing but, by successive elaborations, several of the models have gradually acceded to and accommodated low-involvement processing (Engel *et al.* 1995; Howard 1989), which may influence capacity for recall without requiring prior evaluation (Hawkins and Hoch 1992). The style of consumer decision-making has also provided important evidence of the cognitive framework within which consumer behaviour develops (Bagozzi and Foxall 1996; Bettman 1979, 1986; Bettman *et al.* 1991; Foxall 1993c, 1994d, 1994e).

The theoretical underpinnings of consumer psychology thus anticipated the social cognition movement of the 1980s and 1990s (Fiske 1993; Ostrom *et al.* 1981; Wyer and Srull 1986, 1989, 1994a, 1994b), including the possibility that implicit cognitive events influence social behaviour (Greenwald and Banaji 1995; Janiszewski 1988; Schwartz and Reisberg 1991). Prior to this development, cognitive psychology was little concerned with attitudinal and intentional outputs of information processing, while social psychology largely avoided cognitive concerns (cf. Eiser 1980, 1986). In anticipating the advent of social cognition, consumer researchers made theoretical and methodological advances, notably in the area of attitudinal–intentional–behavioural consistency, which are contributions to social psychology as well as to consumer research. In choosing to study attitudinal–behavioural relationships, consumer psychologists recognise the import of the pivotal component of social-cognitive models of consumer choice. For, if attitudes (and certain other prebehavioural elements of information processing) are not consistent with and predictive of observed consumer behaviour then the whole enterprise must be called into question – as must our understanding of what marketing management is and does.

Marketing Response to the Social-Cognitive Consumer

It is hardly surprising, therefore, that the study of social cognition is now inextricably intertwined with consumer psychology: social cognition theories furnish the dominant paradigm for consumer psychology, while numerous academic consumer researchers have reputations in both fields (e.g. Bagozzi 1992; Folkes and Kiesler 1991; Kardes 1994; Petty *et al.* 1991; Petty *et al.* 1994; van Raaij 1991). Consumer psychology is also closely allied with behavioural and psychological economics (Earl 1988a, 1988b, 1990; Lea 1992; Lea *et al.* 1987; Lewis *et al.* 1995; MacFadyen and MacFadyen 1986; van Raaij 1988). But it is social cognition which occupies centre stage in the drama of consumer psychology.

The prescribed organisational response to the social-cognitive consumer underpins all serious marketing texts and treatises, and is particularly apparent in those that combine analysis of the consumer with guidance for marketing management (e.g. Assael 1995; Foxall and Goldsmith 1994). The near-ubiquity of such managerial prescriptions makes their detailed rehearsal here superfluous. However, relating patterns of consumer behaviour at each stage of the product life cycle to marketing strategies has perhaps been most thoroughly accomplished by Howard (1989), who traces consumer decision-making and marketing response through three phases, a brief description of which may be useful for those unfamiliar with consumer research and marketing thought. First, the introduction of a new brand into a new product class at the beginning of such a cycle engenders extensive problem-solving on the part of buyers who, by definition, have no experience of the item and must establish its meaning largely on the basis of prepurchase deliberation. Next, the introduction of subsequent product versions in the form of competing brands during the growth stage of the cycle prompts limited problem-solving in which novel offerings are compared with existing choices about which much more is now known. Finally, as the product reaches its maturity, numerous brand additions require no more from the consumer than routine problem-solving as additions to the range of brands are judged according to very familiar product attributes and, on the whole, brands whose characteristics are commonplace are selected on recognition.

The managerial tools available to persuade the consumer (which constitute the marketing mix of product, price, promotion and distribution) are employed at each phase to effect cognitive changes in the consumer which guide his or her decision-making accordingly. Information supplied by the marketing organisation influences the consumer's confidence, brand recognition and attitude; brand recognition also comes to influence confidence and attitude directly (cf. Brown and Stayman 1992). Confidence and attitude then determine intention, which in turn determines purchase.

Attitude and related cognitive events and processes are clearly central to this approach, on which so much consumer analysis and marketing theory rests. As a result, it is vital to examine critically and in detail the assumption that behaviour is attitudinally consistent.

Attitude-Consistent Behaviour

Attitude is generally understood in social psychology as a mediating variable corresponding to mental processes or states that account for the consistency of an individual's favourable–unfavourable and cross-situational responses towards an object. Petty *et al.* (1994: 70) state that 'attitude is a general and relatively enduring evaluation of some person (including oneself), group, object, or issue.' A degree of endurance implies that long-term memory acts as a repository for the evaluation that the individual has attached to the attitude object; and generality indicates that it is an overall or global appraisal.

Their basic definition is borne out by Eagly and Chaiken (1993: 1), who refer to an attitude as 'a psychological tendency that is expressed by evaluating a particular entity with some degree of favor or disfavor' (cf. Olson and Zanna 1993; Tesser and Shaffer 1990). 'Psychological tendency' denotes an intrapersonal state, and 'evaluative' encompasses all varieties of evaluative responding: overt or covert, and – an espousal of the traditional tricomponential view of attitude structure and function – cognitive, affective or behavioural. Attitudes develop out of evaluative responding of one of these three kinds, are mentally represented in memory, and are activated in the presence of the object to which they refer with the effect of shaping further behaviour towards it (Eagly and Chaiken 1993).

Indeed, it is not the behaviour involved in the formation of attitudes that has received the lion's share of attention from attitude researchers and theorists, but that to which attitudes are understood to lead. Since the pioneering conceptualisation and measurement in the third and fourth decades of this century (Bogardus 1925; Likert 1932), attitude has been portrayed as an organocentric predisposition to behave consistently towards the object to which it refers wherever it is encountered. The verbal statements by which attitudes are recorded in response to questionnaires have been assumed to express accurately the underlying 'real' or 'true' attitude held in mind and thus predict and explain its non-verbal manifestations.

Foundational definitions of attitude therefore emphasised its motivating capacity: in Allport's (1935: 810) words, an attitude is 'a mental and neural state of readiness, organized through experience, exerting a directive or dynamic influence upon the individual's response to all objects and situations with which it is related'. The tacit assumption was then, as it generally is now, that to know an individual's attitude was equivalent to being able to predict his or her actions (Fazio and Zanna 1981: 162). The attitude–behaviour relationship came to be most contingent in those definitions that claimed that only if consistent behaviour followed from measures of cognition, affect or conation could an attitude be held to exist (Doob 1947; Fazio 1986: 205; cf. Pieters 1988; Pieters and van Raaij 1988; van Raaij 1988).

Attitude psychology thereafter has a familiar history: while its most optimistic phase culminated in the mid-1960s, its most successful era extends from the mid-1970s to the present. The objectives of attitude study naturally embrace far more than the prediction of behaviour but, within social psychology and consumer research, and especially in the analysis of social cognition in which both fields have a current interest (Wyer and Srull 1994a, 1994b), the external validity of attitude measures continues to maintain a central position. Marketing models of consumer choice require the demonstrability of attitude-consistent behaviour (Foxall 1983; cf. Castleberry *et al.* 1994).

The evidence for attitudinal–behavioural consistency that has accrued during the last twenty years or so can be fully comprehended and interpreted only through a short detour into the period of pessimism that intervened between those of optimism and success. The original objective of attitude psychology, of predicting behaviour towards an object from measures of a person's attitude towards that object, became problematical as a result of Wicker's (1969) review of forty-two mainly experimental studies of behaviour with respect to various attitude objects. Wicker lambasted the notion that attitudes and behaviour were empirically consistent on the grounds that correlations were typically small, even if statistically significant. His oft-quoted conclusion was that 'taken as a whole, these studies suggest that it is considerably more likely that attitudes will be unrelated or only slightly related to overt behaviours than that attitudes will be closely related to actions' (Wicker 1969: 65). Not only were the correlations between attitudes and behaviour low – few exceeded .3 and the average was about .15: even the direction of causality between the variables was in doubt (as it remains: Bagozzi, in press).

Fishbein summed up the position:

> what little evidence there is to support any relationship between attitudes and behaviour comes from studies showing that a person tends to bring his attitude into line with his behaviour rather than from studies demonstrating that behaviour is a function of attitude. (Fishbein 1972)

The evaluation of the empirically based evidence for attitudinal–behavioural consistency led then, to pessimistic conclusions: published studies indicated at best only very weak relationships between attitude towards an object and behaviours performed with respect to it; attitude change was not an inevitable precursor of behavioural change; and attitudes might be nothing more than post-behavioural epiphenomena. But the disappointment was quickly to lead to innovations in methodology and conceptualisation that have since then revolutionised the field (Upmeyer 1989). Two broad courses of research have been pursued since the beginning of the 1970s in the attempt to come to terms with the critical conclusions of Wicker and others.

The approach associated predominantly with Fazio and Zanna (e.g. 1978a, 1978b, 1981) retains the original problem of demonstrating a relationship of consistency between global attitude towards an object and behaviour enacted towards that object. By contrast, that associated predominantly with Fishbein and Ajzen (e.g. 1975; Ajzen 1988; Ajzen and Fishbein 1980) and, by extension, with Bagozzi and Warshaw (1990) has adopted a narrower route to the conceptualisation and measurement of attitudes and behaviours, and has concentrated on identifying and implementing the methodological developments necessary if the latter are to be accurately predicted from the former. Fazio's (1990) *ex post facto* categorisation of these approaches suggests that they are complementary (cf. Olson and Zanna 1993). The 'global' approach has dealt with attitude elicitation that is apparently spontaneous, reliant on little if any mental processing and leading directly to action. The information processing associated with it is reminiscent of, though not identical with, the peripheral route to persuasion of the elaboration likelihood model (Petty and Cacioppo 1984a, 1984b), which continues to inspire empirical work in consumer research (e.g. Davies and Wright 1994; MacKenzie and Spreng 1992; Miniard *et al.* 1992; Schumann *et al.* 1990), and of the heuristic processing proposed by Chaiken (1980). The 'reasoned' approach has concentrated on the mental processing involved in deliberating on the consequences of undertaking an action before forming an intention to do so. It assumes a level of information processing more reminiscent of the central route to persuasion (Petty and Cacioppo 1986a, 1986b) and of systematic processing (Bohner *et al.* 1995).

Spontaneous Processing

This avenue of investigation retains the objective of predicting specific behaviours from general measures of attitude towards an object. While, as we shall see, many researchers have adapted the underlying problem by seeking whatever measures correlate with behaviour, Fazio (1986; Fazio and Zanna 1981) focuses on the original general-to-specific problem of correlating global attitude measures with specific behaviour criteria.

While some attitude–behaviour correlations are low using this approach, some are high, and an important goal of this research programme has been to understand *when* attitudes correlate with behaviour. It is the non-attitudinal variables, which people fail to take into account when they form and report attitudes towards targets, that confound attitude–behaviour consistency. Therefore, these investigators have argued that non-attitudinal factors be taken into consideration in the prediction of behaviour from attitudes to objects. The variations in correlations between attitudes and behaviours depends on the variability in non-attitudinal factors from situation to situation, which is considerable. That is, non-attitudinal factors *moderate* the relationship of attitude towards an object and behaviour towards that object (Eagly and Chaiken 1993).

Attitudes as Object–Evaluation Associations

Fazio (1986: 214) defines an attitude as involving 'categorisation of an object along an evaluative dimension': specifically, an attitude is an association between a given object and a given evaluation (Fazio 1989: 155; Fazio *et al.* 1982). This definition of 'attitude' corresponds to the affective component of the tricomponential portrayal of this construct preferred by other researchers and consisting of cognition and conation as well as affect.

The simple idea that an attitude is an association suggests that the strength of attitudes, and hence their capacity to influence behaviour, will vary, just as the strength of any relationship which is the result of associative learning will vary (Fazio 1989: 155). Fazio's model of the attitude–behaviour process thus attempts to answer the question '*When* is attitude related to behaviour?', rather than the more pervasive *why?* question. It assumes that social behaviour is substantially determined by the way in which the individual perceives the immediate situation in which the attitude object is presented, as well as the way in which he or she perceives the object itself.

Situations are generally ambiguous, and the individual's definition of any particular situation depends on how he or she interprets it. Behaviour is guided by perceptions of the attitude object, but also by perceptions of the situation in which it occurs: that setting is said to determine the event. For instance, behaviour towards a particular person (attitude object) naturally depends on the individual's perception of him or her; but the style of that behaviour will differ according to whether the attitude object is encountered in his or her home, or in a store, or at a party, or in church.

> It is this definition of the event – perceptions that involve both the attitude object and the situation in which the object is encountered – that the model postulates to act as the primary determinant of an individual's behaviour. (Fazio 1986: 208).

When Attitudes Guide Behaviour

The extent to which an attitude guides behaviour depends on the manner of its formation. Attitudes formed from direct experience with the attitude object are expected to differ from those stemming from indirect experience (e.g. word of mouth, advertising) in terms of their capacity to predict behaviour. Especially when they have to articulate an attitude, e.g. to a researcher or to fill out a questionnaire, people draw on past experiences that 'are organized and transformed in light of current contingencies' (Rajecki 1982: 78; see also Schwartz 1978); moreover, even enquiries about intentions can influence behaviour (Morwitz *et al.* 1993).

There is corroborative empirical evidence that the attitudes of people who have had direct experience with an attitude object (target) correlate moderately with subsequent attitude-relevant behaviours; attitudes where such experience is lacking correlate only weakly. Attitude–behaviour consistency is higher when the preceding sequence has been behaviour-to-attitude-to-behaviour, rather than when it has been simply attitude-to-behaviour.

Whether an attitude guides behaviour depends also on the accessibility of the attitude from memory (Berger 1992; Kardes 1988; cf. Bargh 1994). Attitudes formed behaviourally lead to a stronger object–evaluation bond than those formed indirectly, and are as a result more easily accessed from memory. This is consistent with Bem's (1972) view that the difficulty people encounter in assessing their attitudes (their evaluations of an object) is overcome by engaging in behaviour with the object or by observing their own behaviour with it. Information gained through behaviour or behavioural observation is more trustworthy than that presented by another person or medium (Stayman and Kardes 1992).

Dealing with Direct Experience

A feasible deduction from Fazio's demonstration of the significance of direct experience with the attitude object is that the consequences of relevant past behaviour are responsible wholly or in part for the probability of current responding in the presence of the attitude object. Current behaviour could then be explained as having come under the stimulus control of the attitude object, such control having been established through the reinforcement resulting from previous experience with the stimulus.

In other words, the entire episode might be depicted as operant conditioning, and investigation might be directed towards identifying the consequences of behaviour that accounted for its future probability. However, the explanation that has predominated is cognitive: attitudes formed through direct experience are held to be more accessible from memory than those formed indirectly. And accessibility, measured as verbal response latency (i.e. the speed with which the attitude is activated or recalled in the presence of the attitude object), is hypothesised to be directly proportional to behaviour change (Fazio and Zanna 1981; Fazio *et al.* 1989; Fazio *et al.* 1982). The strength of an attitude, its capacity to influence behaviour in the presence of the attitude object, increases with such structural attitude qualities as clarity, confidence, stability and certainty (Bargh *et al.* 1992; Doll and Ajzen 1992; Downing *et al.* 1992).

An attitude's strength is also increased through its repeated verbal expression (Fazio *et al.* 1982), though repeated expression is also related to attitude polarisation (Downing *et al.* 1992; Smith *et al.* 1994). Accessible attitudes are, moreover, activated automatically in the presence of the attitude stimulus – without conscious and volitional cognitive processing (Eagly and Chaiken 1993: 197; see also Bargh *et al.* 1992; Blascovich *et al.* 1993; Fazio 1994; Haugtvedt and Petty 1992; Myers-Levy 1991; Tesser *et al.* 1994).

Not all of the evidence supports this: there are contra-indications that *all* attitudes are automatically activated in the presence of the attitude object, regardless of their accessibility (Bargh *et al.* 1992). Prior knowledge about the attitude object also increases attitudinal–behavioural consistency, presumably because such knowledge is attained through direct experience (Eagly and Chaiken 1993: 200–1; cf. Tripp *et al.* 1994). As will be documented, there is empirical evidence that such verbal repetition increases the chance that the evaluative behaviour described as an attitude will become a self-instruction that guides further responding.

Deliberative Processing

Compatibility

Many familiar conclusions of attitude researchers in the era since Wicker's review (1969) and his call (1971) for the abandonment of the attitude concept derive from the application of Fishbein's (1967) intentions model which gave rise to the theory of reasoned action (Fishbein and Ajzen 1975) and the theory of planned behaviour (Ajzen 1985). The emphasis – as in the case of work by Bagozzi and Warshaw (1990, 1992) – is largely on the methodological refinements required in order to increase the accuracy of prediction.

This group of attitude theories revolves around the belief that the degrees of specificity with which attitudinal and behavioural measures are each defined must be identical if high correlations are to be found between them. Global attitude measures are therefore consistent with multiple-act measures of behaviour towards the attitude object. It follows that the prediction of single acts is only likely to result from equally narrow measures of attitude, those that correspond exactly in level of specificity to the act to be predicted; those, moreover, that are framed as measures of the respondent's attitude towards performing that act in closely designated circumstances (Fishbein and Ajzen 1975).

This is not the initial intellectual problem posed by attitude research (Cohen 1964), but its pragmatic departure from the constrictions inherent in that problem has produced a reformation in the technology of behavioural prediction (Ajzen and Fishbein 1980). Nor is the requirement of situational compatibility confined to measuring attitude towards a specific target behaviour rather than attitude towards an object: Ajzen and Fishbein's (1977) analysis of numerous studies of attitudinal–behavioural consistency revealed that high correlations are probable only when the measures of attitude and behaviour coincide with reference to the precise *action* to be performed, the *target* towards which the action is to be directed, the *context* in which the action would occur, and its *timing*.

A further important recognition was that measures of the cognitive precursors of attitude will be highly predictive only when there is maximal temporal contiguity of the behavioural and antecedent measures (Ajzen

and Fishbein 1980). The greater the temporal gap between attitude or intention and the behaviour to which they refer, and hence the extent of situational intervention that potentially separates them, the lower will be their
correlative consistency. Though this remains a significant problem in all of
the theories reviewed below, it is not necessarily a handicap to prediction.
Even a temporal gap of some fifteen years does not impede prediction in
some cases, though the correlation may be positively influenced by the use
of self-report measures of behaviour (Randall and Wolff 1994). Certainly,
there appears to be abundant empirical evidence that the intention that
immediately precedes behaviour is highly predictive (Ericsson and Simon
1993), and that is all that the models now considered explicitly claim.

The Theory of Reasoned Action

The theory of reasoned action (TRA), which represents a culmination
of Fishbein's and Ajzen's work on the prediction of attitude-consistent
behaviours, incorporates both these observations and several other innovations (Fishbein and Ajzen 1975). The theory predicts not behaviours
themselves but intentions to engage in them, provided, first, that reasons
can be adduced for doing so, and, second, that there is no let or hindrance
to the respondent's doing so. It thus refers to reasoned behaviour that is
under the individual's volitional control. Such behaviour, despite the
authors' caution in delineating the predictive scope of their model, is assumed to approximate intentions towards its performance.

Intentions are, in their turn, determined by two belief-based cognitions.
The first, attitude towards performing the target behaviour, is measured as
the respondent's belief that a particular action will have a given outcome
or consequence, weighted by his or her evaluation of that outcome. Only
salient behavioural beliefs enter into the calculation of behavioural attitude, which is presented as a multi-attribute model:

$$A_B \propto \sum_n b_i e_i$$

(2.1)

where

A_B =   the respondent's attitude towards performing behaviour B;
b_i =   the belief (subjective probability) that performing B will lead to
            outcome i;
e_i =   the evaluation of outcome i;

and

n = the number of salient behavioural beliefs over which these measures are summed (Ajzen 1985: 13).

The second cognitive variable that determines intention is the respondent's subjective norm, i.e. his or her perceptions of the evaluations that important social referents ('significant others') would hold towards the respondent's performing the target action, weighted by his or her motivation to comply with them. Hence

$$N_S \propto \sum_n b_j m_j \qquad (2.2)$$

where

N_S = the subjective norm;
b_j = the normative belief concerning referent j;
m_j = the respondent's motivation to comply with referent j;

and

n = the number of salient beliefs.

The subjective norm is an attempt to capture the non-attitudinal influences on intention and, by implication, behaviour. By permitting this consideration of perceived social pressure to enter the calculation of behavioural intentions, the theory takes account of some at least of the situational interventions that may reduce the consistency of the attitude–behaviour sequence. There is empirical evidence that people actually distinguish behavioural and normative beliefs (Trafimow and Fishbein 1995).

These belief-based measures predict not behaviour itself but the *behavioural intentions* that are its immediate precursor and that it is assumed to approximate to. Hence

$$B \sim I \propto \left(w_1 A_B + w_2 N_S \right) \qquad (2.3)$$

where

B = the behaviour of interest;
I = the respondent's intention to perform B;
A_B = his or her attitude towards performing B;
N_S = his or her subjective norm with respect to the performance of B;

and

w_1, w_2 = empirically determined regression weights indicating the relative importance of A_B and N_S (Ajzen 1985: 13–14).

The initial problem of attitude research has thus been modified further by the assumptions that the relationship between attitude and behaviour is mediated by the behavioural intention which is the immediate precursor of the targeted action, and that behavioural intention is determined by both attitudinal and non-attitudinal factors (Sparks *et al.* 1991). But this approach has proved successful in as much as the prediction of behaviour, albeit under the specialised circumstances to which the theory applies, has ben achieved.

A meta-analysis of studies employing the TRA, reported by Sheppard *et al.* (1988), found an average correlation of behavioural intention with behaviour of .53, while a more recent meta-analysis (Van den Putte 1993) reports an average of .62. Hence, the technological achievement of the TRA is that as long as its variables are measured under conditions maximally conducive to high correlations, which, as noted, refer to conditions of close situational correspondence, high correlations are usually obtained by the TRA.

The theory quickly found a pivotal place in consumer research: at the academic level, for instance, the *Journal of Consumer Research* was dominated by articles on multi-attribute modelling from the mid to late 1970s (Journal of Consumer Research 1994); and commercial market research conferences and journals were similarly concerned throughout that decade. For reviews of early use of the TRA in consumer and market research see East (1990, 1997) and Foxall (1983, 1984, 1996a). The fascination continues (e.g. Ball *et al.* 1992; Berger 1992; Berger *et al.* 1994; Haugtvedt and Wegener 1994; Haugtvedt *et al.* 1994; Mick 1992; Percy and Rossiter 1992; Nataraajan 1993; Yi 1990).

Petty *et al.* (1994) furnish a general evaluation of the TRA: while doubts occasionally arise with respect to some aspect or other of the model,

> a monumental body of research supports the idea that attitudes toward objects, issues, and people become more favourable as the number of likely desirable consequences (or attributes) and unlikely undesirable consequences associated with them increase. (p. 77)

Critique of the TRA

But there are criticisms, too (in the marketing context, see especially Bagozzi 1984, 1985, 1988). Sheppard *et al.* (1988) point out that the TRA deals with the prediction of behaviours rather than the outcomes of behaviours: it is concerned for instance to predict the likelihood of one's studying for an examination, not that of one's passing it. The amount of studying one does is largely under personal volitional control, but whether one's hard studying is accompanied by success in the examination depends on factors lying beyond that control: the co-operation of others in the household or library may not be forthcoming, the books one most needs may not be available, one may not have invested sufficient time and effort in attaining study skills, and so on (Liska 1984). Even if one is fully motivated and puts total effort into the task, circumstances may impede one's performance and achievement of the goal (Ramsey *et al.* 1994; Sheppard *et al.* 1988).

The TRA cannot predict goal achievement, because that outcome relies upon situational factors that make the attainment of a goal uncertain. The TRA also concentrates on the prediction of single, specified behaviours that are not in competition with other behaviours. It thus avoids situations of choice within the class of intended behaviours or consequences (Dabholkar 1994). The attributes taken into consideration in expectancy–value models such as the TRA correspond to attributes of the product class: to the extent that brands within that class are perceptively identical, brand choice may be unpredictable (Ehrenberg 1972). The vast majority of consumers are neither entirely brand-loyal nor store-loyal, and appear always to have more than one brand and/or outlet in mind when shopping for a particular product. The availability of choice, leading to the possible selection of one item or behaviour from alternatives, is a situational constraint. Given the multi-brand purchasing behaviours of consumers (Ehrenberg and Uncles 1995) and their multi-store purchasing patterns (Keng and Ehrenberg 1985), it is doubtful whether such specific behaviours can be predicted by models of this sort.

Most significantly, the TRA has been criticised for not taking into consideration the full gamut of non-attitudinal personal and situational factors likely to influence the strength of the attitude–behaviour relationship or to enhance the prediction of behaviour (Brown and Stayman 1992; Olson and Zanna 1993). The authors of the TRA are adamant that behaviour is determined by behavioural intention and that all contributing influences are subsumed by the two elements that determine it: attitude towards performing the target act and subjective norm with reference to performing that act (Ajzen and Fishbein 1980; Fishbein and Ajzen 1975).

Yet this principle of sufficiency has been proved inaccurate by empirical work that has incorporated additional factors to increase the predictability of intentions and/or behaviour (Bagozzi and Van Loo 1991). Factors not comprehended by the theory which have been found to improve the predictability of behaviour include the following (in general, see Eagly and Chaiken 1993; cf. Shepherd and Towler 1992; Shepherd *et al.* 1992; Towler and Shepherd 1991):

Affect (Bagozzi 1994; Bagozzi and Moore 1994; Bagozzi *et al.* 1996);
Amount of reasoning during intention formation (Pieters and Verplanken 1995);
Attitude functions (Maio and Olson 1994);
Availability of relevant skills, resources and co-operation (Liska 1984; Fishbein and Stasson 1990);
Action control (Bagozzi and Kimmel 1996);
Past behaviour/habit (Bagozzi 1981; Bagozzi and Kimmel 1995; Bagozzi and Warshaw 1990, 1992; Bentler and Speckart 1979, 1981; East 1992, 1993; Fredericks and Dossett 1983; Towler and Shepherd 1991/2);
Perceived control/confidence (Giles and Cairns 1995; Marsh and Matheson 1983; Pieters and Verplanken 1995; Sparks *et al.* 1992; Sparks *et al.* 1995; Terry and O'Leary 1995);
Personal norm (Beck and Ajzen 1991; Boyd and Wandersman 1991; Manstead and Parker 1995; Parker *et al.* 1995; Richardson *et al.* 1993);
Self-identity (Granberg and Holmberg 1990; Sparks and Shepherd 1992; Sparks *et al.* 1995);
Self-schemas (Bagozzi and Kimmel 1996); and
Size and content of consideration set (Pieters and Verplanken 1995).

Behaviour that requires resources, skills and co-operation in order to be enacted is especially problematical. Consumer behaviour usually requires all three, yet restricting the TRA to behaviour that is volitional means it requires only motivation on the part of the individual. Studies that have supported the model have dealt with only simple behaviours that require little if anything by way of resources and skills. Fishbein and Ajzen argue that such considerations have an effect on intention and thus were taken care of in their model.

Also, Fishbein and Ajzen stress that the intention that matters for purposes of prediction is that obtaining immediately before the opportunity to engage in the behaviour arose. Understanding what occurs between intention and behaviour has become a big part of predicting actions (Eagly and Chaiken 1993).

The Theory of Planned Behaviour

The theory of planned behaviour (Ajzen 1985) incorporates just one of these additional variables. *Perceived behavioural control* is posited – along with attitude towards the act and subjective norm – to determine behavioural intentions. East (1997) points out that researchers such as Marsh and Matheson (1983) who included a measure of confidence in the TRA were anticipating the development of the theory of planned behaviour.) Further, on those occasions when perceived and actual behavioural control coincide or are closely approximate, perceived behavioural control is expected to exert a direct determinative influence on behaviour. The theory thus applies to behaviours over which volitional control is limited. This is in contrast to the TRA, which is adamantly a theory for volitional behaviour.

Moreover, the extent to which perceived behavioural control adds significantly to the prediction of intentions is apparent from Ajzen's (1991) analysis of the results of several studies employing his theory, which shows that the average multiple correlation was .71. Moreover, a comparison of the theories of reasoned action and planned behaviour (Madden *et al.* 1992) involved a spectrum of ten behaviours from those rated comparatively difficult to control (e.g. shopping) to those rated comparatively easy (e.g. renting a video). The inclusion of perceived behavioural control in addition to the reasoned action variables resulted in a significant increased in explained behavioural variance. As predicted by the theory of planned behaviour (TPB), perceived behavioural control was more important in the case of the behaviours rated as low in controllability. Manstead and Parker (1995: 72) conclude that the TPB has improved on the predictive performance of the TRA and extended the range of behaviours to which it can be applied.

The wide range of applications to which the TPB has been put leads East (1997) to the view that it has now substantially superseded the TRA. These applications include:

Addictions (Godin *et al.* 1992; Morojele and Stephenson 1992);
Avoidance of accidents (Richard *et al.* 1994);
Blood and organ donation (Giles and Cairns 1995; Borgida *et al.* 1992);
Class attendance and scholarly accomplishment (Ajzen and Madden 1986);
Collective action (Kelly and Breinlinger 1995);
Recycling (Boldero 1995; Taylor and Todd 1995);
Complaining (East 1996);
Contraceptive use and sexual behaviour (Boldero *et al.* 1992; Chan and Fishbein 1993; Dewit and Teunis 1994; Kashima *et al.* 1993; Morrison *et al.* 1995; White *et al.* 1994; Richard 1994; Richard *et al.* 1995);
Control of infant sugar intake (Beale and Manstead 1991);
Entrepreneurial behaviour (Desroches and Chebat 1995);
Excessive drinking (Schlegel *et al.* 1992);
Food acceptance and choice (Dennison and Shepherd 1995; Raats *et al.* 1995; Sparks and Shepherd 1992);

Gift purchasing (Netemeyer *et al.* 1993; Sahni 1994);
'Green' consumerism (Sparks and Shepherd 1992; Sparks *et al.* 1995);
Health care (Anderson *et al.* 1995; DeVellis *et al.* 1990; McCaul *et al.* 1993);
Internet use (Klobas 1995);
Intention to play with video games (Doll and Ajzen 1992; Netemeyer and Burton 1990);
Job seeking (van Ryn and Vinokur 1990);
Physical exercise (Ajzen and Driver 1992; Courneya 1995; Godin *et al.* 1993; Harrison and Liska 1994; Kimiecik 1992; Norman and Smith 1995);
Leisure behaviour (Ajzen and Driver 1991, 1992);
Risky driving (Parker *et al.* 1995; Parker *et al.* in press; Parker *et al.* 1992);
Share applications (East 1993); and
Voting (Watters 1989).

Critique of the TPB

The TPB is, nevertheless, problematical on several grounds of conceptualisation and method. Like its immediate predecessor, the TPB assumes temporal contiguity between intention and behaviour, so that precise situational correspondence is still essential to accurate prediction (Netemeyer *et al.* 1991). The operationalisation of the theory remains beset by the problem of whether perceived behavioural control should be measured directly or by the recording of control beliefs (Manstead and Parker 1995). Moreover, as Eagly and Chaiken (1993: 189) point out, the assumption of a causal link between perceived control and intention presumes people decide to engage in a behaviour because they feel they can achieve it. This raises problems in the case of antisocial or negatively self-evaluated behaviours such as risky driving (Manstead and Parker 1995).

Another, potentially more important, technical problem is that the theory introduces only one new variable when we have seen that other factors – habit, perceived moral obligation, self-identity – may also predict behaviour over and above the terms of the TRA. The theory is based on the principle of sufficiency, though the number of variables involved has been increased by just one from the TRA: there is continuing evidence that factors such as self-identity and moral judgement add predictive power over and above the measures formally incorporated into the TPB (see, for instance, Raats *et al.* 1995; Sparks *et al.* 1995). Manstead and Parker (1995) argue strongly that personal norms and the affective evaluation of behaviour may account for variance in behavioural intentions beyond that accounted for by the TPB (cf. Allen *et al.* 1992).

PRIOR BEHAVIOUR

Prior behaviour, in particular, is an independent determinant of intention and behaviour, and several of the extra-TRA variables, including perceived behavioural control, are presumably related to prior behaviour (e.g. Morojele and Stephenson 1992; see also East 1997; Foxall 1996a, 1997a; cf. Thompson *et al.* 1994; Thompson *et al.* 1995). East (1997) argues that 'experience elaborates the belief basis of planned behaviour constructs'. As the consumer progresses from novice to experienced buyer, his or her behaviour is influenced more by attitudes towards the behaviour and perceived behavioural control and less by subjective norm (East 1992).

The consumer who lacks specific and detailed knowledge of, say, a product falls back on simple notions or heuristics: social pressures to act in a particular manner will be more easily known or guessed than the benefits and costs of executing a novel behaviour (East 1997). This is supported by the finding that extrinsic cues such as product price and appearance are used in decision-making by consumers with little or no direct experience of consuming the item (Rao and Monroe 1988); moreover, the less consumers are familiar with a product, the more they tend to infer its quality from its price and to have lower price limits suggesting that they have little idea of the product qualities worth paying for (Rao and Sieben 1992). East (1997) interprets this to mean that 'experience seems to result in detailed product knowledge that is used to change the way in which consumer judgements are made'.

East (1992) also presents evidence that novice computer buyers rely disproportionately on subjective norms and contends, though without direct evidence, that experienced computer users would scarcely be expected to base their decisions on social pressures rather than behavioural attitudes and perceived control. Moreover, there is empirical confirmation in the case of television viewing intentions that subjective norm is the stronger influence among novices (who lack experience and knowledge of the service, that was breakfast-time broadcasting) as compared with experienced viewers (whose intentions were more predictable from behavioural attitudes) (East 1992). Further evidence comes from a study showing that non-users of mineral water, as compared with users, tend to be far more strongly influenced by subjective norm (Knox and de Chernatony 1994).

East (1997) presents further testimony to the importance of past behaviour by showing that a measure of this variable correlates more highly with behavioural attitude and perceived behavioural control than with subjective norm; his study included applying for shares in a privatised utility, four redress-seeking behaviours, theatre-going, complaining in a restaurant, taking out a pension scheme, and playing the National Lottery. The data also indicate that the inclusion of a measure of past behaviour in a regression equation predicting intention from the TPB variables reduces the beta weights to a greater degree for behavioural attitude and perceived behavioural control than for subjective norm. Subjective norm, after all, is unlikely to be affected by or to increase in salience as a result of experience. One approach to the problems remaining in the TPB has been to investigate how people formulate plans and translate intentions into behaviour, something the theory fails to address (Eagly and Chaiken 1993). It is, however, a theme confronted by the theories of self-regulation and, especially, the theory of trying.

3 Why Not Try Behaviour?

THE THEORY OF TRYING

An attempt to uncover the factors responsible for the translation of intentions into behaviour was made by Bagozzi (1986, 1992, 1993; Bagozzi *et al.* 1992a, 1992b) in the theory of self-regulation. The novel thinking behind this approach is that attitude provides only a measure of the extent to which an individual is affectively involved with a behaviour: his or her motivation to act in the specified way depends on the desire to engage in the behaviour. It can be hypothesised, therefore, that desires would show a stronger effect on intentions than would attitudes, that attitude affects would ideally disappear, and that if desires contain explanatory content over and above that provided by subjective norm and past behaviour then they will predict intentions, even though these additional variables are included in the measure of antecedents to intention (Bagozzi and Kimmel 1995).

Bagozzi and Warshaw (1990) argue that goal attainment is determined by trying, i.e. cognitive and behavioural activities that mediate the expression of an intention to achieve a goal and its actual achievement. Trying thus incorporates the effectual tasks on which the attainment of a goal depends (Eagly and Chaiken 1993: 190). This is, therefore, a behaviour-based approach which takes into consideration the planning people engage in order to achieve remote goals. Moreover, as a later section elaborates, it is precisely what the behaviour analysis of rule-governance concentrates on.

The theory of trying is intended to explain the link between intention and behaviour by investigating the striving people undertake in order to perform a behaviour or attain a goal, especially a difficult one (Bagozzi and Kimmel 1995: 5). It assumes that when individuals *try* to achieve such a goal they discern it as potentially burdensome to the extent that it has only a probability of success; i.e. they are concerned about the likely outcome in view of the expenditure of effort that performing the behaviour will entail. They will specifically be concerned with the possibilities of two final consequences – succeeding, having tried, and failing despite trying – and they will certainly incur the intermediate consequences inherent in the process of striving itself.

This approach differs from the theories of reasoned action and planned behaviour in three respects. First, those theories measure attitude as an overall and unidimensional construct, averaging the effects of separate component attitudes and thereby masking their individual effect on intention, which may differ from situation to situation. The three component attitudes, confirmed in a study of respondents' trying to lose weight (Bagozzi and Warshaw 1990) are towards (i) success, (ii) failure and (iii) the process of striving. Second, the theory of trying posits a novel idea of the manner in which attitudes operate in influencing intentions: attitudes towards success and failure will result in intentions to engage in a particular behaviour to the degree that expectations of success are high and expectations of failure are low.

Bagozzi and Warshaw (1990) found evidence for the interaction of attitude towards success and expectations of success, and of a significant main effect of attitude towards the process; they found mixed support for the interaction of attitudes towards failure and expectations of failure. Third, the theory of trying explicitly includes the effect of past behaviour on current trying. Despite Ajzen's (1987: 41) denial of the usefulness of including past behaviour in causal theories of human action, numerous studies indicate the importance of this variable. Bentler and Speckart (1979) compare the TRA with (a) an alternative model that incorporated, in addition to the usual TRA variables, a direct causal path from attitude to behaviour that was not mediated by intention, and (b) a further model that also added a new independent variable, *past behaviour*, which was assumed to affect behaviour both directly and via intention. This final model provided the best fit with the data: direct paths from attitude to behaviour and from past behaviour to behaviour were supported. Attitude and past behaviour explained variability not explained by intentions, though drug consumption, the focal behaviour investigated, is not necessarily volitional (Eagly and Chaiken 1993).

Evidence on Past Behaviour

Other studies have shown that measures of past behaviour improve predictions of behaviour over those provided by attitudes/subjective norm/intention alone: e.g. giving up smoking (Marsh and Matheson 1983; Sutton *et al.* 1987); studying and exercise (Bentler and Speckart 1981); students' class attendance (Ajzen and Madden 1986; Fredericks and Dossett 1983); voting (Echabe *et al.* 1988); seat belt use (Budd *et al.* 1984; Mittal 1988; Sutton and Hallett 1989; Wittenbraker *et al.* 1983); blood donation (Bagozzi 1981; Charng *et al.* 1988); and consumer behaviour (East 1992, 1993, 1996).

It is apparent from these studies that past behaviour influences current behaviour without being mediated by intentions, and that past behaviour may influence intentions without being mediated by attitude or subjective norm. Bagozzi and Warshaw (1990) measured past behaviour in two ways, namely frequency and recency, both of which were expected to impact the target act under investigation; of the two, only the frequency of past behaviour was expected to impact intention to perform the act. They reported that both the frequency and recency of past trying had a direct influence on subsequent trying; moreover, frequency also influenced intentions to try to lose weight.

Comparative Studies

Bagozzi and Kimmel (1995) compared all four of the theories considered thus far in a study of two activities thought to have low perceived behavioural control: exercising and dieting. In the case of the TRA, intentions entirely predicted exercising and dieting responses but, while intentions for both were predicted by attitudes, subjective norms predicted intentions for neither. Their test of the TPB revealed that exercising was predicted by perceived behavioural control but not by intentions; however, intentions but not perceived behavioural control predicted dieting. Results for the prediction of intentions were also mixed: perceived behavioural control predicted this variable in the case of exercising but did not achieve this in the case of dieting.

The direct influence of perceived behavioural control is thus substantiated for exercising; but neither the hypothesised direct effect nor the hypothesised indirect effect of perceived control on dieting was confirmed. Attitudes again predicted intentions for both actions, but subjective norms failed to do so in either instance. As predicted by the theory of self-regulation, desires strongly influenced intentions for both behaviours; intention to exercise was impacted by attitude but not intention to diet; moreover, subjective norm again failed to predict intention in either case. However, behaviour was significantly related to intention for both exercising and dieting. When past behaviour measures were used to augment the theory of self-regulation, both frequency and recency significantly impacted behaviour, but the effect of intention on behaviour became non-significant.

The findings provide mixed evidence for the theory of trying. While intention predicted dieting but not exercising, the measures of past behaviour, frequency and recency, each had a significant impact on both behaviours. A significant interaction between attitude towards success and expectation of success was found only in the case of exercising; frequency and subjective norms also had a significant effect for this behaviour, but neither the attitude towards the process nor the interaction of attitude towards failure and expec-

tations thereof fulfilled the hypothesised relationships. Intentions for dieting were functions of frequency, subjective norms, and attitudes towards the
process of striving, but neither of the hypothesised interactions was confirmed.

Madden and Sprott (1995) report a partial confirmation of Bagozzi and
Kimmel's results. They compared the TRA, the TPB and the theory of trying in two contexts: renting a video cassette, which represented high volitional control, and obtaining a good night's sleep, which represented low
volitional control. The TPB's predictions of intention exceeded those of
the TRA, but were no more predictive of behaviour once intentions had
been taken into account. In the case of the theory of trying, Madden and
Sprott failed to confirm Bagozzi and Warshaw's (1990) finding that frequency and recency of past behaviour significantly affected trying. Intentions to try appear to subsume these effects for these admittedly familiar
behaviours: indeed, past behaviour in the form of recency of trying impacted significantly on intention in both cases.

The inclusion of a measure of past behaviour improved on the predictions
of behaviour generated by the TRA and TPB in the case of sleeping but not
in that of video rental. Past trying frequency improved predictions of intention for both behaviours over those produced by the TRA and TPB, a confirmation of the results reported by Bagozzi and Kimmel (1995). A test of the
TRA and an augmented version of that model containing measures of the
frequency and recency of past behaviour as covariates (Bagozzi and
Warshaw 1992) also indicate the importance of past behaviour as an explanatory variable. The investigation demonstrates the capacity of the TRA
to predict some behaviours under some circumstances when it is not augmented by measures of past behaviour. In the case of losing weight, the
theory performed as expected: behaviour was predicted by intentions, and
intentions were predicted by attitude and subjective norm. Neither attitudes
nor subjective norm predicted behaviour, i.e. the effect of each on behaviour
was fully mediated by intention. However, the other behaviour examined,
initiating a conversation with an attractive stranger, was not predicted by
intentions; attitude predicted intention but subjective norm had no impact
upon it. Moreover, behaviour was directly influenced by attitude.

These results on the whole are not consistent with the relations hypothesised by the TRA (Bagozzi and Warshaw 1992: 628). When the
measures of past behaviour were added to the analysis, neither of the behaviours investigated could be attributed to processes of reasoning or volition (Bagozzi and Warshaw 1992: 630). For neither behaviour was
there an influence from intentions to behaviour; nor did attitude have a direct effect on either behaviour. 'The theory of reasoned action therefore

fails to explain behaviour, once we control for the effects of frequency and recency of past behaviour' (ibid.) Intentions to lose weight or initiate a conversation were unstable after the partialling-out of frequency and recency effects, indicating that neither behaviour can be attributed to volitional control. 'Significantly, strong recency effects are found for trying to lose weight . . . and initiating a conversation . . . No other determinants of behaviour are found . . .' (ibid.).

Bagozzi and Warshaw (1992: 631) conclude that because of the failure of attitude, subjective norm and intention to act as antecedents of behaviour, doubt is cast on their role in the explanation of human action. In a reversal of the explanatory sequence presumed by the TRA, their results indicate that intentions and attitudes arise out of behaviour.

Dealing with Prior Behaviour

Authors of deliberative processing models have generally sought the rationale for the relation between past and current behaviours by invoking a cognitive framework. Hence, it is proposed that frequency effects on intentions operate when attitudes fail: either because the information needed to form a belief and/or evaluation is absent or because it is unclear (Bagozzi and Warshaw 1992: 605). Inability to access or comprehend one's attitude will similarly increase the salience of frequency effects for intention formation. Frequency might exert a direct effect on behaviour when the individual has formed no plan of action, even though his or her attitude and intention are in place, or when choice involves a multitude of similar options, or when there is no time pressure to act. But, in addition, 'frequency effects might reflect desires or cognitive urges' (ibid.; Bagozzi 1991). Frequency effects on behaviour are also likely when 'cognitions and evaluations are primitive or undergoing change', or because the behaviour in question is 'mindless or scripted, such as biting one's fingernails' (ibid.; Abelson 1981; Langer 1989b). (This is precisely the kind of behaviour that, according to Catania (1992a) is contingency-shaped rather than rule-governed; see the following discussion of instructed behaviour.)

Further, an inability to activate intentions, caused by absence of control, situational interventions, or 'internal impediments', may stand in the way of a conscious intention's activating behaviour (Bagozzi and Yi 1989; Bagozzi *et al.* 1990; cf. Warshaw *et al.* 1990). Frequency of past behaviour can also substitute for actual control (Ajzen and Madden 1986; Beale and Manstead 1991). Recency acts upon intentions by increasing availability and anchoring/adjustment biases into reports thereof (Tversky and Kahneman 1974). Recent behaviour exerts a disproportionate influence on the perceived likelihood of an event; and on the anchor value used to estimate subjective probability of an event; both influence one's intention to perform it.

When intentions do not automatically lead to behaviour, recency of behaving may act to 'capture any residual automatic reactions that are triggered by conditioned releasers or stimulated directly by learned dispositions to respond' (Bagozzi and Warshaw 1992: 606). Finally, situational factors may just block an intended behaviour and recency effects may operate by suggesting alternative paths to the goal.

In summary, past behaviour will predict current when cognitive determinants are absent or ineffective or goal attainment is blocked; and when behaviour is either mindless or scripted or incapable of fulfilment even though it is attitude-driven or intentional. The analysis also carries the implication that routine (mindless/scripted/low-involvement) behaviour is to be accounted for by behavioural variables, while novel (high-involvement) behaviour is to be accounted for by cognitive variables. As the following section on the behaviour analysis of choice and decision-making indicates, however, there is no reason to accept this. Either behavioural explanation can cover both or the behavioural and cognitive approaches to explanation should be seen as complementary rather than supplementary: cognitive accounts for proximal causation, behavioural for distal.

SYNTHESES OF ATTITUDE–BEHAVIOUR RELATIONSHIPS

Several attempts have been made to produce syntheses of the evidence on spontaneous and deliberative attitude–behaviour relationships and the cognitive processes inferred to underlie them; though see Eagly and Chaiken (1993: 204), who argue that these approaches cannot properly be considered as alternatives. Several of these attempts have highlighted the questions of *when* each method of processing is relevant and the possibility that they may work in tandem.

MODE: Motivation and Opportunity as Determinants

Fazio (1990) points to two ways in which attitudes guide behaviour – spontaneously and through deliberation – and argues that one or other of these processing modes will be activated according to the circumstances of motivation and opportunity present.

Deliberative processing is probable when the expected costliness of the prospective behaviour induces rational evaluation of the merits and demerits of assuming a given course of action. At this time, motivation to avoid the expense of making and acting upon a poor judgement overrides the spontaneous mechanism whereby attitudes might be activated from memory without cognitive effort. Assuming that an opportunity to deliberate is available, the individual can be expected to engage in extensive prebehavioural mental deliberation.

Where the motivation to avoid heavy costs misjudgment is low and/or an opportunity to deliberate is not forthcoming, attitudinal influences on behaviour will occur via spontaneous processing. The extent to which attitude influences behaviour in these circumstances reflects the strength of evaluative association that has been built with respect to the attitude object, through direct experience or by means of verbal rehearsal of the attitude. Provided that this association is sufficiently strong, the individual's definition of the event will be wholly or predominantly attitude-determined. When the attitude association is weak, however, this definition of the event will be based mainly on non-attitudinal factors: behaviour towards the attitude object will then depend predominantly on the salient features of the attitude object itself and the situation (Fazio 1990: 93–4).

HSM: The Heuristic–Systematic Model

A broadly similar spectrum underlies Chaiken's (1980) heuristic–systematic model (HSM), which arrays processing strategies on the basis of the amount of cognitive effort they involve. The extremes of the processing continuum she proposes are *systematic* processing, which is potentially effortful, requiring the evaluation of multiple interpretations of the situation before a definitive impression is formulated, and *heuristic* processing, which requires minimal information handling, relying on established rules to make sense of the current situation.

On the understanding that individuals minimise effortful activity, systematic processing is likely only when the person is highly motivated and has the cognitive capacity and resources to engage in it. Nevertheless, individuals are also assumed to balance effort minimisation with the confidence they feel in their social perceptions. When heuristics based on experience can be substituted for systematic processing, they will be activated by elements of the current situation that signify their relevance (Bohner *et al.* 1995).

Decision-making may, however, result from the simultaneous activation of both processes, reflecting both 'content-related thinking' (systematic) and 'cue-related evaluations' (heuristic) (van Knippenberg *et al.* 1994). Recent reviews of the empirical work prompted by the HSM can be found in Eagly and Chaiken (1993); in addition, Bohner *et al.* (1995) present the most recent version of the model, and review research that has applied the model in the spheres of mood, persuasion and minority influence.

Eagly–Chaiken Composite Model

Eagly and Chaiken (1993) present an integrative model of the attitude–behaviour relationship, which incorporates both the attitudes towards objects ('targets') implicated in spontaneous processing and the attitudes towards behaviours implicated in deliberative processing. Each kind of attitude is operational at a different stage in a dynamic sequence leading to behaviour. Attitude towards a behaviour is determined by *habit* (successive instances of an action that occur automatically or at least in the absence of self-instruction); *attitude towards the target*; and three sets of outcomes: *utilitarian*, i.e. rewards an penalties expected to follow from the performance of the behaviour, *normative*, i.e. the endorsement or denunciation expected of significant others towards the action, plus the self-administered rewards like pride, and punishments like guilt, resulting from internal moral rules; and, when these self-administered consequences relate to the self-concept, *self-identity*.

Attitude towards behaviour impacts in turn upon intention, which impacts upon behaviour. Intention is also partly determined by normative and self-identity outcomes; and behaviour, by habit and attitude towards behaviour (Eagly and Chaiken 1993: 209–11). This is corroborated by the functional approach to attitude theory and research taken by Shavitt (1989), who proposes that an object may evoke one or more of three functions: *utilitarian* (coffee, for instance), which arises from the reinforcing and punishing outcomes of using the item; *social identity* (e.g. a wedding ring), which communicates social status, identity and prestige; and *ego-defensive/self-esteem* (e.g. one's appearance). Shavitt has shown that many objects evoke a single attitude function and that promotional appeals based on the appropriate function for each product are more persuasive than appeals based on different criteria.

The Elaboration-Likelihood Model of Persuasion

Petty and Cacioppo (1986a, 1986b; see also Petty *et al.* 1991, 1994) are concerned to understand under what circumstances individuals yield to a persuasive message such as an advertising appeal. They posit two routes to persuasion, namely the central and the peripheral; these differ in the extent to which context and personality influence the probability that the individual will elaborate the message by means of conscious information processing. When such elaboration likelihood is high then the central route is brought into play; when low, the peripheral.

Central route processing is an effortful endeavour to uncover any worth in the message. It requires mental exertion in which previous experience is examined along with relevant knowledge in the process of evaluating the usefulness and validity of the message. This is an active procedure, in which the information provided by the would-be persuader is carefully inspected. As a result of this active information processing, the individual forms an attitude that is both clear and supported by evidence.

By contrast, the peripheral route to persuasion recognises the limitations of human cognitive capacity, the impossibility of devoting substantial mental effort to the evaluation of all messages. It leads to attitude change that is far from being based on extensive thinking about the claims made about the attitude object. The individual does not allocate costly resources of time and cognitive effort to evaluating the claims of the message, but rather employs accumulated knowledge of the rewards, punishments and affective responses that have followed previous experience with the attitude object. Classical and operant conditioning may provide such rapid appraisals of the object, which are expressed in terms of inferences drawn from self-observation (as in Bem's 1972 example: 'I must like brown bread; I'm always eating it') or heuristics grounded in abundant practice ('You get what you pay for') or stereotyped reactions ('He's a Manchester United supporter: I'll steer clear of him').

THE IMPORT OF PRIOR BEHAVIOUR

The Precedence of Cognitive Explanation

Prior Behaviour as an Explanatory Variable

So much in the preceding account points to the determinative role of prior behaviour that this variable apparently has the potential to modify the paradigm for attitude research, shifting the emphasis from intrapersonal sources of explanation towards a behaviour-based perspective. More than being just an additional influence that increases attitudinal/intentional-behavioural consistency or accounts for inconsistency, prior behaviour has a determinative influence on behaviour in as much as its inclusion in models has direct implications for the predictive and explicative power of cognitive variables and may even render them redundant. As will be shown, its influence on 'intentions' can be interpreted in a behaviour-analytical account as an influence on verbal behaviour that acts as an instruction to further responding.

The pressure of the evidence is for the incorporation of prior behaviour more fully into explanations of behaviour. However, although prior behaviour is finding a place at the level of measurement, the implications of the empirical findings for this factor impinge little on the epistemology of attitude researchers and theorists. By and large, they have opted for a cognitive framework to embrace the influence of prior behaviour on current responding. The non-attitudinal variables considered by Eagly and Chaiken to moderate attitude towards an object and behaviour towards that object include 'vested interest' (which is surely an aspect of learning history), personality, including moral reasoning level, and having a doer self-image (both of which can be conceptualised as arising in the individual's learning history). But these authors do not consider these further, let alone as denotive of a history of reinforcement and punishment, because they do not fit into a unified theoretical framework.

Rather, they press on with their assumption that 'attitude–behaviour correspondence is affected by the nature of the attitude and by the implications that that attitude is perceived to have for the behavior that is assessed' (Eagly and Chaiken 1993: 194). One might be forgiven for detecting that the social-cognitive paradigm has been allowed to select the approach to explanation. Even authors who speak of learning history as determinative (Eiser 1987; Eiser and van der Pligt, 1988: 41) refuse the full operant alternative to cognitivism.

Cognitive Rationale of Prior Behaviour

Some reviewers have been willing to accommodate behavioural as well as cognitive precursors of attitude as factors that increase attitudinal–behavioural consistency. Eagly and Chaiken (1993: 202) sum up their extensive review of the factors involved in generating such consistency:

> Attitudes that are based on more input are likely to relate more strongly to attitude–relevant behaviors, whether this input is behavioral or cognitive. Thus, research on behavioral experience has shown that increased behavioral input increases attitude–behavior correspondence, and research on prior knowledge has suggested that increased cognitive input has the same impact. Unfortunately, research on affective experience is lacking, but increased input from this source may similarly increase attitude–behavior correspondence.

Yet this approach, though it tries to incorporate both behavioural and bias cognitive influences even-handedly, is limited in two ways by its implicit acceptance of a cognitive reference structure.

First, there is an overwhelming inclination towards explaining attitudinal–behavioural consistency in cognitive terms. The general thrust of the evidence gained subsequently to Wicker's (1969) review, and the disappointment and consternation it generated have tended towards the importance of including non-cognitive factors in the prediction of behaviour. But current attitude theory does not reflect this sufficiently. Extra-attitudinal cognitive factors were, of course, always implicated in the quest for greater consistency, but seminal contributions have emphasised situational and behavioural influences (Foxall 1983, 1984, 1996).

The implication of the tight situational compatibility required of measures of target behaviour and measures of its antecedent cognitive predictors (Ajzen and Fishbein 1977) is that situational factors are highly significant for the correlational consistency of attitudes/intentions and behaviour. Only when the situational influences governing both the prebehavioural and the behavioural variables are functionally equivalent are high correlations found. That the intertemporal period between prebehavioural and behavioural measures must be minimal if high correlations are to be found corroborates this view by pointing to the undesirability of unexpected situational demands reducing the predictive value of measured intentions (Foxall 1983, 1984, 1996a).

Fishbein and Ajzen's (1980) claim that situational factors that intervene between intention and behaviour can be ignored for purposes of prediction since the changes are likely to cancel one another out and thus not influence the predictive accuracy of the intention also requires comment. While the problem of prediction has been overcome – albeit only to the extent that, for the individual, the predictive intention is that which immediately precedes the opportunity to behave in accordance with it – that of explanation remains. For there can be no claim to have explained behaviour in terms of its antecedent reasons if situational interventions can play so large a part in the determination of behaviour (Sarver 1983).

This is no deterrent to Fishbein and Ajzen, whose insistence on attributing behaviour to intentions – and in turn to attitudes and subjective norms – reveals a deliberate predilection to interpret behaviour by reference to underlying causative mental dispositions. The practical importance of predictive methods closely following theoretical expectations is clear from the marketing of new consumer products, in which process about 80 per cent of innovations fail at the point of market acceptance even when their launch has been preceded by sophisticated market research based on the measurement of prospective consumers' attitudes and intentions. Only behaviour with the product, including product tests and test marketing, predicts trial-and-repeat purchase with any acceptable degree of accuracy (Foxall 1984).

But the point here is that context and situation deserve a more central place in the explanation of behaviour, which is denied them by the partiality inherent in acceptance of the pre-eminence of the cognitive paradigm. Yet the reasons why past and current behaviour are consistent are discussed by attitude theorists in predominantly cognitive terms: the possibility that the consistency is due to environmental influences does not appear to enter their research agenda. Moreover, the tripartite comprehension of attitude prevails as the paradigm for further investigation and explication.

Second, although Eagly and Chaiken mention in passing a behaviouristic approach, their apparent understanding of the possibilities thereof seem severely limited. They accept, for instance, that including measures of past behaviour is reasonable from a behaviourist standpoint that holds that 'behavior is influenced by habit, or more generally, by various types of conditioned releasers or learned predispositions to respond that are not readily encompassed by the concepts of attitude and intention' (Eagly and Chaiken 1993: 179).

But this avoids the fact that the explanatory power of past behaviour is frequently sufficient to make cognitive variables superfluous; that a behaviour-analytical theory may be capable of explaining or interpreting the evidence on attitudinal–behavioural consistency in full; and that in any case the reason for including a behaviourist perspective is to identify the consequences that past behaviour has produced to account for the consistency of that prior responding and thus to use those consequences to predict future behaviour.

Prior Behaviour as Habit

Another tendency is to refer to repetitious behaviour as habit. Triandis (1977, 1980) defined habit as 'situation-specific sequences that are or have become automatic, so that they occur without self-instruction' (Triandis 1980: 204). In similar vein, Eagly and Chaiken (1993: 180) comment that 'the concept of habit implies that a behavior has become so routinized through repetition that a person has ceased to make any conscious decision to act yet still behaves in the accustomed way'.

Another way of putting this is that habitual behaviour is that maintained by direct contact with the contingencies of reinforcement rather than instructed through verbal behaviour. The alternative paradigm to which this description belongs suggests a means by which the import of prior behaviour may be more fully understood. However, this is not the usual emphasis in attitude theory and research. Ronis *et al.* (1989: 218) refer to a habit as an action that has been carried out with such frequency that it has become automatic; its performance is devoid of conscious thinking.

A great deal of consumer behaviour is apparently of this kind: see Ehrenberg and Uncles (1995). How is such behaviour to be explained? Unfortunately, it is often 'explained' in terms that are frankly tautological. Hence Ronis *et al.* (1989: 217) argue that 'the continued repetition of behaviors is often determined by habits rather than by attitudes or beliefs'. But this is meaningless given their definition of habit: a habit, as they understand it and as the word is used in everyday discourse, *is* the repeated behaviour. Such behaviour must be accounted for – unless we think it is uncaused – by reference to other factors; in an operant account, for instance, it would be ascribed to the contingencies of reinforcement. These authors attribute the causative habits to repeated behaviour (p. 219), an assignation that completes the tautology of their argument. Eagly and Chaiken similarly refer to habits as 'nonattitudinal determinants of behavior' and as one of several 'psychological tendencies that regulate behavior' (Eagly and Chaiken 1993: 216, 671).

Ronis *et al.* (1989: 216–18) uncontroversially point out that the explanation of habit requires that attention be given to two component processes: *initiation*, namely that in which the behaviour comes about, requiring decision-making; and *persistence*, which implies automaticity, lack of conscious direction. They associate attitudes with initiation, but not persistence. A decision, almost by definition, involves conscious thought and reflection on one or more alternatives to the chosen behaviour. They also point out that initiation (novel behaviour) is predictable from attitudes, while persistence is not; that prior behaviour is also a strong predictor of novelty; and that habit predicts future behaviour more effectively than intentions (Ronis *et al.* 1989: 221).

In other words, attitudes correlate with habitual behaviour under some circumstances, not others. In a behaviour analysis, there is evidence that non-verbal behaviour is consistent with rules in the long term only if the contingencies bear out the rules. Moreover, note that the behaviour-analytical demonstration is that behaviourist explanation can account for both decision and habit: it is not the case that behaviour analysis is confined to habit while decision is accounted for as social-cognitivism.

BEHAVIOUR AND ATTITUDES

According to the social cognition interpretation, consumer behaviour is the result of information processing in a social context. It is attitude-consistent either because prior experience of the object is sufficient to allow evaluations to control behaviour spontaneously, or because, in the absence of such experience, the individual must deliberate, examining the likely consequences of each course of action apparently available and consciously selecting one that he or she intends to perform if circumstances permit. Most consumer behaviour contains elements of both spontaneous and deliberative processing. The tendency of adherents to this paradigm is to interpret evidence for the environmental control of behaviour in terms of additional cognitive processing.

But the factor that emerges again and again as predictive of current behaviour is neither attitude nor intention but *preceding* behaviour. Moreover, this neglected but clearly central explicator has two components. The first is the set of similar overt motor responses performed by the individual in the past, i.e. what attitude theorists and researchers including Fishbein, Ajzen, Bagozzi and Warshaw have referred to as past behaviour or prior behaviour. This stream of similar responses cannot be considered in the absence of the consequences it has produced and their implications for the probability that similar behaviour of the same kind will be emitted again. In the terminology of behaviour analysis, and on the assumption that they are similarly reinforced, these responses belong to the same operant class, and their future rate of emission depends upon the learning history of the individual.

The second sense in which preceding behaviour may be understood is that of the verbal behaviour that instructs the current responding of an individual This verbal behaviour can consist of instructions or rules articulated by someone else, or of the self-instructions generated by the individual for himself or herself. These verbal discriminative stimuli are the antecedent source of the rule-governed behaviour of humans: such behaviour is distinguished from the contingency-shaped behaviour of non-humans and, on occasion, humans. The broader category of verbal behaviour, which includes both the rule-provision of the speaker and the rule-compliance of the listener, allows radical behaviourism to investigate and interpret the phenomena of thinking, reasoning, problem-solving and deciding that have traditionally fallen within the purview of cognitive psychology (Skinner 1974; Ribes 1991, 1992). The paradigm that offers understanding of the role of instructed behaviour and that underpins the argument made here is behaviour analysis.

Our need is for a paradigm that takes account of the import of behaviour itself. The account of consumer behaviour we have just left draws our attention to the significance of prior behaviour in the analysis of current consumer choice, to the need to consider the context in which behaviour has been learned in order to interpret properly its present meaning, and to the necessity of understanding the ways in which environmental influences shape and maintain patterns of consumer behaviour over time. All of these criticisms of social cognition derive from work within that paradigm, though there does not appear to be recognition among its practitioners that, cumulatively, these findings might render their perspective untenable for the comprehensive modelling of consumer behaviour.

If we are dissatisfied with social-cognitive accounts of consumer choice, we may react constructively in two ways. One is to improve the techniques we are using; for instance, increasing the number of variables we employ to predict a response, or expanding the accuracy of our measures by relying more on observation of the behavioural target rather than on respondents' self-reports of what they have done. As long as we wish to continue to work within the social cognition paradigm then this process of amelioration is inevitable. The thrust of attitude and consumer researcher's effort has been so directed: from early attempts to establish statistical consistency between measures of attitude-towards-the-object and behaviour-towards-the-object, through the theory of reasoned action, the theory of planned behaviour, the theories of self-regulation and trying, to the more radical reformulation in terms of spontaneous processing. Moreover, while these attempts might not be definitive in resolving the problems of attitudinal–behavioural consistency, they are forceful in identifying the situational coherence required for the comprehension of verbal and non-verbal behaviours.

The other approach to any professional disappointment we may feel with current attempts to understand and predict consumer behaviour is to take an altogether different approach. But this does not make radical behaviourism, a paradigm founded upon antithetical assumptions about the causation of human behaviour, the obvious choice as the alternative framework of conceptualisation and analysis. Why, then, are the following chapters devoted to it?

LOOKING AHEAD

Radical behaviourism is an approach to the analysis of behaviour that emphasises behaviour itself, rather than its alleged intrapersonal determinants, be they mental (information processing, attitudes, intentions neural (physiological processes), or conceptual (hypothetical constructs purportedly existing only in the mind of the observer). Moreover, radical behaviourism seeks to explain the occurrence of behaviour in relation to the outcomes produced by similar behaviour in the past – notably, the rewards and sanctions that affect the probability of such behaviour's being repeated in similar circumstances. That is, its explication of behaviour relies on events that happen *in the environment* rather than within the individual.

An obvious stratagem, therefore, is to turn to the consideration of a paradigm that claims to understand behaviour in context and that has been dedicated for well over half a century to the practical demonstration that 'the variables of which behaviour is a function lie in the environment' (Skinner 1977: 5) and to the philosophical grasp of its findings to that apparent effect. Not because this way lies Truth but because our intellectual quest requires it. Radical behaviourism is not even the sole perspective on behaviour that seeks to relate it to its consequences. Social learning theory (Bandura 1977, 1986) and social exchange theory (Homans 1974) are but two of the alternatives, each of which owes its emphasis on the environment to radical behaviourism and yet takes account of cognitive processes in its own way. Perhaps our search for a novel approach will lead to one of these or to a close relative. But there are certain advantages in beginning with the more extreme position presented by radical behaviourism.

By examining the claims of this approach to have dealt successfully with the extra-personal explanation of behaviour, and by working with it in the specific context of consumer behaviour rather than as an abstract philosophy, we will be able to evaluate those claims in terms of their capacity to elucidate consumer choice beyond the point to which social-cognitivism has brought our understanding.

Although we approach it positively, it would be naïve to think that radical behaviourism will not ultimately prove to have shortcomings of its own. Every system does. But we are not seeking utter certainty: rather we want as full a view of human behaviour as possible and the more explanatory systems we take into consideration, critically evaluating one from the standpoint provided by another, then the more comprehensive will that view become. It may emerge that the very problems we encountered in social cognition are common to radical behaviourism, or that it has shortcomings of its own with which to impede consumer research. The kind of consumer research, academic as well as commercial, which is concerned with selling soap (or brotherhood) will probably not benefit from our peregrinations. But, if consumer psychology and marketing research are to hold their own in the academy, we must undertake them. Moreover, our excursions abroad are a vital source of inspiration if we are to maintain our own sense of intellectual excitement, as students of human economic behaviour, in the face of the dull strictures our disciplines would impose upon us and the shaping of the academy by those who do not do such work. Such consideration must, nevertheless, be upon the pragmatic level of judgement rather than that of philosophical comparison. Every system of thought is both supported and destroyed by philosophical criticism, which seems to provide no enduring answers nor to convince anybody of anything for long, let alone change the views of whole scientific communities, which remain as fragmented as ever. (There is no need to consult the history of philosophy for proof of this: the numerous philosophical arguments that have littered the pages of marketing and consumer behaviour journals, conference proceedings and books since the early 1980s are ample demonstration: none has apparently informed subsequent empirical or theoretical research to any appreciable degree.) There are always grounds, at this level, to reject what is yet useful. Thank goodness: for it is the variety of our ontologies, methodologies and epistemologies, and their critical interaction, that ensures scientific progress, or at least the growth of knowledge.

Decisive shifts of perspective do not occur in the social sciences – even in psychology, which so wants to be a paradigm science. Tides come and go, but each continues to say something relevant to our scientific endeavours. We may come to reject radical behaviourism in it present form or to reformulate it more usefully. But at least we shall have done so not because its death was announced in a psychology or philosophy text written by someone else but because we appreciate its value as well as its drawbacks and, therefore, what we can do with it as consumer researchers.

The possibility that behaviourism can provide an appropriate general methodological framework for consumer research fills many people with dread. For behaviourism seems to deny the very humanness of our subject matter (Webster 1996). This would be true of radical behaviourism were it the stimulus–response psychology it is usually taken to be (Lee 1988). An ontologically credible behaviourism must be capable of dealing with the private events such as thoughts and feelings that this paradigm is most frequently represented as ignoring. Indeed, it must take them as central to its subject matter and, on this point, radical behaviourism is ontologically distinct from the stimulus–response formulations of classical conditioning.

Part III
Behavioural Science in Marketing

Established psychology is laboratory-based, often takes animals as its subjects, and shows little direct interest in the mundane particulars of human conduct. The psychology of the content of conduct espoused here depends [by contrast] on investigators observing and interpreting events outside the laboratory. It is a local psychology, a psychology of the contingencies that operate under particular historical conditions in particular domains of action. In addition, it is a psychology committed to illuminating the work requirements of various domains and the costs and benefits of various acts for each of the participants in these domains. Most of all, it is a psychology that builds directly and explicitly on our ordinary and specialized experience of the way in which these various domains actually work.

(Lee 1988: 149)

4 A Science of Behaviour

RADICAL BEHAVIOURISM

A Somewhat Exaggerated Death

In spite of the widespread belief that behaviourism has been superseded in the course of 'the cognitive revolution' (e.g., Baars 1986; Mandler 1985; cf. Keehn 1996; Kimble 1996), some schools of behaviourist thought currently exhibit a considerable intellectual dynamic, especially in the analysis of thinking, reasoning and decision-making, areas of human endeavour widely considered to fall exclusively within the province of cognitivism (e.g., Blackman and Lejeune 1990; Modgil and Modgil 1987; Richelle 1993; Reese and Parrott 1986; Davey and Cullen 1988; Lowe, *et al.* 1985; Chase and Parrott 1986; Hayes and Chase 1991; Hayes, *et al.* 1993; Guerin 1994a; Hayes, 1994; Hayes and Hayes 1992a).

This chapter is concerned with *radical behaviourism*, but employs a number of additional terms as virtual synonyms. Vaughan (1989: 97) says, 'The field of behavior analysis is the area of philosophy, research, and application that encompasses the experimental analysis of behavior, applied behavior analysis, operant psychology, operant conditioning, behaviorism, and Skinnerian psychology.' Radical behaviourism is the philosophy of psychology which unites all of these (Skinner 1974).

Far from being a supplanted paradigm, radical behaviourism is a flourishing area of intellectual activity in both its neo-Skinnerian and post-Skinnerian accentuations (e.g., Alessi 1992; Fallon 1992; Hayes *et al.* 1993; Kimble 1994; Lee 1988, 1992; Morris 1993a, 1993b; Rachlin 1992, 1995; Skinner 1980; Staddon 1993; Thompson 1994). In particular, theoretical and empirical work on verbal behaviour has transformed radical behaviourism since the fundamentals of operant conditioning were tentatively applied to marketing and promotions in the 1970s and 1980s. Much of this work has implications for consumer research (Foxall 1987).

First, it facilitates a comprehensive radical-behaviourist interpretation of consumer behaviour, which incorporates the verbal antecedents and consequences of consumer choice, both overt and covert. Previous use of this paradigm in marketing and consumer research has generally assumed that its explanatory system can be extrapolated from the non-human animal laboratory, where supporting evidence has accumulated, to complex human behaviour such as purchase and consumption. However, an operant analysis of complex human behaviour need not rely upon principles of contingency-shaped behaviour gained from laboratory research with non-humans: it is now possible to incorporate the distinctively human capacity for language and rule-governed behaviour. Consequently, operant analysis need not be restricted to simpler, routine consumer behaviours while a cognitive account is necessary for more complex behaviours based on decision-making and problem-solving. A behaviourist analysis may prove capable of handling both.

Second, study of the relationship between behaviour and its controlling environment promises to supply a much-needed systematic understanding of the situational influences on consumer choice. As noted above, because of the emphasis in consumer research on the social-cognitive determinants of consumption, the field currently lacks an integrated model of consumer behaviour in the context of its social, physical, temporal and regulatory surroundings. Radical behaviourism, a discipline concerned almost entirely with the explanation of behaviour as an environmentally determined phenomenon, can be expected to contribute importantly to the required understanding. The advent of research on consumers' verbal behaviour means that this comprehension can incorporate the social influence of rule provision.

By presenting an understanding of consumer choice as influenced by environmental considerations, a behaviour analysis, whether experimental or interpretational, has the potential to fill a cavernous gap in consumer research that currently lacks a coherent explication of situational control of consumer choice. However, mention of this paradigm in marketing and consumer research has usually tended to presume that its explanatory system can be extrapolated unadorned from experimental research with non-humans to complex human interactions such as purchase and consumption. A behaviour-analytical account of human behaviour must take full measure of the situational and speciational peculiarities of the context in which that behaviour takes place. Such an exposition must be conversant with the experimental analysis of human behaviour and the ramifications of radical-behaviourist interpretation (Foxall 1995a). Both require that particular attention be accorded the human capacity for verbal control of behaviour.

Third, consideration of radical-behaviourist explanation of consumer behaviour permits discussion of a number of epistemological issues that are germane to contemporary debates about the nature of 'scientific' and 'interpretive' approaches to consumer research. By showing how an interpretation of consumer choice would proceed within a highly developed behavioural science paradigm, such analysis reveals the strengths and weaknesses of a specific ontology and methodology for consumer research and facilitates comparison with other modes of inquiry and explication. For example, the divergent ways in which social-cognitive and operant approaches interpret the role of previous behaviour in the shaping of current responding provides insight into the varied perspectives available for comparative consumer research.

The remainder of this chapter is structured as follows. First the ontological and epistemological bases of radical behaviourism are discussed, because these may be unfamiliar to many readers. By way of contrast with the cognitive psychology of attitudes and intentions reviewed in the previous chapter, recent developments in behaviourist theory and research are described with special reference to verbal behaviour and the proximal causative role of private events. The differences between social-cognitive and operant interpretations of thinking and reasoning, and their relationships to overt consumer behaviour, are drawn out by relating the recent work on attitude–intention–behaviour consistency to the role of instructed behaviour in behaviour analysis. Finally, the components of the consumer situation are elucidated and incorporated in an operant model of consumer choice, the behavioural perspective model (or BPM).

A Science of Behaviour

Description as Explanation

Radical-behaviourist explanation is descriptive: a response has been explained when the environmental stimuli that predict and control its rate of emission have been identified and their relationship to the response delineated. In practice this means that the radical behaviourist explains behaviour by reference to the contingent relationships of a response and the consequences it produces in the presence of an antecedent stimulus (Skinner 1969; cf. Malott 1986). The 'three-term contingency' represented in this statement comprises the central explanatory device of the paradigm:

$$S^d \to R \to S^r \tag{4.1}$$

and

$$S^d \to R \to S^p \tag{4.2}$$

where S^d is a discriminative stimulus, R is a response, and $S^{r/p}$ is a reinforcing or punishing (consequent) stimulus (Skinner 1953: 110; for historical and philosophical reviews of the paradigm, see Chiesa 1995; Hineline

1990; 1992; Iversen 1992; Morris and Midgley 1990; Morris *et al.* 1990; Smith 1986; Zuriff 1985).

An *operant response* is any arbitrarily defined bit of behaviour, the rate of repetition of which can be systematically related to its consequences. An operant consumer response is, therefore, typically, browsing, paying, taking home, preparing, eating, often sequenced in chains such that each response becomes a discriminative stimulus for the next. A set of responses (or chains), each of which is maintained by a similar pattern of reinforcement, constitutes an operant class.

A *discriminative stimulus* signals the likelihood of reinforcement or punishment that is contingent upon the performance of a particular response. It is thus an element of the environment in the presence of which the individual's behaviour is differentiated; i.e. he or she tends to emit those responses that have previously been reinforced rather than those that have not. Behaviour comes under *stimulus control* when it is performed in the presence of a discriminative stimulus, even when a reinforcing consequence is not forthcoming on every occasion.

The *consequences of an operant response* are either reinforcing or punishing. A *reinforcing stimulus* is a behavioural consequence that results in the increased frequency of the response that produced it. *Positive* reinforcement occurs when the consequence is received by the individual: receiving money for work is likely to result in one's doing more work. *Negative* reinforcement still describes an increase in the rate of a response, but the consequence has to be avoided or escaped: taking aspirin for an incipient headache is reinforced by the avoidance of or escape from pain. Negative reinforcement thus averts an *aversive stimulus*. If an aversive consequence is suffered, however, it reduces the probability that the behaviour that produced it will again be performed in similar circumstances (as defined by discriminative stimuli). Being reprimanded for misbehaviour is to receive an aversive stimulus, which is known as a punisher, and the procedure in which the behaviour that produced it comes to occur less often is punishment.

An individual's *learning history* is the sum total of his or her emitted behaviours and their consequences under particular conditions (usually ones similar to the conditions under which his or her behaviour is to be predicted and controlled). So the learning history summarises the cumulative contingencies of reinforcement and punishment under which the individual has previously behaved.

The term *contingencies of reinforcement and punishment*, redescribes the relationships among discriminative stimuli, the response(s) whose probability they influence, and the consequences of performing such response(s). The most usual representation, noted above, is the three-term contingency.

There is no reason, however, why the paradigm should be limited to three terms. Since discriminations may be conditional on the presence of additional stimuli, there is in principle no limit to the number of terms that may be required to explain an particular operant response. The thrust of the empirical science pursued within the radical-behaviourist framework is thus a search for *functional relationships* that identify the effects of environment on behaviour. Radical behaviourism is pragmatic rather than realist in its ontology. The criterion for judging the functional relationships so identified is entirely practical: do they permit the prediction and control of behaviour? The underlying philosophy of science is not that of logical positivism but the biological expediency of Mach (Moore 1985).

The Role of Theory

Since behaviour is understood in radical behaviourism as a function of the consequences of similar behaviour in the past, any causal reference to attitudes, intentions and other prebehavioural mental, neural or hypothetical entities is redundant (Skinner 1971: 18). Such theoretical entities that exist in some realm other than that in which the behaviour in question is observed are mere 'explanatory fictions', inferred from the behaviour they purport to explain and thus leading only to a circular account. Nor is the antecedent discriminative stimulus an initiating cause of behaviour (Skinner 1988a): it simply signals the availability of reinforcement contingent upon the emission of the appropriate response. Its significance as a setting variable derives from its role in the individual's learning history. When learning has occurred, behaviour may come under the proximal control of the antecedent (discriminative) stimulus in the temporary absence of the reinforcing consequence. The variables of which behaviour is ultimately a function are the environmental consequences such behaviour has produced in the course of that learning history (Delprato and Midgley 1992; cf. Morris 1991).

There is, however, a form of theory that radical behaviourism embraces, that established on the basis of accumulated data. It takes the form, therefore, of empirical generalisation. However, to date, little theoretical work has been undertaken on this basis by radical behaviourists.

An Interpretation of Behaviour

Radical behaviourists have long recognised that their account of complexity amounts to an interpretation, albeit based upon principles gained in simpler,

more amenable contexts (Skinner 1969: 100). Radical behaviourist interpretation proceeds as 'an orderly arrangement of well-known facts, in accordance with a formulation of behavior derived from an experimental analysis
of a more rigorous sort' (Skinner 1957: 11). That formulation provides some
part of the 'warrant of assertibility' (Dewey 1966) of radical behaviourist interpretation and, as the accumulated evidence for operant conditioning in animals and humans in laboratories and field settings attests, it is a persuasive
warrant (Guerin 1994a). But it necessarily differs from the more rigorous
accounts of simpler operant behaviour: it cannot be complete, for instance,
in so far as it alludes to contingencies that can often be inferred rather than
observed and measured: 'merely useful', its truth or falsity cannot be ascertained
with the certainty available to the experimentalist (Skinner 1988a: 364).

It is doubtful, however, whether radical behaviourism differs in this respect from any other science – no critic of behaviourism is suggesting the
overthrow of evolutionary biology or astrophysics because they interpret
where they cannot control. And radical behaviourists claim their interpretations superior to those which have no experimental warrant at all, or
those based on the explanatory fictions of centralist theories.

The epistemological basis of behaviour analysis, radical behaviourism, is
thus a philosophy of science that shares its ontology with a system of interpretation. This emphasis on interpretive behaviour analysis is often overlooked in popular accounts and critiques that identify radical behaviourism
closely with rigorous laboratory experimentation and with the application
of a scientific method derived from Machian positivism to the relatively simple operant behaviour of non-humans (Todd and Morris 1992; cf.
Phillips 1992). The results it gains there are, it is said, uncritically extrapolated to the human sphere, leading to prescriptions for social control and
cultural engineering unsupported by either direct empirical evidence or a
coherent theory of human behaviour. This view overlooks two relevant considerations.

The first is the large proportion of operant research which nowadays
involves human participants, especially in the context of verbal behaviour. The second is the role of interpretation in operant accounts of complex behaviour. Research on verbal behaviour is reviewed below, but the
subject of radical behaviourist interpretation requires elaboration at this
point. Interpretation is necessary wherever the elements of the three-term
contingency, though possibly observable, are not amenable to public confirmation and when they cannot engender the degree of prediction and or
control that can be secured in the laboratory.

Hence interpretation is indispensable when the precise consequent and
antecedent stimuli that control complex behaviour are not consensually

obvious. For example, what attributes of the product class are sufficient for reinforcement of purchasing to take place? What are the exact discriminative stimuli under the control of which eating chocolate occurs? Interpretation is also required to account for phenomena that are observable by only one individual, private events such as *my* thoughts and feelings. I can only infer that the behaviour of another person is controlled by similar stimuli that are private to him or her (Mackenzie 1988; Skinner 1988b). Interpretation is equally inescapable when self-rules are elusive to the observer (and perhaps to the actor). Sometimes only an interpretation that infers such rules from overt behaviour can fill in the gaps. This leads, however, to a circular account, because the proximal causes of behaviour are deduced from the behaviour itself (and, therefore, some behaviour analysts reject this approach, maintaining that only phenomena that can be reduced to experimental control have a place in a science of behaviour).

A Theory of Behaviour

The fact is that, despite the protestations of most of its adherents, radical behaviourism is a theory of behaviour (Foxall 1996a: Chapter 15). Radical behaviourists' ignorance or denial of the theory-ladenness of observation notwithstanding, there is ample evidence that Skinner's philosophical studies prior to his taking up graduate studies in psychology (not having previously studied this subject) prepared him well for a career as a behaviourist. These included the works of Bacon, Bridgeman, Watson and Russell. Although none of these predisposed him to see operant conditioning when it presented itself, though the work of Thorndike would have been instrumental here, Skinner's explanation of his findings was available to him in embryo at least before he ever observed a squirrel (the rats and pigeons came later).

Second, we have noted that the inclusion in radical behaviourism of 'private events' is inferential as far as their use in the interpretation of other people's behaviour is concerned. The ontological assumptions made by Skinner and other radical behaviourists is further interesting in that thoughts are interpreted as behaviours (as they may well be, but there is no way of demonstrating this except on the simplistic assumption that behaviour is 'what an organism does', which is rejected as inadequate by Skinner himself (Skinner 1988b).

The distinction between respondent and operant behaviours, the first elicited in a stimulus–response manner, the latter spontaneously emitted by an organism, their subsequent rate of recurrence determined by the consequences of the first performance, is also a bold ontological step. Most human behaviour is thereby recast as operant, while the subject matter of classical conditioning is interpreted as physiological reflex.

The automatic reinforcement assumed by Skinner (1957) to strengthen such responses as listening to music is a theoretical entity: unobservable, incapable of being brought into an experimental analysis. But then *all* interpretation is necessarily theoretical in as much as it involves translating from one sphere of behaviour to another.

Selection by Consequences

The essence of Skinner's explanatory account, theoretical and interpretive, is the homologic device, 'selection by consequences', which links operant conditioning with evolutionary biology on one hand and cultural evolution on the other. Within the radical-behaviourist paradigm, selection by consequences is as pervasive an *interpretation* in the animal operant laboratory as it is in operant accounts of behaviour that is not amenable to laboratory analysis.

Thus, one way in which behaviour analysis seeks to establish the plausibility of its accounts of both animal and human behaviours is by employing the evolution of biological species through natural selection as an analogue for the procedure in which operant behaviour is selected by the environment (Skinner 1981). Operant conditioning has also been portrayed by its adherents as an evolutionary process in its own right, one whose causal mode is selection through consequences. The essence of evolutionary explanation lies in the inferred action of a selective environment on the continuity of the form, function and behaviour of an organism or organisation and the species to which it belongs.

Evolutionary biology deals with the selection of organisms that are adapted to living and reproducing in a specific local environment. Such an organism, its form, function and behaviour, constitutes the phenotype which is the result of the organism's genetic composition (genotype) and the action of the environment on that organism during the course of its development (ontogeny). Although the environment acts directly upon the phenotype, the fundamental unit of selection is the gene, because it alone is capable of self-replication and of thereby ensuring the continuity of selected features through their manifestation in the inheriting phenotype through successive generations (Dawkins 1982). Genes contain both genotype and phenotype information.

Variation in the phenotype is closely related to variation in the genotype: though phenotypic variation may be modified by the environment, characteristics becoming statistically dominant during this process are not – in the

Darwinian account – heritable through sexual reproduction except through mutation of genotype or phenotype information. The action of the environment on the phenotype determines the extent to which the genotype potential is expressed. Variation between individuals means that some are better suited (adapted) to a particular immediate environment than are others, and this has implications for (but is not identical with) their genotypic fitness, i.e. their capacity to reproduce successfully. 'Survival of the fittest' refers to the selective action of the environment in which more adapted or adaptable individuals are able to survive and reproduce their advantageous characteristics.

The metaprinciple of 'selection by consequences' is used by Skinner (1981) to describe and relate natural selection, which is shaped and maintained by 'contingencies of survival', and the selection and persistence of instrumental human behaviour in operant conditioning, in which behaviour is shaped and maintained by 'contingencies of reinforcement'. A subset of the latter is cultural evolution, in which behaviours that are of utility to the survival and welfare of social groups and organisations are selected and transmitted, according to their consequences, from generation to generation. This is not the place to consider in full the philosophical evidence for and against this stance. (An extensive review of Skinner's ideas on this score is available in Catania and Harnad 1988.) However, it is pertinent to note three sources of support for the proposition.

First, the evolutionary biologist, Dawkins (1988: 33) points out that in natural selection, 'the replicators are the genes, and the consequences by which they are selected are their phenotypic effects, that is, mostly their effects on the embryonic development of the body in which they sit'. However, in operant conditioning,

the replicators are the habits in the animal's repertoire, originally spontaneously produced (the equivalent of mutation). The consequences are reinforcement, positive and negative [and punishment]. The habits can be seen as replicators because their frequency of emergence from the animal's motor system increases, or decreases, as a result of their reinforcement [or punishing] consequences. (ibid)

The principal causal agency is the environment, which acts to select the consequences of some behaviours but not others and thereby ensures the continuity of that which is selected. Biologist Maynard Smith (1986: 75) also mentions the similarity of the processes:

There is an obvious analogy between operant conditioning and evolution by natural selection. Behaviour becomes adapted to the environment by the reinforcement of spontaneous acts, just as morphological structure is adapted by the natural selection of spontaneous mutations.

Second, the philosopher of social science Van Parijs (1981) identifies the evolutionary process, as it occurs in the social and economic spheres, as that of operant conditioning. He designates this mechanism, which relies on behavioural reinforcement, as 'R-evolution' in contrast to the 'NS-evolution', which characterises the survival of the fittest that occurs in natural selection. Richelle, who unlike Dawkins and Van Parijs is a behaviourist, and a leading philosopher of radical behaviourism, has also written of the compatibility of natural selection and the environmental selection of behaviour:

> There is nothing implausible in the idea that one basic process is at work throughout numerous levels of complexity or in a wide variety of living species. The same fundamental mechanism is called upon in evolutionary biology to account for the simplest and for the most complex living forms. The same is true of the basic principles governing the genetic code. One basic principle is acceptable if it provides for structural diversification. This is exactly what the variation-selection process does in biological evolution. But the observed diversity must not hide the basic process that produces it. The same might be true of behaviour . . . Viewed in this perspective, operant behaviour has little to do with the repetition of stereotyped responses which has become the popular representation of it. It is a highly dynamic process grounded in behavioural variation. Novel and creative behaviour, and problem-solving do not raise particular difficulties in this view . . . (Richelle 1987: 134–6).

Third, evolutionary economics rests on the idea of selection by consequences. Dosi (1988: 13), for instance, refers to the evolutionary process as that in which 'individual and organisational behaviours, to different degrees and through different processes, are selected, penalised or rewarded'. In contrast to the presumption of conditions of static equilibrium which pervades neoclassical economics, evolutionary economics emphasises 'discovery, learning, selection, evolution and complexity' (Dosi and Orsenigo, 1988: 15).

The Dual Nature of Causation

As important as the homology of natural selection and operant conditioning is the dual nature of causation in psychology as well as biology. Goldsmith (1991: 6) observes that 'Virtually every question that one can pose in biology has two very different kinds of answers': proximate and ultimate, which supply complementary explanations. We can extend this to the three levels at which Skinner claims that selection by consequences takes place (see Table 4.1).

Table 4.1   Proximate and ultimate causation in natural selection and operant learning

	Proximate causation	*Ultimate causation*
Natural selection	Biochemical, physiological predisposition, phenotype	Function in adaptation and fitness, genetic predisposition, genotype
Operant behaviour	Discriminative stimuli, especially in humans verbal, rules	Learning history
Cultural evolution	Ditto as provided by group artefacts, group-specific objects, rules, mores, etc.	Social history

All these types of behaviour are the result of contingencies (of survival/reinforcement). But the contingencies are not the cause; they are a description of the behaviour in the environment, i.e. of the functional relationship between the two. The causes of operant behaviour are (i) the (susceptibility to/meaning of) discriminative stimuli acquired in a learning history, and (ii) the learning history itself.

The dual nature of biological contingency is mirrored in the case of operant learning. Proximate causation is the realm of the consumer behaviour-setting, consisting of the usually visible instigators of behaviour. Ultimate causation is found in a history of reinforcement and punishment. The distinction has methodological implications. Experimentation is concerned with the manipulation of proximate causes, especially discriminative stimuli in the operant chamber. Of course, the subject has a learning history, which determines its response to the discriminative stimuli, and, in the case of laboratory animals this learning history is known to the experimenter. Interpretation is concerned with ultimate causation where the learning history is not known (at least not in detail). The gaps must, therefore, be filled in with plausible guesses. The question to which radical behaviourists have given scant regard is what procedure to follow in doing this. However, the associations between proximate causation and experimental manipulation and between ultimate causation and interpretation are not absolute. Where the proximate discriminative stimulus consists in verbal responses, interpretation is inevitable, experimentation impossible. Proximate cause in biology, Goldsmith (1991: 7) states,

> has to do with the characteristics that one can see – characteristics that are the final expression of the genetic program (the genotype) that is present in the fertilized egg from which the organism grew. Explanations of proximate causation are often couched in the language of physiology and biochemistry and are frequently the subject of experimental manipulation.

In operant psychology, proximate cause concerns visible behaviour whose characteristics are the final expression of the individual's learning history. Explanations at this level are often couched in the language of discriminative stimuli, including verbal discriminative stimuli and private events such as thoughts. Proximate causation is amenable to experimental manipulation when the factors responsible for stimulus control are publicly available. But when they are inferred private events, interpretation is inevitable – behaviour analysts sometimes refuse to admit them. Much of the behaviour studied is rule-governed (ultimately contingency-shaped). Emphasis on proximate causation, to the exclusion of consideration of ultimate causation, leads to folk psychology and cognitivism.

According to Goldsmith (1991: 7),

> Ultimate cause, is the province of the evolutionary biologist who is interested in the historical origins of genotypes. Explanations of ultimate cause invoke the concept of adaptation of organisms to their environments as well as evolutionary inferences based on comparative studies of different kinds of organisms. Direct experimental manipulation is not unknown but is usually more difficult to achieve.

Ultimate cause is the domain of the operant psychologist interested in the environmental shaping of a learning history. It too involves consideration of the adaptation of behaviour to its environment, but it is that of the operant class rather than the individual response. Ultimate causation involves interpretation in terms of what is known of operant behaviour in accessible, manipulable settings. This dimension is often subsumed under the general rubric of 'experience', the contingency-shaping of which is ignored.

Evolution, is

in a fundamental sense . . . the sifting of genotypes; however, differential survival and reproduction occur among phenotypes. In the world of interacting organisms, phenotypes are the agents of the genotypes, and it is the phenotypes – the organisms themselves – that compete and whose performance determines reproductive success. Obviously, natural selection can act only if the basis for differential survival and reproduction is heritable. Phenotypic differences that are not the result of underlying genotypic differences therefore cannot serve as the basis for evolutionary change . . . It is for this central reason that we must be concerned with how the genotype becomes translated into the phenotype and with the effects of the environment on this process. (Goldsmith 1991: 25)

Current behavioural responses are the expression of the individual's learning history. It is responses that compete and survive (are reinforced) or die out (extinguish). A major difference between natural selection and operant behaviour is that whereas the former is Darwinian, the latter is Lamarckian: acquired characteristics can be inherited (preserved) as small changes in responses are repeated. Learning during the history of the individual is related to the probability of a current response being maintained as a result of elements of environmental continuity (leading to generalisation), but also through verbal behaviour (rules which describe past and current contingencies).

Learning histories 'replicate' in the sense that they prime the responses that are their expressions. But responses 'reproduce' in the sense that they recur. Both processes require appropriate environmental conditions, the discriminative stimuli and reinforcers that make replication and reproduction more probable. Cultural evolution is therefore the continuation of a social learning history; while operant conditioning is the reproduction of a response.

Understanding the relevance of selection by consequences to the analysis of consumer behaviour and of the operant portrayal of consumer decision-making requires the examination of recent research on the verbal control of human behaviour.

VERBAL BEHAVIOUR

Verbal Behaviour of Speaker and Listener

While the operant behaviour of non-humans is shaped entirely by direct contact with the contingencies (Lowe 1989), that of humans frequently comes under an additional source of control. That control is verbal, as when the actions of a new student are modified as a result of the instructions given by the university authorities irrespective of the student's direct experience of the contingencies to which those instructions refer. The analysis of rule-governed, as contrasted with contingency-shaped, behaviour is a longstanding theme in operant psychology, as is that of verbal behaviour in general (Skinner 1945, 1957, 1969). Nor need this analysis exclude any of the behaviours portrayed in many cognitive accounts as 'information processing'. As Richelle (1993: 144) defines the scope of the study of verbal behaviour:

> Rule-governed behaviour is more on the side of the intellect as opposed to emotion, of logical argument as opposed to intuition, of deliberation as opposed to impulse, of knowledge as opposed to know-how, of word as opposed to deed, of reason as opposed to faith, of truth as opposed to belief, of rationality as opposed to passion, of consciousness as opposed to unconsciousness, of culture as opposed to nature.

Skinner (1957) defined verbal behaviour as behaviour that is reinforced through the mediation of other persons: it impinges upon the social, rather than the physical environment (Moore 1994). Since verbal responding is a behavioural phenomenon, it is defined functionally, not logically, and the style of its analysis does not differ from that of any other operant behaviour (Moore 1994: 289; Skinner 1957). Consonant with the metatheoretical stance of radical behaviourism (Skinner 1945), such functional analysis diverges fundamentally from the formalism preferred by most linguists, including the formal standpoint from which Chomsky (1959) launched his critical review of Skinner's *Verbal Behaviour* (MacCorquodale 1969, 1970; Richelle 1993: 120–8).

Verbal Behaviour initially inspired little empirical work by behaviour analysts, and some segments of the recent upsurge in research on verbal responding are critical of Skinner, not least for his alleged concentration on the verbal behaviour of the speaker and his apparent disregard of that of the listener (Hayes and Hayes 1989; cf. Skinner 1989), but also for his failure to consider reference and postulation (L. J. Hayes 1991, 1994; Parrott 1986), and for the 'unwarranted dominance' of Skinner's book in its acceptance as the sole behaviour-theoretical approach to verbal responding and its consequent overshadowing of other theoretical approaches including relational frame analysis (S. C. Hayes 1994; see also Hayes and Hayes 1992a).

Research on human verbal responding has, nevertheless, flourished during the last several years, permitting theoretical advances. The differences

between humans' and animals' susceptibility to the contingencies themselves is demonstrated by a series of experiments. Non-human choices on
concurrent variable-interval (VI) schedules are described by the matching
law, which states that subjects emit alternative responses with frequencies
in direct proportion to the frequency of reinforcement available for each
response (Herrnstein 1961, 1970); that is

$$R_A = \frac{Kr_A}{r_A + r_B + r_0} \tag{4.3}$$

and

$$R_B = \frac{Kr_B}{r_A + r_B + r_0} \tag{4.4}$$

where

R_A, R_B = the number of responses accorded respectively to A and B,
r_A, r_B = the respective frequencies of reinforcement for these alternatives,

and

K, r_0 = empirically derived parameters, K being the response rate at
asymptote and r_0 the reinforcement rate at half-maximal response
rate that is theoretically equivalent to all of the implicit sources
of reinforcement available in the experimental setting
(Herrnstein 1970; Horne and Lowe 1993).

The matching law may be derived by combining equations (4.1) and
(4.2) as long as K and r_0 are invariant. This law states that the relative rates
of responding on the alternatives A and B are roughly equal to the relative
reinforcement frequencies of the two alternatives:

$$\frac{R_A}{R_A + R_B} = \frac{r_A}{r_A + r_B} \tag{4.5}$$

Expressed as a power function (Baum 1974), this becomes

$$\frac{R_A}{R_B} = k \left(\frac{r_A}{r_B} \right)^a \tag{4.6}$$

where

k, a = empirically derived free parameters.

Human responding has been described in several studies as conforming to these equations (e.g., Bradshaw *et al.* 1981; Bradshaw *et al.* 1976, 1977, 1979; Bradshaw *et al.* 1979; Ruddle *et al.* 1979). Moreover, the potential of the matching law to describe nonhuman behaviour accurately and consistently has been indicated in several applied settings (Epling and Pierce 1983, 1988; Hamblin 1979; McDowell 1981, 1982; Pierce and Epling 1980, 1983; Rachlin 1980; Winkler 1980).

However, some researchers (notably Lowe 1983) have argued that human responding frequently deviates substantially from the matching relationships found for other animals. Horne and Lowe (1993: 53) summarise six experiments involving human performances on concurrent VI schedules by noting that

In our studies, . . . less than half the subjects' performances resembled those typically found in animal choice studies. For many of the remaining subjects, there were not mere 'deviations' from the matching typically observed in nonhumans; rather their performance was qualitatively different and could not be described by the matching equations.

Departures from the matching law have been reported by several other researchers (e.g. Navarick and Chellsen 1983; Oscar-Berman *et al.* 1980; Pierce *et al.* 1981; Schmitt 1974; Schroeder 1975; Takahashi and Iwamoto 1986; Wurster and Griffiths 1979; Schroeder and Holland 1969; Silberberg, *et al.* 1991). Horne and Lowe (1993: 54) comment that

Together with the data from our six experiments, these findings clearly demonstrate that human subjects showing ideal matching, or even a close approximation to it, are the exception rather than the rule in the literature.

Departures such as these are apparently explained by humans' capacity for verbalising the contingencies of reinforcement which they believe to be in operation. Information, accurate or otherwise, about the contingencies operating in experimental settings is provided in the instructions given by the experimenter: use of such information may account for the digressions shown in human behaviour from patterns found in experiments with non-humans (Catania *et al.* 1982; Hayes *et al.* 1986; Horne and Lowe 1993; Lowe 1979, 1983; Lowe and Horne 1985; Matthews *et al.* 1985). Verbal behaviour may thus be invoked in the search for the causes of both the relatively simple behaviours emitted in experimental settings and the more complex patterns of response found in the situations of purchase and consumption. The interpretations of such complex behaviour can and should be submitted to further experimental analysis (Horne and Lowe 1993).

Instructed Behaviour

When a listener's behaviour results from the verbal activity of a speaker, it is said to be instructed or rule-governed. The rule in question acts as a verbal discriminative stimulus that takes the place of the contingencies themselves. (The view that rules are simply discriminative stimuli is not the only interpretation of rule-governed behaviour; cf. Hayes 1989; Horne and Lowe 1993.) The provision of rules is especially pertinent in changing behaviour the consequences of which are delayed, improbable or small (Malott 1989). If it is effective over time, such control requires a degree of consistency between the instructions and the contingencies they describe. But instructed behaviour has noteworthy properties of its own arising from its insensitivity to changes in the consequences of responding (Catania *et al.* 1990; Catania *et al.* 1989).

Instructed behaviour is always subject to two sets of contingencies: the social consequences that maintain the rule-following, and the natural contingencies that eventually take over if the instruction is effective (e.g. Baum 1994). Moreover, if the instructed behaviour is to be effectively learned, the consequences of rule-compliance must be more powerful than the natural consequences that would follow trial-and-success behaviour in the absence of the instruction. Since these natural contingencies are often remote, delayed and weak, learning from them alone (i.e. in the absence of instructions) would be slow or dangerous – as in the case of learning to drive a car – or possibly never-acting. This may supply part of the reason why instructed behaviour is often insensitive to changes in the natural contingencies. Shaped behaviour does not show this insensitivity: the acquisition of a practical skill such as glassblowing must, in many of its aspects, be directly shaped by hands-on experience that confers positive environmental consequences.

Functional Typology of Rule-Following

The functional categorisation of rule-following presents difficulties, though that suggested by Zettle and Hayes (1982), paralleling somewhat Skinner's (1957) definitions of the functional units of the behaviour of the speaker, has found support and prompted both empirical and theoretical investigations (Hayes 1989; Hayes and Hayes 1989; Chase and Danforth 1991; Malott 1989). Skinner posited two such units in particular, manding and tacting.

The *mand* denotes the consequences contingent upon following the instructions of the speaker or of imitating his or her example. Much advertising consists of mands – 'Buy three and get one free!' 'Don't forget the fruit gums, mum' – which indicate contingencies that are under the control of the speaker. *Tacts* present a contact with part of the environment and, depending on learning history, a potential for behaviour on the part of the recipient. A trade mark or logo may be followed by making a purchase or entering a store. Zettle and Hayes suggest the following units of analysis for the recipient's responding that match these phases of the prompter's behaviour or presence.

Corresponding to manding is *pliance*, which is rule-governed behaviour controlled by consequences that the speaker (or his/her agent) regulates (or claims to regulate). The rule, known as a *ply*, refers, therefore, to the social consequences of compliance or non-compliance: 'Keeping my breath fresh will get me more dates.' Corresponding to *tacting* is *tracking*, which is instructed behaviour that, according to the rule, is under the control of the non-social environment. A *track* specifies the arrangement of contingencies within that physical or temporal context: 'If I turn left at the next intersection, I'll come to Sainsbury's.' 'If I arrive by five, the shop will still be open.'

A third functional unit of listener behaviour has no corresponding unit for the speaker: the *augmental* (Zettle and Hayes 1982) is a highly motivating rule that states emphatically how a particular behaviour will be reinforced or avoid punishment. 'Just one more packet top and I can claim my watch!' The reason for the difficulty of defining plying and tracking exclusively is that a single rule often embodies elements of both (Poppen 1989): sometimes both elements of such a rule require the same behaviour to be performed (in which case the rule is a *congruent*); sometimes there is conflict (when the rule is known as a *contrant*).

Private Events

Contrary to general opinion, radical behaviourism provides a coherent interpretation of so-called cognitive phenomena such as thinking, reasoning and decision-making (Skinner 1945, 1974; see Catania 1992b). Indeed, counter to the predominant view that the behaviouristic paradigm has been superseded by cognitivism largely as a result of the former's incapacity to deal with cognitive phenomena, a substantial proportion of recent work in the theoretical and experimental analysis of behaviour has focused on verbal behaviour (S. C. Hayes 1989; Hayes and Chase 1991; Hayes and Hayes 1992b; Hayes *et al.* 1994).

An account of private events cannot be separated from the subject of radical behaviourist interpretation in general. Radical behaviourism differs from methodological behaviourism in its embracing private events as a part of its subject matter (Moore 1994; Baum 1994) Moreover, they are not treated as unobservables, though private events such as thoughts and feelings are observed by only one person. Radical behaviourism *infers*, however, that other people have private events which act as verbal discriminative stimuli for their behaviour (Mackenzie 1988). But this is a far cry still from the treatment of unobservables by social cognitivists: to the radical behaviourist such 'mental way stations' (Skinner 1963) are no more than explanatory fictions that bring inquiry to a premature end by diverting attention from the ultimate causes of behaviour which lie in the environment.

Some behaviour analysts have cast private events as possible proximal causes of behaviour (e.g. Malott and Garcia 1991), though others have argued against this (e.g. Hayes *et al.* 1986), partly on the grounds that only entities that can be manipulated in an experimental analysis of behaviour should be admitted. To assume that private events are proximal causes of behaviour is, nevertheless, to blur the distinction between behaviourist and cognitive modes of explanation (Foxall 1990; Overskeid 1995).

Stimulus Equivalence

Non-humans have proved capable of learning complex relationships if they are appropriately reinforced, but generally do not innovate by initiating relationships they have not been explicitly taught (Lowe 1989). By contrast, even young humans display the emergent behaviour of relating *A* to *C* having been taught that *A* is related to *B* and that *A* is related to *C*. This capacity for transitivity is one of three criteria used to establish *stimulus equivalence*, a phenomenon which appears peculiar to human animals (Dugdale and Lowe 1990). The other criteria are symmetry, i.e., matching *A* to *A*, and reflexivity, i.e., matching *B* to *A* having learned that *A* relates to *B* (Catania 1992a; Sidman 1990, 1992). The implication is that these stimuli (*A*, *B* and *C*) belong to the same *stimulus class*, because they evoke the identical response: for instance, a picture of a car (*A*), the written word 'car' (*B*), and the written word 'auto' (*C*) are all likely to evoke the oral response 'car'; but learning stimuli that belong to the same stimulus class is not sufficient for equivalence.

Stimulus equivalence is relevant to rule-governed behaviour in that a rule and the contingencies it describes presumably belong to the same equivalence class, because they are functionally identical (Dugdale and Lowe 1990; cf. Sidman 1990, 1992).

Consistency of Verbal and Non-Verbal Behaviours

Words and events are linked by a web of contingencies arranged by the verbal community (Catania 1992a: 250). The relationship between what a person says and what he or she does is central to the establishment and maintenance of social life. This is the heart of the attitude–behaviour problem, though in a behavioural analysis the problem is reformulated as that of how and when verbal rules come to guide behaviour (cf. Fazio 1986, 1990). These rules may originate in one of two ways. Either the behaviour may be instructed by others or it may be self-instructed as the individual describes the apparent contingencies to him or herself. An individual's behaviour may be changed, therefore, either by instruction or by shaping what he or she says about it; in the latter case, 'one's own verbal behaviour may thus become effective as an instructional stimulus' (Catania 1992a: 251). Of the two, shaped verbal behaviour has a greater effect on the individual's propensity to act than either direct shaping through modification of the contingencies or instruction (Catania *et al.* 1990: 217).

In other words, encouraging a person to formulate his or her own rules by altering the contingencies that govern their verbal behaviour is the most effective persuasive strategy (though the danger of false rules, leading to superstitious behaviour, is ever-present: Ono 1994). The resulting behaviour is then sensitive to the natural contingencies only to the extent that changes in those contingencies result in changes in the corresponding verbal behaviour (Catania *et al.* 1990: 217).

A corollary of this is that only changes in the contingencies that are mediated by verbal behaviour, *self-instructing*, will change behaviour. None of this implies that behaviour formed through instruction does not come into contact with the contingencies. The natural contingencies remain the ultimate causes of behaviour and, therefore, rule-governed behaviour will at some point become contingency-shaped. Perhaps it is from the contingencies that we can ultimately predict behaviour most successfully, as well as explain it. Hence the contingency category analysis of consumer behaviour must include reference both to rules that are the proximal causes of behaviour and the natural contingencies in which their ultimate causes reside.

Attitudes and Intentions as Verbal Behaviour

Guerin (1994a, 1994b) argues that attitudes and intentions can be behaviouristically interpreted. Hence attitudes constitute 'a generalised affective response to stimuli and contexts': the things that individuals report they like, favour or prefer are those that have relatively strong reinforcing effects (1994a: 236). Beliefs, consisting predominantly of intraverbals (an intraverbal is a verbal response occasioned by a preceding verbal response, as when one recites the alphabet) and tacts do not control either attitudes or overt behaviour, any more than attitudes control behaviour. Attitudes, according to Guerin, are simply a commentary on one's behaviour that one makes to oneself, though we should wish to add that they are an *evaluative* commentary (Lalljee *et al.* 1984). But attitudes are not comments on elusive beliefs or latent behavioural processes: rather, the elements on which they provide a commentary are the individual's overt (public) and covert (private) behaviours.

This goes beyond the simpler behaviouristic stratagem of using the term attitude to describe the consistency of behaviour: while this is sometimes a useful approach (Foxall 1983, 1996a), it fails to acknowledge the evaluative nature of verbal behaviour and its capacity to direct other verbal and nonverbal behaviours: i.e. to provide a truly behaviouristic counterpart to the attitude concept of social cognition. The distinction is that between attitudes as verbal behaviour that is contingency-shaped (under the direct control of the environment) – as in saying that 'This book is enjoyable' because I have been reading it and have found it so – and attitudes under social control – as in saying the same thing about a book I have not read but about which my mentor has expressed a favourable view. The result of an operant analysis of such verbal behaviour is a functional view of attitudes. Functioning as tacts, attitudes may be simply reports on the environment, replies to questions, social rituals or self-regulating verbal behaviours that involve self-reinforcement (Guerin 1994a: 237–8). Expressed to others, attitudes may also function as mands.

The so-called 'problem' of attitudinal–behavioural consistency disappears on this view: both attitudinal and non-attitudinal acts are operant behaviours in their own right, each maintained by its own context of contingencies. Consistency cannot, therefore, be expected unless the contingencies happen to be functionally equivalent, perhaps as a result of a verbal community arranging the contingencies so as to produce consistency. Guerin (1994a) identifies the interesting question for behaviourists as that of isolating the effect of attitudes on the person who hears them spoken; since, as the previous section showed, the verbal control of behaviour falls far short of perfection, the surprising thing is that any degree of consistency at all is observable, especially in view of the large repertoires of behaviour that people have and the reinforcement available for inconsistency (lying, for instance: Sato and Sugiyama 1994).

The compatibility required for the predictive success of the TRA and other models that stress deliberative processing thus demands the verbal detailing of specific contingencies rather than the provision of generalised statements about possible outcomes. Such statements of attitude and intention act as verbal instructions to guide behaviour. Actual responding is predictable from them in circumstances where the individual has control over the contingencies of the situation, where he or she is familiar with behaving in that context and the consequences that have previously followed it. The evaluative beliefs elicited by questionnaires based on such theories actually record what the respondent takes to be the contingencies entailed in acting in a particular way (belief strength) and the likelihood of reinforcement/punishment resulting from the performance of the behaviour in question (evaluation).

The summation of these evaluative beliefs entails the combination of the positive and negative aspects of the contingencies, which Guerin (1994a: 244) likens to 'a multiple contingency matching law for verbally governed behavior'. Both the beliefs and their evaluations have their origins in the individual respondent's learning history. Subjective norm similarly records the contingencies laid down by the respondent's verbal community, reflecting social pressure (Guerin 1992). But learning history is significant here and is overlooked by cognitivists only because it is not immediately obvious, leading to the ontological inference that the causes of behaviour must lie within the individual. Guerin (1994a: 245) sums up:

> The TRA brings together the major variables also dealt with by behaviour analysis: verbally governed behaviour, verbal tacts about contingencies and reports of their value, combining the multiple contingencies involved to get an overall prediction, and the verbal community contingencies.

LOOKING AHEAD

The thinking developed in this chapter can be applied to understanding consumer decision-making from an operant point of view. But before this can be done, we must construct a model that comprehends the limitations imposed by the basic operant paradigm and deals specifically with the requirements of consumer behaviour in the terms of the three-term contingency. The formulation of such a model makes it necessary to define them more closely in three respects (Foxall 1990). First, the nature of the setting variables and the influence they exert must be clarified in view of the complexity of the environments in which human economic behaviour takes place. Second, the nature of reinforcement must be refined in the context of human behaviour that, even in the operant laboratory, is multiply motivated. The nature and influence of consumers' verbal behaviour can then be considered.

5 A Theory of Consumer Situation

OPERANT INTERPRETATION OF CONSUMER BEHAVIOUR

The Meaning of Behaviour

Radical-behaviourist interpretation is a matter of locating behaviour; that is, of reconstructing the contingencies that produced it, without the aid of experimental method. This might easily be misunderstood as imposing external order on observed actions of sentient beings; indeed, operant accounts of contingency-shaped behaviour are often criticised for omitting the actor's 'subjective' experience of situations. In fact, behaviourists have tackled this question of individual reaction by accounting for a person's behaviour within the situation; the account includes consideration of the individual's verbal behaviour, the rule-governance of his or her earlier activities, and the continuity of behaviour over time. This is achieved by reference to the individual's environmental history (Skinner 1974: 77), for the meaning of an operant response is to be found in what has preceded it. According to Skinner – note that the concept of meaning expounded later differs from his – the meaning of an act is not found in the current setting: neither in the discriminative stimuli that compose the setting, nor in the responses that take place there, nor in their outcomes. Rather, it is located solely in the history of exposure to similar contingencies that have brought behaviour under the control of the current situation (p. 91).

Meaning is thus defined in terms of the function of a response, not – as the structuralists would have it – in its topography. And function is determined by the individual's learning history. The meaning of a response is found in the past contingencies that control the topography of current behaviour and empower current discriminative stimuli (Skinner 1974: 91). Thus topographies of behaviour may resemble one another closely, but the meanings of the behaviours may differ markedly. Two customers may buy ties from the same assistant, one right after the other, but the meaning of doing so can be quite different if the first tie is bought as a present (and therefore controlled by a history of gift-giving) while the second is bought for personal use (and controlled by a history of wearing 'ordinary' ties to the office). The meanings do not depend on the reinforcer (the type of tie) but on these histories of buying, giving, wearing, and their outcomes.

The Behavioural Perspective Model

The BPM is a neo-Skinnerian model of situational influence on consumer behaviour in which the responses of consumers are held to be determined by the contingencies of reinforcement under which they are emitted (Skinner 1938, 1953, 1974). Consumers' approach and avoidance/escape behaviours, as well as emotional responses (or, at least, the verbal behaviour by which they are described) are posited to be functions of situational influence: i.e. of the scope of the consumer behaviour-setting defined by the behaviourally contingent reinforcement signalled by the setting elements as they are mobilised by the consumer's learning history (Figure 5.1). The meaning of the behaviour that is emitted in those circumstances is uniquely a product of the interaction between the discriminative stimuli that comprise the behaviour-setting and the individual's history of reinforcement and punishment in similar settings (Foxall 1995b). Consumer behaviour can, therefore, be contextualised in a manner absent from cognitive consumer research in which the mainsprings of overt behaviour are sought in intrapersonal information processing. In the BPM, the consumer's behaviour is located at the intersection of his or her learning history and the current behaviour-setting. These co-ordinates define the *consumer situation*, a device that explains consumer behaviour by locating it in space and time (Foxall 1992b, 1993b).

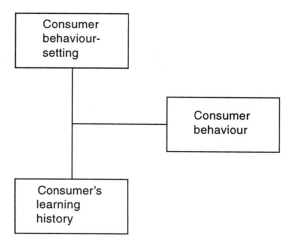

Figure 5.1   Outline BPM

The behavioural perspective model (BPM) proposes that consumer behaviour is situated at the intersection of the behaviour-setting in which it occurs (the spatial perspective) and the learning history of the consumer (the temporal perspective) (Foxall 1990). The resulting synomorphic construct of the *consumer situation* has been used to interpret observed patterns of consumer behaviour, including purchase and consumption, saving and domestic asset management, the adoption and diffusion of innovations and 'green' consumption (Foxall 1993a, 1994a, 1994b, 1994c, 1995c). The interpretation proceeds essentially in terms of the three-term contingency, albeit critically appraised and re-presented in line with the provisions outlined above (Figure 5.2).

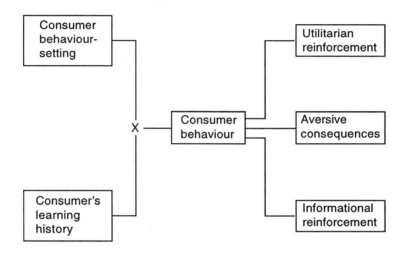

Figure 5.2   Summative behavioural perspective model

Each of the elements of this summation facilitates the interpretation of consumer behaviour as a situationally influenced activity. The resulting model, which complements the social-cognitive interpretations of consumption which currently dominate consumer research (Kardes 1994; Foxall 1997a), introduces to consumer research a three-stage operant interpretation of consumer choice.

The following discussion develops the model through three stages of interpretive detail that successively elaborate the basic representations of Figures 5.1 and 5.2 and locate consumer response with increasing specificity. The first is the *operant classification* of consumer behaviour, which explores the role of different sources of reinforcement in establishing the equifinality class to which an operant consumption response belongs. The second is the allocation of a consumer response to a particular *contingency category*; this means extending the idea that consumer behaviour is located at the intersection of a learning history and a behaviour-setting by showing (a) how these combine to determine the *scope* of the setting, and (b) how consumer-behaviour-setting scope and operant classification are used to locate consumer choice in terms of the overall pattern of environmental contingencies maintaining it. The third, the exploration of the *consumer situation* further elaborates this intersection and shows how the process of consumer decision-making is a function of the spatial/regulatory and historical components of consumer-behaviour-setting scope.

OPERANT CLASSIFICATION

The Consequences of Behaviour

Lee (1988: 135–7) proposes as the first question of operant interpretation, 'What is this person doing?' This is an inquiry into the consequences being produced. Equivalent forms of this question are: 'What is this act?' and 'What is the meaning of this act?'. The traditional answer as we have seen, would be couched exclusively in terms of the individual's learning history. Unfortunately, unlike the learning history of the rat or pigeon whose entire lifetime has been altruistically given over to advancing the experimental analysis of behaviour, that of the middle-aged consumer in Harrods is not empirically available. We might be able to surmise a certain amount, and the consumer might be able to tell us an uncertain amount, but we shall be left wondering whether we have elucidated the current act in terms of a reconstructed environmental history with any validity.

And yet we cannot simply observe the current behaviour and its outcomes in order to uncover its meaning. The problem is that of equifinality. We have already seen that topographically similar responses may produce disparate consequences; so may topographically dissimilar responses belong to the same equifinality class. Ordering a book by mail has a form that is entirely distinct from asking for the same item in a bookstore, but both are functionally equivalent if they have the same outcome. Operant interpretation requires that, in addition to whatever evidence is obtainable for reconstructing the individual's learning history, elements of the current behaviour-setting and the kinds of reinforcement or punishment they prefigure as consequent upon specific responses should also be taken into consideration.

The behavioural perspective model of consumer choice indicates the form which an answer to Lee's question would take in the context of consumer behaviour. Isolating the operant classes relevant to consumer behaviour is not just a case of saying which responses produced 'similar ends'. It can be more sophisticated than that, identifying the sources of reinforcement appropriate to a set of responses that binds them together as an operant.

The Dual Consequences of Consumer Behaviour

Three frequently overlapping disciplines – economic psychology, behavioural economics, and psychological economics – are vitally concerned with the argument that human economic behaviour is not fully explicable in terms of neoclassical economic rationality. Such behaviour also displays a social psychological consistency and rationale, which a full explication of consumer choice must take into account (Katona (1951, 1975; Scitovsky 1986).

Aggregate consumer demand certainly conforms broadly to the strictures of utility theory, and even individual consumer behaviour fulfils the laws of demand in the general sense that consumers seek utilitarian benefits and usually settle for more value than less; but they do not do so always, and there are often 'lapses' that do not lend themselves to an exclusively economic explanation. Any explication of the totality of consumer behaviour must recognise that it is under the dual control of, on the one hand, its utilitarian/economic consequences and, on the other, those additional outcomes that consist in social status and the feelings reported self-esteem.

Economists have usually ignored or been unable to deal professionally with the social psychological causation of consumer behaviour (Mason 1988; see also Earl 1988a, 1988b, 1990). The behavioural perspective model is founded upon two variables that capture the social psychological influences on consumer behaviour. Each of these variables is based on a conception of social psychological influence relative to a significant counter-influence. First, the concept of consumer behaviour-setting scope contrasts social with individual influences on responding. For consumer behaviour-setting scope indicates how far persons other than the consumer control the settings in which consumption occurs. This continuum thus provides a measure of personal versus social locus of control. Second, the ratio of instrumental informational reinforcement allows social psychological influences (informational reinforcers) to be contrasted with economic influences (utilitarian reinforcement). For the ratio of utilitarian to informational reinforcement indicates how far the consequences of a consumer's actions are supplied by others (in the form of social approval or socially-learned feelings of self-esteem) rather than by the requirements of the consumer's biological and innate individual constitution. Despite the protestations of some behaviour analysts (e.g. Guerin 1994a) that feedback is not reinforcement, because of the post-response delay in its presentation, its capacity to reinforce behaviour cannot be denied. Such delay is, in any case, the province of verbal behaviour, of rule-governance, and of the question of stimulus equivalence on which informational reinforcement undoubtedly depends (Foxall 1997a).

Bifurcation of Reinforcement

The consumer behaviour-setting – a store, a library, an opera-house, or a crack dealership – consists of four kinds of such elements or discriminative stimuli: physical, social, temporal and regulatory. These antecedent stimuli signal the possibility of three kinds of consequence. The first is utilitarian reinforcement, which we define as consisting in the functional properties (economic and technical) of the reinforcer, often reported verbally in term of the satisfaction that consuming them brings.

Utilitarian reinforcement consists in the practical outcomes of purchase and consumption – the functional benefit, value-in-use, economic/pragmatic/material satisfactions received by consumers as a result of acquiring, owning and/or using an economic product or service. It is purely instrumental, consisting in itself and for itself; it is concrete and likely to be constant across social systems. Incentives are usually of this kind.

Hence, utilitarian reinforcement arises from the characteristics of the product or service obtained in purchase or used in consumption; this corresponds to the use of utility in economics to refer to 'the direct satisfaction that goods and services yield to their possessors' (Gould and Kolb 1964: 303, 740). Utility theory in economics derives essentially from the psychology of hedonism (Viner 1925; Black 1987; Griffin and Parfitt 1987; Menger 1956). Hence, while utilitarian reinforcement is akin to value-in-use, it derives not only from the functional performance of a product or service but from the feelings associated with owning and consuming it. In addition to the functions performed by a product or service, utilitarian consequences of consumption include the positive affect generated in the process. Utilitarian reinforcement refers, therefore, to all of the benefits derived directly from possession and application of a product or service, it is reinforcement mediated by the product or service; and it inheres in the use-value of the commodity.

Informational reinforcement, by contrast, is symbolic, usually mediated by the responsive actions of others, and closely akin to exchange value. It consists not in information *per se* but in feedback on an individual's performance. Informational reinforcement attests to the level of correctness or appropriateness of a person's performance as a consumer; whereas utilitarian reinforcement stems from economic and functional payoffs of buying and using goods, informational reinforcement results from the level of social status, prestige and acceptance achieved by a consumer by his or her efforts. It is usually publicly determined, judged by others according to the rules, and thus of primarily social significance. In as much as it is mediated by other people, it is verbal (Skinner 1957), consisting in speech, in gestures and – where the individual provides his or her own informational reinforcement and thus becomes the 'other' person – in private thoughts (Skinner 1974).

From the viewpoint of the consumer, informational reinforcement rests on a comparative judgement of how well he or she is using time and energy relative to other uses to which they would be put: 'How well am I exchanging my time and effort for the acquisition of groceries?' If the consumer is being relatively inefficient, he or she may either speed up the shopping trip or postpone purchasing further items. If efficient, they can use the time and energy left over to accomplish something else. From the social viewpoint, the public consumption of a prestigious product or service is exchanged for the goodwill, praise, positive responses and so on of others, i.e., for esteem and social status.

The feedback on the level of performance or achievement of the consumer in which informational reinforcement consists takes one or both of two forms, public and private. Public informational reinforcement is the social honour, esteem or status accorded by others for the position achieved or level of accomplishment conferred on the consumer for his conspicuous acquisition, ownership, or use of products and services. It may be positive, when the product or service is valued by the social group, or negative, when it is despised. Private informational reinforcement consists in the individual's own evaluative reaction to his performance: it may take the form of a verbal 'slap on the back', a silent or at least solitary 'Well done!' given oneself by oneself. It may also be accompanied by such collateral (though not epiphenomenal) responses as feelings described as pride and self-esteem. These responses may act as reinforcers in the BPM framework, though strictly speaking in a radical behaviourist interpretation they are ascribed only the status of responses. Public or private, informational reinforcement is symbolic, representative, referential, cultural; the behaviours it reinforces are likely to differ sharply from social system to social system.

In short, *utilitarian* reinforcement refers to the acceptance of positive benefits of purchasing, owning or consuming economic products and services (goods); these benefits are functional, conferring material satisfactions, the utility of orthodox microeconomic theory. Utilitarian reinforcers are frequently referred to as incentives, both in general discourse and in applied behaviour analysis. *Informational* reinforcement is performance feedback, an indication of how well the consumer is doing. It may confer social status and/or self-satisfaction, or may simply constitute a reference point denoting progress to date. Informational reinforcement is associated with verbal behaviour, because the meaning of the behaviour is always mediated by a person who is usually someone other than the actor but may perhaps be himself or herself. There is empirical evidence that utilitarian and informational reinforcement have separate influences on behaviour not only in human operant experiments conducted under laboratory conditions (Wearden 1988), but also in token economy studies and in the field experiments of applied behaviour analysis directed towards the reduction of environmentally deleterious consumption (Foxall 1995b, 1996b).

The distinction between utilitarian and informational sources of reinforcement is empirically supported (Foxall 1996a). First, there is the empirical finding that human operant performance in the laboratory is often relatively insensitive to material reinforcers such as points, money and food but highly sensitive to performance feedback in the form of graphs and listings of achievement, especially relative achievement in a competitive setting (Wearden 1988).

Second, research into environment-impacting consumer behaviour has found that reinforcers of two distinct kinds influence the rate at which consumers will ride the bus or share transportation rather than use private cars, reduce domestic energy consumption, and avoid destructive waste-disposal. One class of reinforcer, 'incentives', is primarily utilitarian: prizes, money and gifts, for example, while another class, 'feedback', is informational: records of the amount of electricity saved, miles foregone, personal recognition. While the first class consists in direct benefits of altered consumption patterns, the second is symbolic, conveyed verbally (including words and gestures) and has a wider, social significance. Moreover, a considerable volume of field-experimental findings indicates that these classes of reinforcer have separate and distinct effects on rate responding (Cone and Hayes 1980).

Finally, there are aversive consequences, which, if suffered, reduce the chance of this behaviour being repeated. A defining characteristic of economic behaviour, since it includes a reciprocal transfer of rights, lies in its being simultaneously reinforced and punished (Alhadeff 1982; see also Chapter 4). It incurs reinforcement and punishment as direct and specific consequences of its being performed. Economic behaviour is determined by the interaction of two response strengths: approach and avoidance, each of which is dependent upon the consumer's learning history, the quality and quantity of reinforcement, reinforcement schedules, and so on (Alhadeff 1982).

Contingency- and Rule-Derived Reinforcement

The usual functional distinction made of reinforcers is between primary and secondary. *Primary reinforcers* such as sexual gratification, water and food are effective from birth and for almost all species. Their effectiveness is not contingent upon their relationship with other reinforcers; the apparent biological determination of these inherent reinforcers has led to their being known as *natural*. *Secondary reinforcers* acquire their capacity to influence the rate of behaviour in the course of the individual's experience; their power to do so depends upon their being repeatedly paired with primary reinforcers. An example is money, with which many primary reinforcers can be obtained. Some authors (e.g. Lieberman 1993, pp. 204–6) also speak of *social reinforcers*, including praise, affection and attention, which are a combination of primary and secondary reinforcers.

A more useful functional distinction in the present context is between *contingency-derived reinforcers* and *rule-derived reinforcers*. Contingency-derived reinforcers are both primary and secondary. Their effect is apparent in the contingency-shaping of behaviour; it derives from the impact that behaviour has directly upon its environment. These reinforcers are generally associated with pleasurable effects for the individual who is in a state of reinforcer deprivation (though behaviour analysts usually avoid the notion that something is reinforcing because it is pleasant). But evolution has required that most acts whose rate is influenced by primary reinforcers have pleasant outcomes: eating sugar and avoiding pain, for instance. Secondary reinforcers such as foods, furniture, housing, and music usually also have a utilitarian effect. Contingency-derived reinforcers are, therefore, *utilitarian* reinforcers. (Though, in human contexts, rules may be implicated in the pairing of primary and secondary stimuli.)

Rule-derived reinforcers have their effect only by virtue of being specified in rules – e.g. social groups rule that money is a measure of individual prestige as well as a medium of exchange. None of these derives its reinforcing power from 'nature'; none is a reinforcer from the organism's birth. They are only useful/reinforcing in so far as they are symbols, i.e. as they point to something else – a level of performance, success, access to a job, etc. Rule-derived reinforcers are social and verbal; their effect is on behaviour that is mediated by others (where 'the other' may be the individual himself or herself). Such instructed behaviour, the verbal behaviour of the listener, is reinforced by the individual's level of achievement of socially (or personally) prescribed goals; the behaviour consists of pliance or tracking. In the case of pliance, the informational reinforcement derives from the praise, recognition, acknowledgement extended by the mediating individual(s) to the rule-follower. (Informational punishment would be the result of non-compliance or counter-compliance.) In the case of tracking, the informational reinforcement derives from consonance between the physical environment as it is experienced and as it was described by the mediating individual (who may the behaver). (Informational punishment would result from a lack of such consonance.) These reinforcers are always secondary. They derive power from the social status and/or self-esteem conferred as a result of the behaviours they maintain. Rule-derived reinforcers are, therefore, *informational* reinforcers.

It may be worth emphasising here that no one-to-one mapping of primary/secondary reinforcement onto utilitarian/informational reinforcement is implied by this reasoning. Primary reinforcement emphasises utilitarian but may, in humans at least, have an informational component. Human awareness and competitiveness can, for instance, make success in survival a matter of status. Secondary reinforcement involves both utilitarian and informational reinforcers: by definition, the required pairing requires both; by demonstration, consumer operants comprise elements of each. Social/verbal reinforcement emphasises informational consequences but entails the emergent utilitarian consequences included in social status and self-esteem. Table 5.1 summarises.

Table 5.1   Sources of reinforcement

Contingency-derived	Primary reinforcement	Utilitarian (plus informational)
Contingency-derived (may be rule-assisted)	Secondary	Utilitarian and informational
Rule-derived	Social/verbal	Informational (plus utilitarian)

Hence the most we can deduce with respect to the distinction between contingency-shaped and rule-governed behaviour is this: the former is shaped and maintained *predominantly* by utilitarian reinforcement, the latter *predominantly* by informational reinforcement.

Nor should the impression be given that we are speaking here of utilitarian and informational reinforcers as inalienably distinct entities as though there were some things or events that always and invariably reinforce via utility while others always and invariably reinforce informationally. We are speaking of the functions of reinforcers. Function is always determined by the situation. Most things or events that are consequences of behaviour have both utilitarian and informational functions: jewellery is mainly informational but also performs a utilitarian function; air conditioners are principally utilitarian but may add to one's social status. (This applies especially in a West European country where they are relatively scarce as compared with the US. Even in North America, an air-conditioned car may confer some status; it certainly does in Britain.)

Primary and secondary reinforcers are often differentiated on the basis of the speed with which they cease to reinforce. Primary reinforcers are permanent and universal in their effectiveness; but there is no logical reason why secondary reinforcers should be either: money may give way to bartered goods as a means of exchange in some circumstances; horse-drawn carriages are seldom as functionally useful in industrial societies today as they were in the rural societies of a century ago. Informational reinforcers are more contingent still upon social usages: fashions, forms of address, fad products, etc., quickly cease to reinforce and may punish when they no longer confer membership of a group. Powdered wigs may, alas, be gone forever.

Moreover, the effects of utilitarian and informational reinforcers may be mutually strengthening. Since informational reinforcement is contrived and symbolic, its power stems ultimately from its pairing with contingency-derived or utilitarian reinforcement. It reinforces only in so far as it is linked with the reinforcers provided by the contingencies themselves, only as the rules it reflects are consonant with those environmental contingencies. Hence the behaviours that confer informational reinforcement lead ultimately to pleasure just as surely as do the utilitarian reinforcers with which they are associated. Where those utilitarian reinforcers are secondary, they are effective only as they are related to primary reinforcers. This is only to say that the ultimate reinforces are always primary – natural, non-contingent, biological. The BPM classification of consumer operants reflects this: all four operant classes of consumer behaviour are reinforced by a combination of utilitarian and informational reinforcement rather than by one or other of these.

Since this is a functional classification of reinforcers, any particular item such as money might have both utilitarian and informational effects. Money has generally been regarded as a secondary reinforcer that derives its power from the primary reinforcers that can be acquired with it. But it can also play the role of an informational reinforcer: social status and self-esteem both stem from the performance feedback provided by a high salary or bank balance. Operationally, therefore, the interpretation of the meaning of money will depend upon the situation under investigation. Furthermore, operational measures of utilitarian and informational reinforcement (whether these are being used in a quantitative analysis or qualitative interpretation of consumer behaviour) must reflect the pleasurable/utilitarian and social/personal functions of reinforcers respectively. That is, we should look for expressions (verbal and non-verbal) of pleasure or usefulness in order to identify utilitarian reinforcers; and for considerations of status/self-esteem in order to identify informational reinforcers.

Operant Classes of Consumer Behaviour

We can now elaborate our understanding of the nature of an operant class as applied to consumer choice. An *operant class* of consumer behaviour consists of a set of responses that, irrespective of their topographical similarities or dissimilarities, correspond in terms of the pattern of reinforcement which maintains them, i.e. the configuration of relatively high/relatively low utilitarian reinforcement and relatively high/relatively low informational reinforcement associated with their continuance.

The actual procedure by which these four classes of behaviour were initially derived is as follows (see Foxall 1990). On the basis of the BPM reinforcer variables, four theoretical classes were known to be possible: high, high; high, low; low, high; and low, low. Broad kinds of consumer behaviour were allocated to each of these on the basis of the definitions of utilitarian and informational reinforcement and the responses maintained by 'incentives' and 'feedback' in the applied behaviour analysis of environmental conservation. Only when this had been done satisfactorily were labels attached to the operant classes.

The first operant class suggests behaviours that supply high levels of incentive and high levels of status/esteem. Activities leading to personal accomplishment seem to belong here: for instance cultural pursuits that confer social status in addition to the intrinsic pleasures of engaging in them.

Consumer behaviours maintained by a high level of utilitarian reinforcement but, relatively speaking, a low level of informational reinforcement suggest entertainments, pleasures, the amelioration of one's own suffering; in short the hedonistic activities involved in increasing one's pleasure and/or decreasing one's pain.

Where informational reinforcement is high but utilitarian relatively low, the characteristic behaviours indicate saving and collecting. Incremental acquisition is not without its satisfactions from day to day or week to week and ultimately such behaviour depends upon the utilitarian benefits of having the products in question. But the behaviours of gradually saving and collecting are maintained from week to week or whatever by feedback on performance: How much interest has my saving attracted? How many more points do I need for the bonus gift? How soon do these magazines transform themselves into an encyclopaedia?

Finally, there are behaviours maintained by relatively low levels of both utilitarian and informational reinforcement. These ought to include activities that are routine or mandatory, the minimal consumer responses one needs to effect to stay alive or duties one must perform to continue to exist as a citizen.

These four operant classes of consumer behaviour can be described, respectively, as accomplishment, hedonism, accumulation and maintenance (summarised by the acronym AHAM). (In order to avoid tedium, the qualifying 'relatively' is henceforth omitted, though utilitarian/informational reinforcements are always relative, as are open and closed consumer behaviour-settings). Table 5.2 summarises the classification.

Table 5.2   Operant classification of consumer behaviour

	High utilitarian reinforcement	Low utilitarian reinforcement
High informational reinforcement	ACCOMPLISHMENT	ACCUMULATION
Low informational reinforcement	HEDONISM	MAINTENANCE

An understanding of the probable consequences of current consumer behaviour, which have through prior generation presumably brought the consumer to the current behaviour-setting, is intended as a response to the problem of equifinality. Each of these classes is an operant equifinality class: placing the behaviour in question in one or other of these is the first stage in locating that behaviour. Only by isolating these consequences, an act that partly supplements and partly acts as a surrogate for a full reconstruction of the consumer's learning history, can we propose an answer to Lee's second question of operant interpretation, 'What has been done?'. In other words, 'What ends have been achieved?' and 'How is the action effective?'.

Figure 5.3 summarises the *operant classification level of analysis* within the BPM framework.

CONTINGENCY CATEGORY ANALYSIS

Consumer Behaviour-Setting Scope

The *consumer behaviour-setting* consists of the current discriminative stimuli that signal reinforcement and punishment contingent upon the emission of a purchase or consumption response. The discriminative stimuli that compose the setting may be physical (e.g. point-of-sale advertising, the product array, a store logo), social (principally the physical presence of co-shoppers, other diners in a restaurant, the waiter, the salesperson), temporal (the hours of opening of a store, the duration of a special offer, Christmas) or regulatory (self- and other-rules that specify contingencies). Rule-governed behaviour is actually a social phenomenon but deserves separate treatment (Guerin 1994a; Hyten and Burns 1986). In addition to the suggestion of several behaviour analysts that operant principles are most clearly visible in the control of behaviour in settings such as a factory, an army or a school, there is abundant evidence for this distinction in the operant literature on consumer behaviour. Token economies are relatively closed settings in which consumer behaviour conforms very strictly to the ordinal utility theory of microeconomics (which is operant), to the extent of being delineable by demand curves. Consumer behaviour investigated in the field experiments of applied behaviour analysis is clearly under environmental control, but not to the same degree.

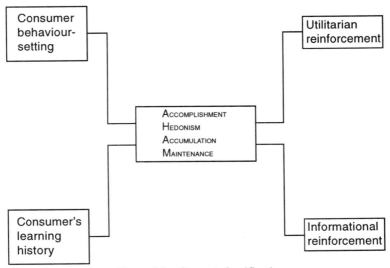

Figure 5.3   Operant classification

The extent to which consumer behaviour can be attributed unambiguously to control by environmental contingencies varies with the *scope* of the setting in which it takes place. The animal laboratory, from which principles of operant behaviourism were derived, presents a particularly closed setting, one in which the elements of the three-term contingency can be objectively identified and behaviour therefore traced unambiguously to its environmental effects. The further behaviour-settings stray from this degree of closedness, the harder it is for the operant psychologist to ascribe activities within them unreservedly to operant conditioning. Even in the animal laboratory, there exists scope for alternative interpretations: in terms, for instance, of classical conditioning or cognitive decision-making. The human operant laboratory, for example, presents a less closed context, one from which escape is relatively easy; while non-humans face no option but being in the setting, human participants on occasion remove themselves from the experimental situation.

The settings in which human consumer behaviour takes place are more open still: though a continuum of such settings is evident, from the relatively closed confines of a large group awareness training session to the relatively open variety store. Closed and open settings may also be distinguished in terms of the verbal behaviour that characterises each. In closed settings, the other-instructions and contingencies are precise: in order to get a passport, a consumer must obey the rules to the letter. In open settings, the consumer has more control over his or her behaviour through self-instructions, and specific other rules are less likely to be determinative.

There may be several other-rule configurations to 'choose' among; further, there is the possibility of behaviour being directly controlled by the contingencies: as one spots new products, devises new ways of finding presents, and so on. Even if the view is taken that most consumer behaviour is rule-governed, open settings allow self-rules to a far greater extent than closed. Moreover, human behaviour that is entirely contingency-shaped is rare. Self-rules, devised and followed by the same individual, are particularly effective instructions, which may be more isolated from the contingencies than other-rules (Catania *et al*. 1990: 227).

Thus *behaviour-setting scope* is the extent to which the current consumer behaviour-setting compels a particular pattern of behaviour (as a national opera house induces people to wear evening dress, remain seated and silent during arias, and applaud wildly at the end; compare a rock concert where one is free to walk about, shout, sing, smoke, eat and drink and do many other things during the performance). The scope of the former is said to be (relatively) closed; that of the latter (relatively) open.

The Role of Learning History

The importance of learning history is amply demonstrated by the repeated finding that prior behaviour is an important determinant of current responding. We have seen that it is not sufficient to attribute the influence of prior behaviour simply to 'habit', which is to redescribe it rather than explain it. The continuance of behaviour is to be accounted for by the consequences it produces and whether or not a stream of behaviour is continued into the near future depends on the stimulus control that influences it and the maintenance of the pattern of reinforcement that is its distal cause.

The deliberative processing models such as the TRA are centrally concerned with the self-reported consequences of behaving in a given way, which constitutes a personal summary of the respondent's learning history. The elicitation of subjective norm beliefs and evaluations is also indicative of a history of rule-compliance. The spontaneous processing models emphasise direct experience with the attitude object, which both constitutes a learning history in itself and serves to establish the attitude object as a discriminative stimulus for further responding. The rehearsal of attitude statements, especially if they have their origin in other-instructions, constitutes prior verbal behaviour, which also exerts an environmental influence on the probability of current responding.

The potency of a learning history is manifested within a particular behaviour-setting: prior learning establishes what will act as a discriminative stimulus in that setting by embodying the consequences, reinforcing and punishing, of earlier behaviour in the presence of the relevant setting elements. The functional approach to attitude theory and research taken by Shavitt (1989) corroborates the BPM by indicating several functions of behavioural consequence in controlling verbal and non-verbal current responding (usually via preceding verbal behaviour/instructional control). The bases of the attitude functions she proposes appear closely related to the nature of the reinforcement associated with these products – utilitarian (utilitarian) and informational (social identity). The distinction between utilitarian and informational reinforcement is consonant with that between the utilitarian and social identity functions of attitudes (Shavitt 1989). Shavitt argues that the function of a person's attitude towards an air conditioner is principally utilitarian

> because one's attitude toward it should be based largely on rewards (e.g., comfort) and punishments (e.g., high energy bills) intrinsically associated with it . . . One's attitude toward an air conditioner should guide behaviors that maintain the rewards and avoid the punishments associ-

ated with this object (e.g., using the air conditioner on a hot day, turning it off at times to conserve energy). (p. 324)

However, an individual's attitude towards a wedding ring performs contrasting functions:

One's attitude toward it should be based largely on what it symbolizes. Furthermore, wedding rings are worn (in public) primarily to communicate information to others about the wearer, and one's attitude toward wedding rings and what they symbolize should guide this behavior. (ibid.)

The components of Eagly and Chaiken's (1993) composite model of attitude–behaviour relationships are also supportive of the BPM: all of the determinants of attitude towards behaviour – habit, attitudes towards the target, utilitarian, normative and self-identity outcomes – are indicative of learning history. Habits form only if the behaviour of which they are composed is sequentially reinforced; attitudes towards target develop only through experience; and, although conceptualised as expectations of what will result from behaving in a specified way, the outcomes can result only from environmental history, either in the form of contingency-shaping or through instruction. Moreover, utilitarian outcomes closely resemble the utilitarian reinforcement of the BPM, while normative (including self-identity) outcomes are akin to informational reinforcement.

The BPM links past behaviour, behaviour-setting elements, and outcomes by arguing that learning history primes elements of the setting to act as discriminative stimuli for utilitarian and informational reinforcement/ punishment contingent upon the performance of specific responses. The BPM provides an alternative, non-cognitive synthesis of empirical results gained in both attitude research and operant investigations of instructed behaviour.

The BPM Contingency Matrix

The second stage, then, in locating consumer behaviour is to summarise the probable effect of behaviour-setting stimuli on the probability of an approach or avoidance response currently taking place. The BPM proposes eight general contingency categories defined by the operant class to which the situated behaviour in question belongs and the scope of the behaviour-setting in which it occurs (Figure 5.4). Allocating consumer behaviour to one or other of these on a functional basis (i.e., in terms of the consequences produced and the stimuli that signal them) takes place, then, at a second level of analysis.

By employing dichotomous variables to represent the causative elements of the model, actual consumer situations can be categorised among eight contingency configurations, depending on whether the consumer behaviour-setting is relatively closed or relatively open, whether utilitarian reinforcement is relatively high or low, and whether informational reinforcement is relatively high or low.

A *contingency category* summarises the contingencies of reinforcement pertaining to a set of consumer situations. It thus presents in outline the pattern of reinforcement that typically maintains the response in question, and the scope of the consumer behaviour-setting in which it occurs. Since pattern of reinforcement is defined by the relative levels of two sources of reinforcer, utilitarian and informational, there are eight contingency categories (shown in the BPM contingency matrix, Figure 5.4).

The BPM contingency matrix suggests a *functional* typology of consumer situations: the placing of any particular consumer behaviour within this scheme depends on the pattern of utilitarian and informational reinforcement that maintains it. Saving up belongs in CC5 because it is primarily maintained by expressive reinforcement, secondarily by instrumental. The behaviour is best regarded as 'accumulation'. But collecting antiques would be CC1 or CC2 because it is 'accomplishment': behaviour maintained by high levels of both instrumental and expressive reinforcement.

The consumer situations and behaviours assigned to each of these eight contingency categories are defined functionally rather than morphologically, and topographically identical behaviours may be assigned at different times to difference operant classes and contingency categories depending on the interpretation of the combination of contingencies maintaining them. The labels employed in Figure 5.4 are, therefore, ultimately arbitrary, though they have proved useful in the interpretation of consumer behaviour (Foxall 1994a). Some topographically similar behaviours can be allocated to more than one contingency category, depending on the particular environmental determinants that are to be emphasised. Status consumption involves both aspects of expressive reinforcement: status and/or self-esteem. Collecting, for instance, may not be a public affair: personal (private) reinforcement may be to the fore as the joy of acquisition and ownership, etc.

The BPM was initially conceived primarily as an interpretive device. In this section we explore how it might be applied to the description of consumer behaviour as it relates to the environmentally located contingencies that apparently maintain it. In other words, despite the qualification made

Behaviour-setting scope

	Closed	Open
ACCOMPLISHMENT (high utilitarian, high informational)	Contingency category 2 *Fulfilment*	Contingency category 1 *Status consumption*
HEDONISM (high utilitarian, low informational)	Contingency category 4 *Inescapable entertainment pleasure*	Contingency category 3 *Popular entertainment*
ACCUMULATION (low utilitarian, high informational)	Contingency category 6 *Token-based consumption*	Contingency category 5 *Saving and collecting*
MAINTENANCE (low utilitarian, low informational)	Contingency category 8 *Mandatory consumption*	Contingency category 7 *Routine purchasing*

Figure 5.4   The BPM contingency matrix

above that the BPM operant classification and the contingency matrix are based upon functional possibilities rather than upon final taxonomies of consumer behaviours, is it possible to allocate broad examples of consumer choice to each of the contingency categories, at least on a provisional basis? Single responses such as browsing, inspecting, signing, paying, transporting, preparation and using are to be found within any of the categories, but do more molar patterns of consumer behaviour *reasonably* belong to specific classes and categories, given the logic on which the classification and the matrix were constructed? There is no harm in making the attempt so long as our surmising is at some stage open to empirical examination.

Therefore, arbitrary or useful as they must ultimately be, the following generalised descriptions of consumer behaviours and situations that appear to belong to each of the contingency categories provide a summary of consumer choice in relation to the contingencies that maintain it.

Accomplishment

'Accomplishment' in an open setting consists in general in the *purchase and consumption of status goods*. A familiar instance is pre-purchase consumer behaviour for luxuries and radical innovations such as TV satellite dishes, video recorders, exotic vacations, and home computers. These behaviours, including window-shopping and browsing, involve search for and comparative evaluation of information about many products and services. Most of the items in question are possessed and used for the pleasure or ease of living they confer, the well-being they make possible for the individual: they thereby provide extensive hedonic rewards. But they are often status symbols, and their conspicuous consumption also strengthens the behaviour in question. They attest directly, and often publicly and unambiguously, to the consumer's attainments, especially economic. Goods in this category are usually highly differentiated – by novel function in the case of innovations, by branding in the case of luxuries.

In a closed setting, 'accomplishment' can be generally described as *fulfilment*. In such a context, it comprises personal attainments gained through leisure, often with a strong element of recreation or excitement as well as achievement. This category refers to the material contribution to *fulfilment* and could include both the completion of a personal development seminar such as Insight and gambling in a casino. Gambling in so closed a setting is an activity maintained by both hedonic and informational consequences. In addition, few consumer behaviours are maintained so thoroughly by social rules. All these elements of the setting unambiguously signal both the positive consequences of approved approach behaviours and the potentially punishing implications of escape or avoidance responses which flout established rules and gaming conventions. Although several games may be available in the casino, there is one principal reinforcer: winning. Pleasure and social approval stem mainly from success, though a certain amount of enjoyment and prestige may be derived from being part of a somewhat exclusive social group and conforming to its code of behaviour. Closely defined acts must be performed in order to participate, including obtaining membership, dressing appropriately, and entering the game at the right time and in an acceptable manner.

Hedonism

In an open setting, this behaviour generally consists of *popular entertainment*. Obvious examples are watching television game shows, which provide near-constant hedonic reward, and the reading of mass fiction, which contains a sensation on almost every page. Personal cassette players and VCRs have made such reinforcement more immediate to the point of its being ubiquitous. Mass culture presents frequent and predictable, relatively strong and continuous hedonic rewards, which are not contingent on long periods of concentrated effort. Indeed, the arrangement of reinforcers is such that viewing, listening or reading for even a short interval is likely to be rewarded. Informational feedback is more obvious on some occasions than others, as when game shows allow the audience to pit their own performances against that of the competing participants, but it is not the main source of reward.

Hedonism in closed settings consists as a generalisation of *inescapable entertainment* and amelioration. The behaviours in question are potentially pleasurable but – in this context – may be irksome because they are unavoidable. As a result, consumption of these products and services may be passive rather than active. An example is the situation in which long-distance airline passengers must purchase meals and movies along with their travel. The meals are usually consumed, like the in-flight movies that follow them, without alternative. The setting, which cannot be other than highly restrictive if one is to arrive safely, is further closed by the pulling of blinds, the disappearance of cabin staff, the impossibility of moving around the plane, and the attention of one's fellow passengers to the movie. To try to read or engage in other activities may invite censure.

Accumulation

In an open setting, 'accumulation' is generally described as *saving and collecting*. For example, purchases for which payments are made prior to consumption – instalments for a holiday that can only be taken once the full amount has been paid. Another example is payments into a Christmas club. Discretionary saving, with the intention of making a large purchase once a certain amount has accumulated, would fall into this category, too. Promotional deals requiring the accumulation of coupons or other tokens before a product or service can be obtained also belong here. The important reward, in every case, is informational: feedback on how much one has accumulated, and thus how close one is to the ultimate reinforcer.

Accumulation occurring in a closed setting may be described, in general terms, as *token-based buying*. This also involves collecting – through schemes in which payment for one item provides tokens that will pay for another. Although some examples of this are quite recent, the practice is simply an extension of the familiar prize schemes open to collectors of cigarette cards or trading stamps. For example, the 'airmiles' earned by frequent flyers on domestic and international airlines constitute informational reinforcers (Chesanow 1985). Some hotels also offer gifts to customers who accumulate points by staying there frequently. The collection of these tokens is reinforced by gaining additional free air travel or hospitality, or by access to different types of reinforcer such as prizes. Purchase and consumption of the basic product, the air travel or accommodation originally demanded, are maintained by both the intrinsic hedonic rewards they embody and the feedback on progress that is being made towards the ultimate incentive. The setting is said to be relatively closed, because the first item would probably be purchased anyway in some form or other and the consumer's income constraint makes it likely that the second or backup reinforcer would be obtained only in this way.

Maintenance

In an open setting, 'maintenance' may be generally described as *routine purchasing and consumption*. This includes the regular buying of goods necessary for survival. For example, the habitual purchasing of grocery items at a supermarket. Consumer behaviour in these circumstances is indeed routine: it occurs as if reinforcement were available only at fixed intervals. Further, contrary to the usual depiction, the frequent consumer of – say – baked beans is highly rational, having tried and evaluated many brands in the relevant product class. But his or her behaviour is not static: again in contrast to the received wisdom of the marketing texts, comparatively few such consumers are brand-loyal in the sense of always choosing the identical brand in a long sequence of shopping trips. There is so much choice that the consumer enjoys considerable discretion among versions of the product (Ehrenberg 1972).

Maintenance is generally characterised in closed settings as *mandatory purchase and consumption*. It includes all forms of consumer behaviour necessary to remain a citizen: the payment of taxes for public and collective goods, for instance; less extremely, it includes payments into pension schemes linked to employment, payments of endowment insurance premiums linked to mortgages. To this extent, maintenance is the consumer behaviour inherent in pursuing the normal business of citizenship. In the workplace, it may include the enforced use of areas under smoking bans (Owen *et al.* 1991), which, for smokers, represent a severe limitation on behaviour (though for non-smokers, particularly the allergic, they constitute an opening of the setting, a measure that permits a wider range of behaviours).

We can better understand the BPM in terms of these analytical developments by representing it as in Figure 5.5. At this second level of analysis it is important to take account of the punishing utilitarian and informational consequences of consumer behaviour. Although these do not enter into the operant classification of consumer behaviour, in so far as they are signalled by discriminative stimuli, they are important determinants of the scope of consumer behaviour-settings.

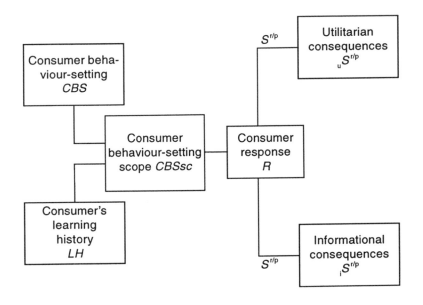

Note:
$S^{r/p}$ is the process of reinforcement or punishment; u stands for utilitarian, and i for *informational*.

Figure 5.5   Consumer behaviour-setting scope

THE CONSUMER SITUATION

The third level of interpretive analysis is that of the consumer situation. The significance of this construct requires its distinction from that of consumer behaviour-setting scope. A *consumer behaviour-setting* comprises the discriminative stimuli which signal the likely consequences of emitting a particular response, i.e. the probable levels of utilitarian and informational reinforcement, and that of aversive outcome. In other words, it provides a summary of the reinforcement and punishment contingent upon the performance of the requisite response. This is an abstract definition, general and theoretical, because it is dependent on other variables (the consumer's learning and evolutionary histories, for instance) in order to have a concrete influence on behaviour (Foxall 1993b).

Consumer behaviour-setting scope is the extent to which the consumer's current behaviour is narrowly determined by elements of the behaviour-setting in which it is located. It is determined not only by the elements of the behaviour-setting (social and physical surroundings, temporal frame, regulatory frame) but by the consumer's history of behaving in similar settings and the consequences of having done so. Consumer behaviour-settings of varying scope may be arrayed on a continuum of closed–open consumer behaviour-settings, with the most closed setting controlling the nature of the consumer's responses entirely and predictably and the most open setting having minimal external control over behaviour that is accordingly much more difficult to predict. Hence, the proposed route from environment to behaviour is as shown in Figure 5.6.

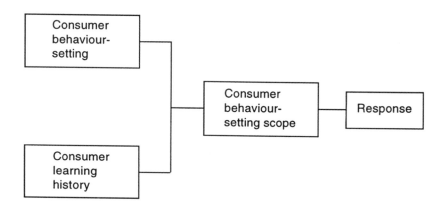

Figure 5.6   Consumer situation 1

This is a somewhat more operational idea of the immediate determinant of consumer response: consumer behaviour-setting *scope* comprehends both the setting and the consumer's learning history, which 'activates' the setting elements, converting some of them from neutral stimuli into discriminative stimuli that bring behaviour under stimulus control. However, this is still a rather abstract depiction of environment–behaviour relationships. To that extent and, since these concepts are not unobservables posited at some other realm than observed behaviour, both consumer behaviour-setting and consumer behaviour-setting scope may be considered examples of the kinds of descriptive theoretical entity that can organise collections of facts, for which Skinner (1947) called. Note that the contingency analysis involved in deciding upon the scope of a consumer behaviour-setting is on a macro-level: strictly speaking, from it we can predict the operant class to which the consumer's response belongs.

However, a *consumer situation* is a particular (concrete, real world) consumer behaviour-setting and a learning history. It is delineated by the synomorphic presence of a given individual (who embodies a behavioural learning history and an evolutionary history) and a specific consumer behaviour-setting, e.g. John Smith at the barber's. This is a more empirically available entity, not in the sense that it comprises data while the preceding notions of consumer behaviour-setting and consumer behaviour-setting scope were hypothetical constructs, but in as much as it is amenable to direct observation in and of itself rather than a précis of empirical relationships at a disaggregated level. It is a description of a situation that has potential for influencing/determining behaviour or making it more predictable.

Diagrammatically, we can, at this more concrete level of analysis, substitute the consumer situation for consumer behaviour-setting scope in our causal chain (see Figure 5.7).

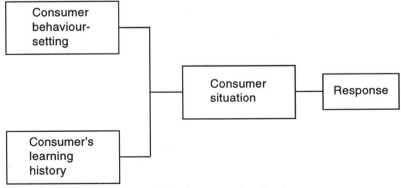

Figure 5.7   Consumer situation 2

Consumer behaviour is located at the meeting place of the consumer's learning history and the current consumer behaviour-setting. This intersection is the consumer situation. Both of its components are necessary to the operant reconstruction of the meaning of a particular response or behaviour pattern to the consumer. The consumer's learning history determines what can act as a discriminative stimulus of current behaviour; that learning history thereby also determines what is a potential reinforcer or punisher. But that learning history, which shapes the individuality, the unique response potential, of the consumer, is activated by the consumer behaviour-setting. It has no meaning in itself and can confer no significance on the current behaviour of the consumer unless an opportunity to act presents itself: that opportunity is afforded by the current setting which primes the learning history's capacity to shape current consumer choice. When this has occurred, whatever consumer behaviour takes place is a function of the interaction of historical and current environments: it can be located in time and space.

In practice, this third and most detailed level of analysis relates particular consumer responses – browsing, evaluating, buying, using – to the elements of the consumer situation in which they arise. In accounting for the approach, avoidance and escape responses of consumers, this micro-level interpretation involves identifying the discriminative stimuli that compose the setting, the consequences to which they point, and, as far as is feasible, the learning history of the individual. Ultimately, the purpose is to understand the meaning of the observed pattern of behaviour for the individual consumer.

Since direct empirical access to the consumer's learning history is denied the observer, an operant interpretation often necessarily concentrates on those environmental factors that can be observed or inferred, notably elements of the behaviour-setting. The assumption is – and all interpretive systems rest upon an act of faith – that the reinforcing consequences that these setting elements prefigure are broadly those that have shaped and maintained similar behaviour in the past; such (setting) elements and (behavioural) consequences can thus be used as a guide to the predisposing/inhibiting nature of the consumer's learning history. But there is no reason why the resulting account cannot be checked, corroborated, and amended by the individual's own recollection of that history; no reason why the consumer's verbal account cannot provide the interpretation; no reason why the operant interpretation cannot be 'thick' rather than 'thin'. The sole criterion is our resulting understanding of 'how the action of interest makes a difference to the person's life. That is, what does the action produce or present that would not be produced or presented otherwise?' (Lee 1988: 137). The framework could easily accommodate a fourth interpretive level to embrace the detailed, self-described and analysed experience of an individual consumer related to the organising environment. Figure 5.8 incorporates the consumer situation into the BPM.

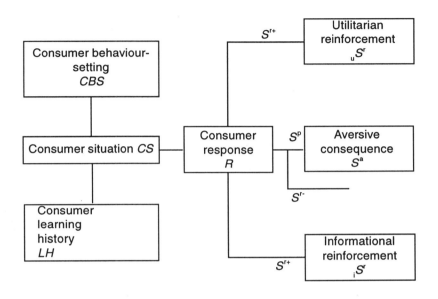

S^{r+} is the process of positive reinforcement;
S^{r-} is that of negative reinforcement;
S^{p}, that of punishment.

Figure 5.8   Consumer situation 3

THE INTERPRETATION OF CONSUMER DECISION-MAKING

An integral part of the consumer situation is the extent and nature of consumer decision-making required before an operant response is emitted. The preceding analysis of verbal behaviour and the BPM interpretation permit this aspect of consumer choice to be covered now in detail.

Consumer Decision-Making as Behaviour

How do the mechanisms for decision-making and persuasion proposed by Fazio's MODE model (1990), the 'elaboration likelihood model' (Petty and Cacioppo 1984a) and the 'heuristic–systematic model' (Chaiken 1980) relate to consumer decision-making in behavioural perspective? In the

BPM interpretation, 'motivation' is supplied by the individual's learning history or lack thereof. It is this that determines the likelihood that the outcome of a particular action will be relatively costly or rewarding and which leads to more or less prebehavioural reviewing of the contingencies, i.e. the probability of particular positive and aversive outcomes emerging from each of the behaviours available. (See Table 5.3.)

Table 5.3 Behavioural and cognitive approaches to decision-making

	Low experience/ high cost	High experience/ low cost
Behavioural perspective model (b.p.m)	Other-rules. Consumer's lack of a relevant learning history prompts search for other-rules.	Self-rules. Acquisition of a learning history from which self-rules can be extracted.
Elaboration likelihood	Central route	Peripheral route
MODE	Deliberation	Spontaneity
Heuristic-systematic processing	Systematic processing	Heuristic processing

Such review is not mental processing: it is behaviour, verbal behaviour which is often private. Where deliberation takes place it consists of a review of rules, self-rules generated on the basis of direct learning experience of the contingencies, and other-rules provided by those whose instructions have proved accurate and reinforcing if followed in the past and/or who themselves have relevant experience of the consequences, which can be publicly ascertained. Self-rules correspond to the attitude towards the act of the Fishbein–Ajzen formula: how would one identify learning history through self-report other than by asking what an individual believed would be the outcome of acting in a given way in specific circumstances and weighting this by that same individual's appraisal of those consequences? Questions that elicit attitude towards the act may be equally understood as indicating a history of reinforcement.

The rules revealed in this manner ('Eating fresh greens every day will result in a clear complexion') are akin to the tracks identified by Zettle and Hayes (1982): they specify how to get to a particular goal point. By this time, behaviour is 'scripted' (Langer 1989a, 1989b), following not from conscious intentions or plans but under the control of self-rules and/or immediate stimuli.

Other-rules correspond to the subjective norm of the Fishbein–Ajzen model: acting as plys, they specify the social consequences of compliance or non-compliance with a specified course of action. Evidence for the progression from other-rules, via deliberation, experience and self-observation, to action based on self-rules is provided by research on the TPB by East (1992, 1997), reviewed above. (A comparative review of the cognitive and behaviourist approaches to problem-solving is found in Reese 1994; cf. Chase and Bjamadottir 1992; Reese 1992a, 1992b; Ito 1994.)

The probability of a particular response depends also upon the non-regulatory components of the consumer behaviour-setting, the physical, social and temporal discriminative stimuli given meaning in any particular setting by the individual's learning history. Where they have figured in the past as controlling antecedents, they will now act to signal the kinds of consequences that are contingent on each possible response. They will thus play an integral role in prebehavioural deliberation, each setting the occasion for behaviour, with predictable results in the form of positive and aversive consequences.

When the learning history of the individual is such that known consequences have followed regularly and unimpeded from specific acts, the discriminative stimuli in the current setting will provide signals that quickly result in the performance of the requisite behaviour; when the individual has little appropriate learning history, or the history is ambiguous with respect to the kinds of reinforcer or punisher likely to result from behaviour, the magnitude of these consequences and their probability, greater deliberation including the formulation, weighing and use of rules will be normal.

The self- and other-instructions activated to a greater or less extent in either deliberative or spontaneous processing, plus the power of current discriminative stimuli – conferred in a history of reinforcement and punishment – determine the probability of a specific response. The immediate prebehavioural verbal self-instruction or prediction the individual is capable of making (on the question of introspection entering into rule formulation, see Moore 1994; on that of self-editing in rule formulation, see Hyten and Chase 1991; cf. Vaughan 1991) – equivalent to what deliberation theorists call behavioural intention – is another kind of rule, an augmental, i.e. the proximal motivating factor leading to the consummation of a particular act.

Behaviour formed through direct experience is contingency-shaped: its persistence is due to continued reinforcement and its emission is likely to come under the stimulus control of the physical, social and temporal elements of the behaviour-setting. Such behaviour may be described as 'spontaneous' or 'automatic' – finger tapping, for instance – when it is entirely under the control of these historical and current contingencies (Catania 1992a). However, it is unlikely that a great deal of human behaviour is formed and maintained entirely through the direct action of the environmental contingencies.

Humans are rule-formulating animals and routine/habitual behaviour is likely to be guided by self-rules, formed through experience and observation, and taking the form largely of tracks. Private tracking probably controls a great deal of repetitive consumer behaviour such as weekly or monthly supermarket shopping. Although such behaviour as brand choice shows 100 per cent loyalty in only a small minority of the users of a product class, most consumers' multi-brand purchasing is confined to a small repertoire of tried and tested brands in each class (Ehrenberg and Uncles 1995). Brand choice within this repertoire may look haphazard, but it is far from random. It differs from finger tapping in that it is highly functional and economically/consumption rational, and most consumers have no difficulty in describing the rules employed in finding and selecting brands of fast-moving consumer goods, as protocol analysis readily shows.

Self-rules in the form of tracks are undoubtedly analogous to global attitudes towards the object – in this case a known subset of substitutable brands within a product class – which are easily/automatically elicited by the discriminative stimuli in the purchase setting. Formed through repeated purchasing, observation and imitation, including a long period of consumer socialisation, they are readily available to guide immediate, familiar purchasing in the presence of such antecedent controlling stimuli as the label on a can, a familiar brand name or a logo. This resembles the spontaneous processing in the presence of a known attitude object identified by Fazio as prerequisite to unpremeditated, automatic, routine processing.

Behaviour instructed by the rules provided by others is formed through indirect experience: TV advertisements, neighbours' recommendations, parents' approbation, and so on. Such rules are most likely to be effective when the listener's relevant learning history is minimal or non-existent and/or when the behaviour-setting in which he or she is acting is closed (the latter a function of how much control the speaker has over the setting). Other-instructions are far more likely to be productive in situations unfamiliar to the listener, when a novel course of action is commended – perhaps buying a radically innovative product or moving house or just trying a new make of computer disc. Such behaviours usually require some degree of deliberation, because since no self-rules exist to 'spontaneously' guide action. Depending on previous rule compliance and its outcomes, the consumer will be more or less disposed to follow the other-instructions without demur: a friend whose advice has proved worthwhile may be able to offer recommendations that are immediately taken up and acted upon, providing the new sphere of consumption is not too far removed from that previously instructed. But a stranger appearing in a TV commercial may not be able to rely on audience members' having so motivating a reinforcement history with respect to following other-rules. Other-rules of these kinds take the form of plys: in the absence of direct experience on the part of the listener, and especially if the rules come from a remote/unfamiliar/impersonal source, they are more likely to lead to deliberation than immediate action.

The consequent review of the contingencies is interpreted by Skinner (1974) as behavioural, a series of private events in which the ultimate causes of behaviour are scrutinised. Verbal rules towards specific courses of action (like attitudes towards target behaviours in the cognitive theories) may result from this process. The consumer who initially had no self-rules for the proposed course of action (as a result of having little or no direct experience thereof, little or no relevant learning history) eventually may form such rules, translating the plys provided by others into the private tracks necessary to guide particular behaviour in a clearly defined situation (corresponding to that defined in terms of target, action, timing and context by the multi-attribute modellers).

To reach a decision, choosing one action from among several, is to form a behavioural intention in the deliberative models; in the BPM, it appears to involve augmentals, which motivate the individual to behave in a specific manner. Augmentals of this kind result from deliberation and are succeeded by positive motivation, perhaps the outcome of a cost–benefit analysis that indicates that the reinforcing consequences of the proposed act are likely to exceed the aversive, a review of the contingencies that suggests one action will generate greater net benefits than any other.

If the action is performed and reinforced, the plys provided as other-rules gradually become track-based self-rules and, ultimately, the contingencies themselves exert a greater share of control than instructions: the behaviour becomes routinised and apparently habitual. Much behaviour is of course a mixture of contingency-shaped and rule-governed, subject to adjustment as new contingencies arise and as new instructions from others and oneself emerge to be evaluated and otherwise deliberated upon. Guerin (1994a: 192) distinguishes two kinds of decision-making which have the capacity to bring together the findings of social-cognitive research and those of behaviour analysis.

Intuitive decision-making refers to behaving in accordance with the multiple environmental contingencies acting at that time [while] nonintuitive means that decision behavior has become verbally governed in some way and verbal rules are controlling the decision behavior through pliance or tracking.

The preceding analysis goes beyond this, however, eschewing the simple dichotomy it implies. The theory expounded above assumes that, where there is little direct learning history, behaviour is guided by other-rules (especially plys); where there is a well-established learning history it is guided by prior contingency-shaping and the discriminative stimuli of the current behaviour-setting including self-rules (especially tracks). Between the two is a period of contingency-shaping through which the self-rules that come to guide behaviour apparently spontaneously are formulated. At this stage, the non-verbal contingencies that guide current behaviour are notoriously difficult to distinguish from the self-rules that may do so (Hackenberg and Joker 1994; Hayes *et al.* 1986). The choice of explanation is methodologically based: some behaviour analysts refuse to admit variables represented by private events that are not amenable to an experimental analysis of their subject matter (e.g. Hayes 1986); others are willing to interpret observed behaviour in terms of non-publicly available entities of this kind (e.g. Catania 1992a; Horne and Lowe 1993).

Hence, the debate about the direction of causation between attitudes and behaviour is redundant: a consumer who has simply seen an advertisement for a brand will have an attitude in the sense of being able to express some verbal evaluations, perhaps only in the form of echoics (repetitions of what has been heard; Skinner 1957), or possibly some minimal verbal evaluation of the brand. But such an attitude is less likely to act as a self-instruction to guide behaviour than that formed through experience with the brand.

CONSUMER DECISION-MAKING AS RULE FORMULATION

Behaviour-analytical consumer research portrays consumer behaviour as the outcome of environmental consequences, acting either directly or through verbal descriptions (rules). Behaviour is contingency-shaped when the person has much experience of the outcomes of this or similar behaviour. When this is not the case, behaviour is usually preceded by a review of the contingencies described by other-rules (instructions provided by other people). In this process, and through direct behavioural experience, the individual forms personal self-rules about how the contingencies operate. As behaviour comes under the control of self-rules, it appears spontaneous and routine, though it has a long history in which it was shaped by successive approximations to what it has become. Most human behaviour is rule-governed to some extent, but ultimately the contingencies themselves determine what people actually do. Adherents of this viewpoint interpret prebehavioural deliberation not as mental processing but as a behaviour in its own right in which the consequences of acting are reviewed and evaluated.

The behavioural perspective model (BPM) proposes that consumer behaviour is a function of the interaction of the scope of the current consumer behaviour-setting and the individual's learning history. This interaction motivates a specific behaviour by prefiguring the utilitarian and informational consequences it is likely to produce. A relatively closed behaviour-setting involves mainly other-rules that describe not only the contingencies but the social reinforcements and punishments of compliance or non-compliance. Compliant behaviour in these settings is negatively reinforced, while non-compliance is punished.

Relatively open settings involve mainly self-rules. Personal learning history encapsulates an individual's disposition towards complying with the instructions of others (which is activated by the discriminative stimuli that compose a closed setting) as well as the basis for derivation of self-rules (which are activated by the elements of an open setting). Utilitarian reinforcement consists in the utilitarian benefits of purchase and consumption: the behaviour that produces it is contingency-shaped. Informational reinforcement consists in social standing and the achievement of personal norms: the behaviour that produces it is rule-governed. Self-rules appear to refer to the attitudes formed through deliberation other-rules to subjective norms; when self-rules have been employed frequently, the behaviour appears to come under the automatic stimulus control of the behaviour-setting.

Behaviour analysts have surmised that behaviour is rule-governed only on its initial emission; thereafter, it comes under contingency control. The analysis undertaken in this chapter suggests a more elongated process.

At first the consumer has no specific learning history with respect to the consumption behaviour in question. Perhaps presented with a new brand in a new product class, he or she has no accumulated experience or knowledge of buying and using the item and the consequences of doing so. However, in proportion to the consumer's having a learning history for rule-following, other-rules may be sought out for guidance and action. These may take the form of the advertising claims that first created awareness of the innovation; alternatively, they may come from significant others, acquaintances and opinion leaders. Whatever their source, these rules are not passively accepted by the consumer but used as the basis of a sequence of deliberation and evaluation, first of the claims themselves, and their comparison with similar claims for other products and brands, then of accumulated consumption experience. The consumer's actions involved in the trial and repeat purchase/consumption of the product develops a learning history. Moreover, reasoning with respect to personal experience of the item, and the evaluation of this experience, will lead to the formation of self-rules that henceforth guide action without constant deliberation. The consumer has moved from the central route to the peripheral, from deliberation to spontaneity, from systematic reasoning to the application of heuristics. The initial lack of a relevant learning history prompted a search for other-rules; the acquisition of such a history means that self-rules can be extracted from experience. Only the acquisition of such an extensive history can transform the behaviour finally from rule-governed to contingency-shaped, and even then the distinction between self-rule governance and contingency-shaping is not empirically available.

The import of this analysis lies not in its superficially reiterating the sequence of consumer decision-making found in cognitive models of initial and subsequent information processing but in its capacity to account for these phenomena without extensive reliance on theoretical entities posited at a metabehavioural level.

SUMMING UP

Moreover, the analysis invites the integration of consumer research not only with operant psychology but with a wider paradigm, selection by consequences. Goldsmith's (1991) statement of the dual causality found in biological evolution has echoes in Kimble's (1996: 44–50) proposal for a scientific psychology. Kimble argues that 'behaviour is the joint product of relatively enduring *potentials* for, and relatively more temporary *instigation* to, action'. In representing behaviour as a function of potential and instigation, the BPM portrays consumer choice as an evolutionary process. In natural selection, potential resides in the genotype, instigation in the environment, behaviour in the phenotype. In the BPM, potential (ultimate causation) resides predominantly in learning history (though natural selection has also played its part); the instigating environment (proximate causation) is represented by the consumer behaviour-setting; and behaviour is the outcome of their intersection. The environment is that of the behaviour, not the individual (as, in strict behaviourist terms, it is *behaviour* that has a learning history rather than a person), and so it includes bodily states such as deprivation as well as economic and social state variables such as financial means, physical surroundings and interpersonal influence. Potential is determined largely by the role of the utilitarian and informational consequences of prior behaviour; instigation is a matter of the extent to which that learning history transforms the antecedent stimuli of the current behaviour-setting into *discriminative* stimuli; behaviour consists in economic responses that can be allocated to operant classes based on the pattern of reinforcement that maintains them. As has been noted, the potential for behaviour derives from the individual's history of approach and avoidance responses and their consequences.

Nevertheless, while operant consumer research provides ontological diversity, it does not solve the epistemological problems of cognitive explanation. It relies ultimately on the very inference that it seeks to avoid, differing by assuming that proximate causes of another's behaviour lie in those behavioural events that are private to him or her rather than that the causes of behaviour inhere in an unobservable mental realm. The encouragement of ontological diversity nevertheless represents an advance for the consumer research subdiscipline that has sought so little to emancipate itself from the strictures of social cognition.

Part IV
What Marketing Does

Marketing is human behaviour. In affluent societies, it is the behaviour of buyers and managers, directed towards the fulfilment of economic objectives through consumption that is satisfying to consumers and profitable for marketers.

(Foxall 1995b: 68)

6 The Marketing Firm

This part of the book undertakes a functional analysis of marketing, conceived as the intersecting activities of customers and marketers; i.e. it explores what marketing does. In the process of doing this, it defines the nature of the marketing firm. The resulting micropositive account of marketing thus casts economic behaviour in the light of a controlling environment rather than as the actions of autonomous agents (Foxall 1996a). There are three reasons for assuming this perspective.

First, the neglect of the functional approach to marketing behaviour is a serious omission in marketing research. By contrast, the BPM research programme has examined the respective natures of consumer behaviour and marketing management from an operant viewpoint (e.g. Foxall 1990, 1992a, 1995a). The operant psychology from which the model derives permits a detailed exploration of economic behaviour as an instrumental activity, i.e. in terms of its functional relationships to the consequences it produces and their implications for the repetition of that behaviour. Hence, the functional analysis of marketing behaviour promises to increase the overall number of unique perspectives on consumer and marketer behaviour and thereby to contribute to scientific progress by promoting the interplay of theoretically diverse frameworks of analysis and conceptualisation (Feyerabend 1970).

Second, whereas the analysis of marketing management has been generally undertaken within a separate framework of conceptualisation and analysis from that of consumer behaviour, the approach adopted here allows the behaviours of both consumers and marketers to be comprehended within the scope of a single set of behavioural assumptions and concepts. These considerations are important in view of the symbiotic relationship between consumer behaviour and the marketing firm, which has implications for the manner in which these activities are studied.

A central assumption, therefore, is that consumer research is impossible in the absence of a theory of marketing behaviour. An independent psychology or economics of consumption is infeasible: marketing response to consumer choice is a central component of the controlling environment, which must be taken fully into account. The psychology or economics of consumer behaviour requires a psychology or economics of marketing.

(The comprehensive understanding of consumer behaviour requires also that it be placed within the context of social behaviour generally, especially the interpersonal network of relationships that provides perhaps a more significant influence on consumer choice than does the marketing firm.) The required understanding invokes both of these disciplines; neither psychology nor economics alone seems capable of doing justice to the complexity of human economic choice.

Third, this approach is inter-disciplinary in that it draws upon and integrates both economic and psychological analysis. Although the economics of markets and firms forms an important segment of the argument, it is inadequate to account for the complexity of the phenomena now identified as 'relationship marketing' and 'internal marketing'. Psychology, particularly the operant psychology of economic behaviour, is equally necessary in order to elucidate these relationships fully. Hence the discussion is intended as a contribution to the economic psychology which Lea (1992; Lea *et al.* 1987; cf. Van Raaij 1988) argues embraces both psychology and economics.

THE MARKETING FIRM

The subject matter of marketing as a field of study is understood to be reciprocally reinforcing economic behaviour between consumers/suppliers and the marketing firm with which they deal. Part of the reciprocity consists in economic exchanges that can be literally described, though in affluent marketing-orientated economies additional reinforcement not involving such exchange usually accompanies marketing relationships. Thus intra-firm relationships between those responsible for the entrepreneurial (strategic management) function of the organisation and those of its members whom it employs also have characteristics of the marketing relationships so defined, though only if they contain the definitive element of literal economic exchange. It is this crucial distinction between economic and non-economic exchanges, moreover, that elucidates the essential nature of marketing. Before the theme of economic exchange can be treated in detail, however, it is necessary to summarise how an operant analysis of consumer and marketer behaviours elucidates the nature of marketing behaviour and the *raison d'être* of the marketing firm.

This expression does not designate a particular kind of business organisation, to be distinguished from other, presumably 'non-marketing', firms. Rather, it emphasises a characteristic of all firms by alluding to the central purpose of all businesses as opposed to other organisations: to create and retain customers by serving them profitably in a competitive market context. But the origin of firms is usually traced, following Coase (1937, 1988b), to another set of market transactions, those previously undertaken exclusively within the external marketplace but now executed by employees of an entrepreneurial organisation. However, a functional analysis of the firm must begin with the behaviour of its key stakeholder, that which calls it into existence and rationalises its use of resources; that is, with consumer behaviour. A theory of the firm will thus be a theory of an entity that engages in marketing, because any firm is inescapably and essentially embedded in networks of marketing relationships; its nature and function cannot be understood if this point is neglected. 'The marketing firm' is a tautology but one that is necessary in view of the tendency of many social scientists to overlook marketing relationships as a defining characteristic of the firm.

Beyond the Consumer-less Economy

Marketing firms exist under particular economic-structural conditions, those which induce consumer-orientated management by the business as a whole. Consumer orientation is a contingent behaviour appropriate to a particular external economic structure that generates consumer choice. This requires high levels of discretionary income among consumers and competition among suppliers. It also depends upon a situation in which the quantity of a good supplied or capable of being supplied exceeds demand. The managerial style of the marketing firm facilitates, economises and maintains marketing relationships in these conditions; that is its rationale. By contrast, economic theories of the firm often adopt an intra-organisational perspective that stresses relationships based on production rather than the firm's external publics. At worst, they deal with apparently consumer-less economies from which many aspects of marketing are absent. It is astonishing, for instance, that marketing-orientated management, the creation and implementation of marketing mixes to satisfy consumers profitably, is not considered one of the 'economic institutions of capitalism' by Williamson (1985), who also omits, therefore, to deal with the industrial structures that compel this managerial approach, and the demands it makes on the structure and functions of business organisations. Note that while I am using Coase's approach to the nature of the firm as a reference point, several other accounts of the origin of firms and their function exist (e.g. Williamson 1975, 1985; Hart 1995; Easterbrook and Fischel 1991; Demsetz 1995). Unfortunately, all treat consumers as a passive source of demand, which apparently requires no analysis complementary to that of the firm.

But, the myopia of economists apart, intra-firm behaviour is comprehensible only in relation to the external institutions that control the organisation. Microeconomics has been primarily a source of theories of production, which assume away or ignore that the *raison d'être* of the business organisation inheres in its wider environment. That environment provides the reinforcement on which the continuance of the firm depends and for which it was established. The behaviour of members of the firm, its managers and other employees and additional stakeholders, such as its owners and those who invest in its shares, cannot be understood in ignorance of the contingent relationships that bind firm and marketplace together.

Theories of the firm in organisation studies equally assume a limited purview of business–environment relationships, which generally takes consumers for granted, assumes that companies sell products or services to available buyers, and omits the need for marketing as opposed to sales management. Even marketing studies have failed to develop a unified theory of the marketing firm in which the behaviours of consumers and marketers are conceptualised in similar terminology.

It follows that the function of the firm inheres uniquely within the management of marketing transactions and relationships, both 'internal' and 'external'. This includes, first, marketing management, which is responsible for using the marketing mix to manage consumer behaviour-setting scope and to control the reinforcers that maintain consumer choice. Second, it involves the management of intra-firm quasi-marketing relationships, those which, on a Coasian understanding of the origin of the firm, were previously undertaken entirely within the market but have been integrated within the organisational boundaries of the firm. By tracing the interlocking environmental contingencies at these levels, the theory of the marketing firm shows how these contingencies and the behaviours they control encourage organisational responsiveness to the market. We can now describe what the marketing firm does: that is, the nature of the relationships (i) between the marketing firm and its consumers/suppliers, and (ii) between the firm's entrepreneurial function and its other members. These actions necessarily involve behaviour-setting scope management and/or the management of reinforcers ('mutuality relationships') and market transactions that are characterised by literal exchange of property rights ('marketing relationships').

Non-marketing Relationships

The firm also develops relationships with various parties that are not based on market (exchange) transactions and which are not therefore marketing relationships, e.g. public relations to consumers, internal communications (which is not 'internal *marketing*'), and maintaining long-term relationships with customers or suppliers (which is not entirely 'relationship *marketing*'). These non-market activities involve mutual reinforcement (those who claim they involve exchange use this term metaphorically). Hence, it is impossible to understand marketing management, social marketing, internal marketing or relationship marketing without making the distinction between relationships that inhere in mutual setting scope restriction and/or mutual reinforcement, and those that additionally involve real exchange in a marketing-oriented economic system.

This analysis contributes the recognition that the management of market relationships is the essence of firms; firms come into existence because they make marketing relationships possible/more economic. They make it possible to enclose market transactions and thereby to make them more predictable; this is circumscribing market relationships rather than circumventing the market. Production and selling are independent of firms in the sense of being functions whose execution does not require firms; the creation and management of marketing and quasi-marketing relationships, however, are the very essence of the firm's existence. They are what it is for.

MARKETING AS BEHAVIOUR

Economic Behaviour as Operant Response

To ask why the firm exists is to ask what it does. This is to enquire of the consequences of its behaviour (Lee 1988). But in so far as behaviour analysts have been concerned with economic behaviour it is usually that of rats and pigeons which, despite its useful insights, cannot spawn the necessary behaviourist interpretation of complex economic behaviour in humans (e.g. Kagel 1988). However, there are two reasons for optimism. The first is the renewed interest of behaviour analysts in human behaviour which has transformed the experimental analysis of behaviour over the last decade or so, particularly in its drawing attention to the verbal responding of humans (Foxall 1997a). The second is the demonstration that the behaviour of consumers in affluent economic systems can be the subject of an operant analysis based on the interpretive capacity of radical behaviourism (Foxall 1994c).

Operant psychology is therefore particularly relevant to our task, since economic behaviour is instrumentally conditioned. Thus its analysis in operant terms – i.e. as behaviour that operates on the environment to produce consequences that determine its future rate of emission – can elucidate the nature of consumer and corporate behaviour in affluent market-orientated societies. The operant behaviourist paradigm is summarised by the *three-term contingency*, which denotes that reinforcing or punishing outcomes are contingent upon the performance of a specified response in the presence of a discriminative stimulus that sets the occasion for this response–stimulus relationship. The subsequent rate of emission of the response is thereby controlled by the consequences produced by similar responses on earlier occasions.

This formulation summarises the *contingencies of reinforcement and punishment* that comprise the operant approach to explanation. The application of this paradigm in the present context stems from the fact that economic behaviour is operant: it is emitted rather than reflexive behaviour the outcomes of which influence its rate.

Consumer Behaviour in Operant Perspective

The behaviour of human consumers can be comprehended within the general methodological orientation of operant analysis. But, as noted in Part II, the complexity of such activity – in comparison with the simpler economic behaviour of infra-humans which is readily amenable to experimental analysis (Kagel 1988) – requires qualification.

Alhadeff's (1982) operant theory of economic behaviour points out that any consumer behaviour meets with both reinforcing and aversive consequences; the strength of the behaviour (its frequency and its magnitude on any occasion) is the result of tendencies towards approach, leading to such positive reinforcement as possession and consumption of the utilities and information provided by a purchase, and those towards escape, leading to punishers such as loss of cash, an end to prepurchase deliberation that may be satisfying in itself, and forgoing other products. Whether approach – such as purchasing – or escape – such as saving or buying something else – is the outcome depends upon which of these responses is the stronger, i.e. upon the learning history of the individual (Alhadeff 1982; see also Foxall 1990: 65–9).

The *relative strength of potential reinforcement and punishment* is the net outcome signalled by the discriminative stimuli in the current behaviour-setting as contingent upon the purchase or consumption response. Alhadeff (1982) portrays purchase behaviour as a vector of these two strengths or probabilities which the b.p.m represents as a function of the current consumer behaviour-setting as it is primed by the consumer's learning history. The strength of approach depends upon reinforcer effectiveness (which is, in turn, a function of the consumer's level of deprivation), the schedule of reinforcement (and here we must add to Alhadeff's analysis, the possibility that multiple schedules will be in operation in non-laboratory settings), reinforcer delay (the length of time by which reinforcement has followed the response in the past; the longer this interval, the weaker the response), the quantity of signalled reinforcement, and the quality of signalled reinforcement.

The strength of escape depends upon how aversive the loss of money is to the consumer who must pay for the product (and this is itself a function of the reaction of others to previous purchases by the individual), the past results of losing the positive generalised reinforcer, money, and the result of having been prevented from acquiring other reinforcers as a consequence of having bought a particular product, the length of delay between the purchase and such punishing consequences, the quantity and quality of the money surrendered, and the reinforcement schedule (Alhadeff 1982; Foxall 1990: 65–9). The loss is the opportunity cost signalled by the physical and social, temporal and regulatory discriminative stimuli of the current setting.

In summary, the operant analysis of marketing proposes that *consumer behaviour* consists of economic purchasing and consumption activities that are reinforced by utility and informationally, i.e. which recur because of the instrumental and expressive consequences contingent upon them. It provides the fundamental datum of operant consumer research. *Consumer choice* is any behaviour that reduces the aversive consequences of facing a number of apparently functionally equivalent options, i.e those which have similar response strength for the individual. It may involve or be preceded by private deliberation, but this is not the cause of the ensuing behaviour; that behaviour is under the control of the consumer situation.

Marketing Management in Operant Perspective

From this account of consumer choice emerges a novel interpretation of how marketing management works. For, if consumer behaviour-settings actually influence choice, then marketing management ought logically to be found attempting to engineer the components of such settings to increase the probability that consumer behaviour advantageous to the firm will emerge. Those components are the social, physical, temporal and regulatory discriminative stimuli that signal the outcomes of specific behaviours in the setting. Moreover, if consumer behaviour is influenced by the pattern of utilitarian and informational reinforcement thus signalled, then marketing management ought to be found arranging the contingencies that shape and maintain such behaviour.

The extension of the behavioural perspective model to the activities of the firm suggests that a great deal of marketing activity is, in fact, concerned with modifying two main variables that influence consumer behaviour. The first involves managing the scope of the consumer behaviour-setting to increase its attractiveness for the individual and reduce his or her propensity to avoid or leave it without purchasing or consuming. The second is the management of the ways in which utilitarian and informational reinforcers are made available to the consumer.

The marketing mix, comprising the four media through which marketers directly influence consumer behaviour – product, price, promotion and place – can, therefore, be understood behaviourally by the logic of the three-term contingency. Both product and non-product elements of the mix can be defined in operant terms and included in a situational analysis of purchase and consumption. To do this is to recognise that all four elements of the marketing mix are essential components of the consumer situation, presenting discriminative stimuli and reinforcers which guide purchase behaviour, e.g. in the retail setting, and throughout subsequent consumption. The following functional interpretation of the marketing mix leads into a deeper analysis of executive marketing as concerned with the management of consumer behaviour-setting scope and reinforcement.

Operant Analysis of the Marketing Mix

Product

In an operant analysis that incorporates a marketing or brand level of analysis, a product class is defined as a set of reinforcers that, in combination, shape and maintain specific purchase and consumption behaviours; the set of reinforcers is common to the brands that comprise the class, each of which is distinguished by its unique composition. Brands are also distinguished by the discriminative stimuli used by their marketers to differentiate them from competitors; these discriminative stimuli are not found exclusively in the product attributes of the brand but also feature in the non-product marketing mix elements (Foxall 1994d).

The features or attributes of a product or service contain discriminative stimuli announcing the reinforcement that will result from the performance of specified purchase and consummatory responses. Packaging and product shapes, brand names, and labels also perform these functions. They enable the consumer to discriminate his or her behaviour by purchasing the brands of which he or she has positive experience and avoiding the others. All of these effect a partial closure of the consumer behaviour-setting, making the purchase of the brand in question more probable and seeking to exclude consideration of alternatives. But products and services also contain the reinforcing stimuli that make further purchase more probable. They are the principal vehicle through which utilitarian and informational reinforcements are transmitted to the consumer, sometimes at the point of purchase but usually in the process of consumption; and, less frequently and usually not by design, they are the principal means by which punishing consequences are delivered to customers.

Price

Price information contains both positive and aversive stimuli. For most consumers, price is aversive, and effectively closes the setting by putting some items out of reach of many would-be consumers or limits severely the amount that can be bought and consumed. The payment of this price is the major aversive consequence of purchase and consumption. However, for those consumers who are reinforced by conspicuous consumption, a high price may actually be a prerequisite of purchase, a discriminative stimulus that signals high levels of informational reinforcement contingency upon the possession and use of the item. The price still closes the setting given the reinforcement history of such consumers and their current financial status (ability to pay or obtain credit). Additionally, for many consumers price has become an indicator of quality: for them a relatively high price may similarly lead to discriminated purchasing.

Promotion

Marketing communications such as advertising and point-of-sale promotions provide rules, promises, suggestions, prompts and other abbreviated descriptions of the contingencies of consumer behaviour. They are generally elements of the consumer behaviour-setting which they close in the sense of encouraging purchase and consumption of one brand within the product class at the expense of its competitors. However, when advertising and other marketing communications are designed to promote a new brand in an existing product class, they may have the effect of opening the consumer behaviour-setting by offering novelty. They encourage rule-governed consumer behaviour that is not initially dependent upon the actual consequences contingent upon purchase and consumption so much as those (such as the approbation of others) that are contingent upon rule-following (Foxall 1994e). However, they are effective only if the consumer has a tendency to behave already in the specified way, that is a learning history which predisposes him or her towards rule-conformity (Foxall 1997).

Place

The place and time utilities, the creation and delivery of which have long been seen as marketing's function, consist of discriminative stimuli that signal the availability of the reinforcing and punishing properties of the remainder of the marketing mix. The components of a retail outlet portray its downmarket, value-laden or plush ambience, which in turn prefigure the probable prices of the merchandise, the level of customer service that can be expected, the quality of the products and services on offer, and so on. Time utilities indicate the usefulness of the items purchased in the context of the consumer's overall sequence of consumption behaviours. Timing is a central element in determining the usefulness of what is on offer to the consumer. Retail outlets are consumer behaviour-settings that encourage *or deter* purchase; consumption contexts are consumer behaviour-settings that encourage or *deter* usage. Wicker (1987) defines a behaviour-setting as 'a small-scale social system composed of people interacting with one another and with inanimate objects to carry out a regularly occurring, prescribed behavioral sequence or program, within specifiable time and place boundaries'.

The behaviour-setting evolves or institutes means of ensuring that the behaviour programme is maintained; it counters deviation from the programme by means, for example, of reprimands and vetoes inconsistent behaviour by exclusion, for instance. (See also Taylor 1991; Foxall 1994a.) Distribution management can be seen, therefore, as the creation and maintenance of consumer behaviour programmes through the design and conservation of the physical, temporal and some of the regulatory components of consumer behaviour-settings.

MANAGEMENT OF CONSUMER BEHAVIOUR-SETTING SCOPE

Rationale

A considerable amount of managerial action in marketing can be viewed as the attempt to influence the scope of behaviour-settings, making the purchase of whatever the marketer offers more likely (whether this refers to spending on buying a product or consuming a service such as depositing money in a savings account) and making other responses (such as leaving the store, or buying or consuming an alternative offering) less probable. Obvious examples are the provision of credit facilities for consumers who cannot afford the full cash outlay immediately, changing consumers' moods through in-store music, using advertising to promise desirable reinforcers contingent upon buying and using the item, and so on.

Nor is this strategy of *closure* necessarily manipulative (in the worse sense of the word), especially in a competitive environment. Presenting the consumer with a more pleasant retail environment, for instance, or with clearer way-finding aids and more legible shopping mall designs encourages the potential buyer to stay in the marketing environment and to become an actual consumer (Foxall and Goldsmith 1994). The entire marketing mix enters into the attempts of marketing organisations to control the scope of consumer behaviour-settings. Products and services on view in the retail outlet (or its equivalent) are composed of 'attributes', discriminative stimuli that set the occasion for utilitarian and informational benefits subject to the consumer's purchasing and consuming them in specified ways. Purchase, ownership and use are the responses required to translate those attributes into reinforcers. Branding is an attempt by marketers to reduce the probability that consumers will exercise the choice open to them by selecting an alternative, closing the scope of the setting, making purchase of the target brand more probable by customising the product to the purchase and consumption propensities of segments of the consumer market. Price is a discriminative stimulus for punishment – consisting in the opportunity cost to the consumer of alternatives forgone, dependent on the resources available to him or her – but also for quality (utilitarian reinforcement) and value (informational reinforcement). Promotion consists of discriminative stimuli in the form of rules that stipulate the behaviours necessary to acquire and derive maximum advantage from the consumption of the product or service advertised. Advertisements, the most conspicuous of the promotional variables, create verbal behaviour – i.e. provide the plys (other-instructions) to be turned into tracks (self-rules).

This occurs partly through instruction and deliberation but especially and ultimately through reinforcement based on the contingencies, i.e. putting the rules into practice. Moreover, instructions are only likely to work if there is some tendency already to behave in the manner advocated (Skinner 1971). Finally, distribution determines opportunities to purchase and consumer based on the creation of consumer settings in time and space (Foxall 1992a, 1994b).

The following examples are not exhaustive or systematically comprehensive. Their object is to show how marketing management can be partially construed as the manipulation of consumer behaviour-setting scope.

Examples

Retail Design

Within the distribution function of the mix, merchandising techniques that route customers around a supermarket to maximise the number of discriminative stimuli they encounter are attempts on the part of marketers to open or close the consumer behaviour-setting or to affect the relationship between reinforcement and purchase. Often the discriminative and reinforcing stimuli available in stores are arranged so as to maximise consumers' patronage and to shape purchase responses. Such manipulation may be the result of modification of the physical or social environment by means of retail tactics that guide supermarket shoppers past specific products, juxtapose leading brands with complementary items, or employ point-of-sale advertising to encourage unplanned purchasing (contingency category 7: *routine purchasing*). The physical and social settings in which financial institutions such as banks and insurance companies transact business are such that only the serious business of transacting is encouraged. Extraneous activity that might detract from efficiency is punished, principally by the austere, or at least pointed, behaviour of the seller; the environmental stimuli are so arranged as to be closed sufficiently to ensure that the transactions in question are effectively accomplished. However, more subtle means of closing consumer settings are apparent (Bitner 1990, 1992, Ward *et al.* 1992; Zimmer and Golden, 1988).

Wayfinding may thus be deliberately reduced or enhanced by the setting (Foxall and Hackett 1992). The longer a consumer remains in a store such as a supermarket, the more he or she is likely to spend (Foxall and Goldsmith 1994). The decor and atmospherics of shopping environments are designed to attract and keep customers through the delivery of emotional responses that shape and maintain more overt purchase responses (Donovan and Rossiter 1982; Foxall 1997b; Russell and Mehrabian 1976). Store location and shopping centre design are based on some understanding, accurate or not, of the contingencies that control consumer behaviour (Foxall and Hackett 1992, 1994; Hackett *et al.* 1993; Timmermans 1993). Point-of-sale displays, price information and advertising also exert a strong effect on consumer choice (Phillips and Bradshaw 1993), and consumers themselves have long shown signs of transferring their purchase-planning activities from the home to the store environment (Stern 1962).

Over/Under Demand

Retail organisations use both marketing and demarketing in order to respond to their ability to staff their operations (Wicker 1979). Staffing levels (both qualitative and quantitative) are one source of constraint on firms' resource bases, especially in relation to what the psychologists call overpopulation but that we would recognise as over-demand, but the ability to provide products of the right quality and quantity, to advertise their availability, to price them adequately (for consumers, managers, shareowners and other stakeholders) and to distribute them efficiently also influence the extent to which firms can effect closure of the consumer setting. Over-demand typically arises because the density of consumers in a physical setting interferes with the level of service available to satisfy demand. This service level is relative not only to the size of the public present in the locale but also to the level of human and physical resources available to deliver the required service. More significantly, it is relative to the quality of staff and other resources and, particularly, to the implications of the quality and quantity of these resources for the delivery of a demanded level of marketing proficiency. We could suggest many examples of the ways in which marketers respond to over-demand by modifying the scope of the consumer setting in order to increase consumer satisfaction as well as marketing goals. Here are just three examples of the ways in which place has been modified to effect closure.

Closure of the Sales Environment

An example is the efforts of marketers to control the entrance of consumers into the setting. Consumers are sometimes scheduled through an appointments systems or by active demarketing such as a reduction in the volume or frequency of marketing communications. On occasion the standards required for admission are increased through a price increase or requirement that patrons (e.g. in a restaurant) wear suitable clothing. Customers might also be channelled into a holding area (such as a bar in a restaurant if a table is not immediately available). Some consumer behaviours might be banned (smoking, for instance), so that some potential customers are effectively debarred. Another example arises from marketers' attempts to control the capacity of the setting. The size of the setting might be increased or decreased – as when airlines fly larger or smaller planes. Opening hours may be altered. Staff shortages might be compensated for by the installation of automatic teller machines. A third example is related to marketers' control of the time consumers spend in the setting. The service or product might be provided more quickly (e.g. a hairdresser might cut hair faster or food operations in a fast-food restaurant might be automated). Motorists may be allowed only thirty minutes' parking and their return prohibited for a further two hours. The flow of consumers through a service area might be controlled to ensure that bottlenecks do not occur: for example, self-service restaurants may require consumers to place orders at one counter, obtain their purchases from another and pay at a third.

Another selling tactic involves the closure of sales environments once the customer has tacitly agreed to buy. In departmental stores, for instance, purchase agreements, especially those involving the arrangement of credit for infrequent purchases of luxuries or innovations (contingency category 1: *status consumption*), are finalised not in the relatively open store setting in which the merchandise has been inspected and sales claims made, but in separated areas of the store such as offices or corner desks, where behaviour not germane to the agreement is discouraged and the customer is less likely to change his or her mind, and from which escape may be accomplished only with difficulty and embarrassment.

Not all marketer-qualification of the consumer behaviour-setting involves closure. Schemes such as banks' attempts to make account switching easier open up the consumer setting, increasing consumers' choice and, perhaps, welfare. All new product development, long-term price reduction, informative promotional activity and extension of distribution systems has these beneficial effects.

Closure of the Consumption Environment

Managerial control of the behaviour-setting is especially apparent in the case of contingency category 2 (*fulfilment*). In the case of gambling, for instance, access to the casino is strictly determined by its management, who pronounce on membership rights and may deny entry on any particular occasion to anyone who does not conform to the required codes of conduct. The casino managers arrange the physical and, to a degree, social environment (within the law), controlling lighting, lack of clocks, the situation of tables, the clientele, all of which may be manipulated to ensure the continued presence of the punters where they are most likely to gamble: to the extent of serving drinks and even meals at the tables, and providing opportunities to gamble in the restaurants. Although there are such obvious physical encouragements to gamble and movement may be severely restricted on occasion, the most subtle control is social. Quitting, failing to take risks by staking inadequate sums, etc., evoke social disapprobation, which makes escape and avoidance less probable. Similar contingencies are maintained in self-improvement programs such as *est* (Baer and Stolz 1978; for a situational analysis of large group awareness training of this kind, see Foxall 1995a).

MANAGEMENT OF REINFORCEMENT

Rationale

Marketing management also consists in the provision and scheduling of reinforcements/punishments to shape and maintain consumers' trial-and-repeat buying responses. Three broad strategies are practised: the control of schedules of reinforcement; the control of the quality and quantity of reinforcers; and the management of reinforcer delay. Each of these can be applied to understanding better the response of marketing organizations to each of the operant classes of consumer behaviour identified in the BPM (Foxall 1992b).

Once again, the object of the following examples is to demonstrate that marketing management consists partially in the manipulation of reinforcement.

Examples

Reinforcer Effectiveness

The Token Economy.   Marketers make use of token economy principles (Battalio *et al.* 1974), arranging additional reinforcers contingent upon prior purchasing: the practice is simply an extension of the familiar prize schemes open to collectors of cigarette cards or trading stamps (contingency categories 5 and 6: *saving and collecting* and *token-based buying*). For instance, the points earned by frequent flyers on international airlines are informational reinforcers analogous to the tokens earned for prosocial behaviour in therapeutic and connectional institutions (Chesanow 1985; Foxall 1995a). Similarly, hotels sometimes offer gifts to customers who accumulate points by staying frequently. The collection of these tokens is reinforced by gaining additional free air travel or hospitality (an increase in reinforcer quantity) and/or by access to different types of reinforcer such as prizes (an increase in reinforcer quality). Purchase and consumption of the basic product – i.e. air travel or accommodation – are maintained by both the intrinsic utilitarian reinforcers they embody and the informational consequences of buying and using them. These extrinsic, informational reinforcers also act as discriminative stimuli, directing behaviour toward the attainment and consumption of the additional (back-up) reinforcers offered. The use of tokens in this way may not only increase the loyalty of existing consumers but also increase overall demand, at least while the deal is operated.

Retailer-operated loyalty schemes also exemplify the attempted use of token economy principles. Insurance premiums have always reflected the level of risk borne by the insurer; banks and building societies often charge small depositors additional fees or reduce the rate of interest for such savers. Some US retailers offer cardholders varying discounts depending on the amount they spend: most-favoured customers might receive 20 per cent off, reducing to zero per cent for the customer group most costly to serve and yielding the lowest revenues/profits. Consumers who do not 'perform' sufficiently profitably may be dropped from the scheme. It is questionable, however, whether such schemes actually encourage deviation from the usual pattern of loyalty shown by consumers. See Ehrenberg and Scriven (1996); Sharp and Sharp (1996). Indeed, although the principles of consumer loyalty schemes, including frequent-flyer programmes, are well understood, there is a general lack of information about their effectiveness, especially long-term.

Special Promotional Deals. The encouragement of approach and the minimisation of escape may be simultaneously accomplished through promotional deals that make an extraordinary reinforcement (such as a prize) contingent upon repeat purchasing (contingency category 5: *saving and collecting*). The requirement that the promoted brand must be successively purchased before the additional reinforcer is obtained reduces the probability of escape or avoidance such as purchasing an alternative brand. Indeed, products that arrive periodically in parts (such as the weekly and monthly magazines that build into encyclopaedia) are promoted such that non-response (missing even one part) is punished: missed parts may become available again only after a period of time has elapsed and the series is rerun, or they may be obtained at additional cost and inconvenience. Competitions and deals demanding repeat buying to be effective also apparently change the schedule of reinforcement, albeit temporarily, for those customers not already brand-loyal.

The benefits of saving and investing are also necessarily delayed; in these cases, the eventual reinforcements on which consumer behaviour is to some extent contingent can be described through prompts and vicarious reinforcement relating to the gaining of interest and bonuses, and the future level of consumption that will ensue: all strengthen the responses which add up to sustained saving or investment over many years.

Contingent Consumption. A similar process is at work in the maintenance of some mandatory or required consumer behaviours (contingency category 8: *mandatory consumption*). Purchase of a less-desired complementary good such as life assurance is reinforced by acquisition of the principally desired product – perhaps a mortgage – and marketers may be able to increase sales of the former by making the primary product contingent upon it more attractive.

Scheduled Reinforcement

Advertising and Mass Communications. Many communications aspects of *hedonism* are, as noted in Chapter 5, maintained by carefully scheduled reinforcement. Mass culture presents frequent and predictable, relatively strong and continuous utilitarian reinforcements that are not contingent upon long periods of concentrated effort. Competing television channels and other electronic media provide dozens of sources of highly utilitarian reinforcement with some informational content. The portable nature of the technologies involved extends the geographical scope of these behaviours.

The consumption behaviours in question are apparently maintained on low variable interval schedules, though in some instances reinforcement is almost continuous. Mass visual communication presents reinforcers in such a way that the audience's attention is maintained in the face of strong competition from alternative media and pursuits. Although TV advertisements fulfil the primary function of presenting discriminative stimuli which signal the reinforcements contingent upon specified purchase and consumption responses, they also reinforce sustained attention on the part of their viewers. Since they are usually presented in open settings that offer numerous incentives to pursue alternative activities, their use of emotional and social reinforcements is understandable. The constant reduction in consumers' attention spans – evidenced by frequent switching of TV channels and use of split screens to watch two or more programs simultaneously – implies a constant search for reinforcement.

In an attempt to overcome this, some television shows incorporate a sustained presentation of reinforcement for very short periods of responding. An example is the 'happy news' bulletin format, which was pioneered in

California and provides frequent reinforcers so that even a short period of viewing is reinforced and further viewing made more probable. The bulletins are meant to entertain as well as inform; stories are chosen for their amusement value and sensational content and each gets two or three minutes' coverage in a 30-minute broadcast which also contains two three-minute advertising breaks and a five-minute weather forecast – all as exciting as the news items.

When the contingencies are remote, verbal behaviour comes into play (Malott, 1989). The analysis undertaken in Chapter 5 clarifies how verbal behaviour, rule-following operates in these circumstances. It is by providing informational reinforcement as an interim or alternative to the eventual contingency-based reinforcement. Marketing makes use of this, e.g. in the promotion of toothpaste, not only on the basis of its capacity to care for teeth by preventing decay etc. but as a means to social ends: white teeth, 'fresh breath confidence' etc. These are informational reinforcers: they indicate how well a person is looking after his teeth and how socially acceptable his or her behaviour is.

Sales Promotions.   The shorter the time between the emission of a response and the presentation of a reinforcer, the greater the likelihood that the behaviour in question will be repeated in future (Alhadeff, 1982). Reduction of reinforcer delay is, therefore, an integral component of the enhancement of reinforcer quality. Where it is necessary for consumers to await gratification already paid for, e.g., when an expensive exotic vacation that will be taken in August must be paid for some months earlier (Contingency category 1: *status consumption*), both payment and patient waiting are elicited and maintained by the presentation of reinforcers for intervening in the act: letters of acknowledgement and receipt, brochures and books describing the trip, preparatory instructions and meetings or film shows of the destination, and so on.

Marketers often increase the quality and quantity of consumers' purchases by providing promotional deals that provide more for the same price or reduce the price. More elaborate methods involve the creation and scheduling of information to consumers, e.g. when a product paid for now cannot be consumed for some time. Progress reports on expensive furniture that is being handmade over a period of weeks or months, advertisements that remind consumers of the benefits of the exotic vacation they are awaiting, preparatory meetings and detailed instructions pertaining to self-improvement courses are all examples of the use of information to reward a commitment made to *Accomplishment* long before the product or service is delivered.

Reinforcer Delay: Product Sequencing

Much consumer marketing management is concerned with the temporal relationships among products that are consumed in a given setting. For instance, the effectiveness of some reinforcers can be increased by deliberately delaying their availability to the consumer. This is an ineffective strategy when competitors can quickly step in and supply the product – there is no point in making would-be customers wait too long for perishable produce. But if the item in question is a service and if the marketer has been successful in closing the consumer setting then marketing managers may have further scope for increasing total purchasing or consumption through delay. This is especially relevant to consumer operants described as *hedonism*. The consumer who has paid for a cinema or theatre seat, for instance, has entered a relatively closed setting. He or she can of course get up and leave at any time (though there will be costs such as the forfeiture of the entrance money, the disdain expressed by other members of the audience who are inconvenienced, and the loss of an opportunity to see the film, play or act). Films and acts in these establishments are often scheduled, however, so that the most popular or most hyped appears last; the audience is, willingly or not, required to consume less highly demanded products such as a minor movie, new short ballets or playlets, advertisements, less-well-known acts, and so on. Nevertheless, they usually wait, primed for the arrival of the major film, play or top of the bill by the state of deprivation induced over the time interval.

The consumer performs a series of responses, chained together so that each reinforces its predecessor (watching the minor movie is a reinforcer contingent on sitting through the advertisements, for example), while each signals the next and makes watching it more probable. The enjoyment of the final act is actually greater because of the anticipation that has been created, the deprivation that has been skilfully managed.

Consumer behaviours that require systematic collection or the accumulation of a specified number of tokens before a major reinforcement is provided are apparently maintained on a fixed-ratio schedule (contingency category 5: *saving and collecting*). These include purchases where payments are made prior to consumption, e.g. the payment of instalments for a vacation that can only be taken once the full amount has been paid. Indeed, any saving done with the intention of making a large purchase when a certain amount has accumulated would fall into this category. Promotional deals requiring the accumulation of coupons or other tokens before a product or service can be obtained also belong here. In both *saving and collecting* and *token-based buying* (contingency categories 5 and 6), the effectiveness of the smaller, frequently acquired reinforcers is enhanced by the promise of the ultimate reinforcer, which takes the form of a prize, dividend or additional product or service. The next item in the series is always strongly reinforcing, therefore, not through its intrinsic worth but because its acquisition is a measure of the consumer's progress toward the final goal.

Quality and Quantity of Reinforcement: Value for Money

Considerable product marketing is dependent upon the management of the schedule of reinforcement. When a reinforcer is provided every time a particular response is performed, individuals learn the required behaviour quickly – every time the switch is turned, the lights go on – but the response is quickly forgotten or extinguished once the reinforcement ceases. Learning a response is surer when reinforcers are intermittent – every *n*th response is reinforced or a reinforcer is given every *x* minutes as long as the action has occurred at least once in the period. Behaviours learned under these conditions often take longer to get into the individual's repertoire, but they are performed for long periods even when all reinforcement has ceased. Industry has long made use of these effects by making pay contingent on the amount of work done (as in piecework).

An example of this that belongs to the *accomplishment* class of consumer behaviour is gambling in a casino, a fairly closed setting that it may be costly or inconvenient to leave once play has begun. Casino managers have considerable control over access to the informational and utilitarian reinforcement represented by winning by virtue of its determining the schedule of reinforcement in operation (although the rules of a game like roulette may be said to determine the schedule, the casino may have legal discretion over the favourability of the odds to the house, and over the amounts staked). 'Stretching' the variable-ratio schedule in operation, so that progressively more responses are needed to achieve reinforcement, is a particularly powerful means to affect behaviour. The reinforcers are both utilitarian (money, which is a generalised secondary reinforcer, can be spent to acquire numerous primary and secondary reinforcers) and informational (the amount won or lost over time gives accurate feedback on performance). Games of chance are scheduled in such a way that gambling is likely to persist even when nothing has been won for some time. Progressively 'stretching' the schedule of wins to responses has the effect of encouraging long periods of gaming.

Table 6.1 summarises the role of the marketing mix in the management of consumer behaviour-setting scope and reinforcer effectiveness and provides examples, rather than an exhaustive typology, of the marketing techniques employed.

Table 6.1 Typology of marketing mix management

	Management of antecedents (behaviour-setting scope)	*Management of consequences (reinforcer/punisher effectiveness)*
Product	Branding: image, competitive advantage Product range structure Innovation	Multi-product deals Quality/quantity Status enhancement
Price	Price to suggest value/ status	Quality/quantity
Promotion	Advertising	Deals/sales management Advertising (reward)
Place	Instore displays/ managed wayfinding Negotiation setting	Deals promoting return to store/schedule management/reinforcer delay

7 Case Studies of Marketing Behaviour

OPERANT ANALYSES OF MARKETING BEHAVIOUR

The following cases illustrate how marketers combine the management of consumer behaviour-setting scope and reinforcer effectiveness in order to develop and implement an overall strategy. These cases are taken from an earlier work (Foxall 1996a) and have been updated where possible. They are chosen here because, among the many available exemplars of marketing as an operant process, they rely on documentation by other researchers. It must be stressed that marketing is an intersection of the behaviours of managers and consumers: neither group is solely responsible for the behaviour pattern that emerges, because each reinforces the behaviour of the other.

ACCOMPLISHMENT: LARGE-GROUP AWARENESS TRAINING

Introduction

Large-group awareness training (LGAT) stems from the 'Human Potential Movement' which was influenced by Rogers, Maslow and Mayo, by existentialism and by various strands of Eastern philosophy (Finkelstein *et al.* 1982). The movement emphasised that neuroses could be cured through 'self-actualisation' or the development of the individual's full potential. Other sources of input to LGAT include Gestalt therapy, sensitivity training, encounter groups and yoga. While LGAT may appear an unusual focus for the study of consumer behaviour, the movement has a strong commercial footing and, from the beginning, the key criterion of its success has been 'consumer satisfaction' (Finkelstein *et al.* 1982: 516–17).

Various programmes now offer this approach to personal development training – 'Lifespring', 'Insight', 'Relationships' and 'Actualisations', for instance. The oldest, *est*, (standing for Erhard Seminar Training), now known as 'The Forum', has been chosen for analysis here since it is 'the only commercial large group training which has been studied in the professional literature' (Finkelstein *et al.* 1982: 518).

Operant Class

The operant class to which consumer behaviour of this kind belongs (our first level of analysis) is apparently accomplishment, since high levels of both utilitarian and informational reinforcement maintain the responses involved. Utilitarian reinforcement is evident from the ability of the service provided to the consumer: self-management skills, emotional release during the programme, and the resulting capacity to control one's life more effectively after the two compulsory weekends and the voluntary 'post-graduate' meetings that the training offers.

Informational reinforcement takes the form of feedback on the individual's performance in life (pointing out first the unworkability of his or her life to date), on the acquisition of the positive understanding and skills provided by the course, and – through the post-graduate meetings – continued performance feedback as the principles of *est* are put into practice in the real world. Both of these sources of reinforcement appear to influence behaviour strongly relative to their effects in the other operant classes considered here (see also Foxall 1990: chapter 5).

Contingency Category

At the second level of analysis, that of the contingency category, it is apparent that LGAT takes place in a relatively closed setting, that of a hotel ballroom between 8.30 a.m. and about midnight on the Saturdays and Sundays of two consecutive weekends. Trainees also must attend a pre-training evening, when they are introduced to the rules that will govern their behaviour in the ballroom sessions, and a three-hour mid-training session held on the Wednesday evening between the two training weekends.

The rules to which they are introduced at the pre-training session, and which are generally followed throughout the training, require the consumer to forgo alcohol and non-prescription drugs during the sessions, to introduce no watch or other timepiece into the training room, to use toilets, eat and smoke only during breaks, to remain in their seat, until they are called upon, to wear identification tags, and to avoid sitting close to anyone of their acquaintance (Finkelstein *et al.* 1982; Fisher *et al.* 1990; Rhinehart 1976). The degree of pliance induced by the stating and re-stating of such rules and the means by which consumer behaviour in the setting is personally mediated (see below) confirms that *est* takes place in a closed setting compared with other forms of accumulation (e.g. the prepurchase browsing for luxury items in a prestigious department store that is classified as status consumption).

We may, therefore, justifiably refer to *est* and other LGATs as *fulfil-ment*. By contrast, accomplishment in open settings, e.g. browsing for a luxury gift in a prestigious department store, provides the consumer with far more choice among alternative products, brands and stores, and also confers more temporal control.

The essence of the case study of *est* is the identification of its methods of controlling consumer behaviour in the current setting by means of rules and other discriminative stimuli that signal the positive and aversive con-sequences that are immediately contingent upon responses performed 'here and now'. This is the concern of the third level of analysis, that of the consumer situation.

The Consumer Situation

On the first morning of the training, 250 to 300 trainees assemble, wearing tags showing their first names, in a ballroom in which they are seated fac-ing the dais, which contains only blackboards, stools and a lectern. The ground rules are reread by the assistant trainer who stresses their voluntary nature, though by now each trainee has agreed in writing to be bound by them. The trainer who now takes over is clean and smart and projects an air of authority; he or she is in total control. Trainees may address no one but the trainer and then only when called upon.

The trainer terminates the interaction with the trainee by saying 'thank you' (an informational reward, since it may signal that the trainee has under-stood what is being said or has complied with some requirement). This 'thank you' is also a signal for the audience to applaud (a utilitarian reward since it suggests approval and recognition). The rules emphasise the control-ling features of the physical and social environment – social restraints (the power of the anonymous crowd) and physical constraints (the doors to the ballroom are actually locked) and forbid familiar discriminative stimuli such as watches and clocks. At first, the sole behaviour permitted of the trainees is speaking, when permission is granted, to the trainer, and later movements and actions are restricted to what the trainer prompts and allows.

Learning Histories

Some rudimentary conclusions can be drawn with respect to the learning histories of the trainee consumers. According to Fisher *et al.* (1990: 36–8), *est* participants are typically female (60 per cent), heterosexual (>90 per cent), white (>90 per cent), infrequent churchgoers (63 per cent went 'rarely'), middle-income (>66 per cent earned between 12 000 and 50 000 dollars), not living alone (>80 per cent), and highly educated (15 years on average). Trainees are, however, more positively inclined toward self-improvement and change than a control group of peer-nominees; they also have a tendency to report a greater impact on their lives of negative happenings during the preceding year than do members of the control group, even though both have roughly the same number of such negative events (Fisher *et al.* 1990: 38).

More interesting is the re-evaluation and redefinition of their learning histories during and as a result of the seminar training. Its transformation is closely related to the progressive assertion of instructional control by the trainer over trainees (Baer and Stolz 1978: 49). Trainees are encouraged to give up their 'act', their self-images and attempts at self-presentation of their beliefs about themselves, their titles, the rules by which they try to live, their wealth, knowledge of their reputation, techniques of self-defence, etc. The trainer subtracts all of these defences against the new knowledge he or she is trying to inculcate, to wear down the trainee's ideas about the source of his or her personal status and worth. This procedure actually invalidates the trainee's learning history (as he or she is aware of/can verbalise it), especially that based on informational learning, i.e. the result of performance feedback.

Trainees are encouraged to 'give up their act' in several ways (Baer and Stolz 1978: 49–50). First, any self-assertion on the part of a trainee with respect to his or her personal status, position or achievements is immediately punished; the trainee's assertions are ridiculed, he or she is called an 'asshole', and it is pointed out that the trainee's life does not work: else why are they here? Second, the trainer points out that trainees do not know even what they think they do; they do not know how true what they believe about themselves actually is. Third, trainees are led to disbelieve their own minds which are portrayed as 'tricksters'. Fourth, all attempts at escaping the contingencies are punished. Finally, the physical surroundings – a fifteen-hour day spent in a cool room, for instance – increases the probability that the trainer's instructional control will be effectively imposed; few trainees have a learning history that would enable them to cope with the closed behaviour-setting situation in which they now find themselves.

Conclusion

Several tactics allow the trainer to fine-tune the instructional control strategy. He or she first tells them accurately how (bad) they are feeling, increasing the feeling that the instructor is always right. Then, he or she slowly increases their feelings of self-worth. It is all part of the *est* philosophy that the trainee is already perfect, already doing an unexceptionable job of being him or herself; the course aims at 'enlightenment' but this is the realisation that there is actually nothing to 'get', one is already complete, has no need to evaluate him or herself or his or her progress, no need to set up standards for the self or others (Baer and Stolz 1978: 57). It takes time for this full philosophy to be presented and for the trainees to 'get it' – hence the length of the seminar training – but the road to self-realisation or self-actualisation begins now.

Third, the trainer allows no countercontrol: he or she is not open to suggestion, persuasion or coercion from the floor. He or she ignores personal attacks while providing selective reinforcement for the trainee's self-disclosure, 'sharing', and gradually transferring control to the audience, allowing the informational reinforcement of a 'thank you' (which implies some progress has been made) to be enhanced by the utilitarian control exerted by the group's rate of acceptance. As we have seen, the physical, social, temporal and regulatory environment consists of discriminative stimuli that signal all the rewards and punishment within the control of the trainer and their relationship to specific behaviours – by trainees in the setting.

The in-setting training also provides utilitarian reinforcers, which have the effect of further reducing the power of the pre-training learning history and of strengthening the new patterns of behaviour learned during the sessions. Not only are new skills learned; they are accompanied by the emotional release elicited during the nine 'processes' of 'experience algorithms' that trainees undertake with eyes closed. Each of these increases their self-awareness, i.e., leads to a greater understanding of the contingencies that have influenced the trainees' behaviour. 'They immerse the person in feelings, attitudes, sensations, and judgments that might otherwise be avoided. Thus, they allow an appreciation of what the experiences in fact consist of . . .' (Baer and Stolz 1978: 53). The trainee is encouraged to be in a position to articulate the contingencies that have shaped their prior behaviour and emotional reactions, to practice self-management and gain control. In the process of reinventing the self, the trainee establishes or recognises new reinforcers, which strengthen the new self-image he or she has acquired.

HEDONISM: THE MANAGED RESTAURANT EXPERIENCE

Introduction

An example of hedonism is provided by the Benihana restaurant case (Sasser *et al.* 1978: 44–57), on which the following account is based. Each restaurant in the Benihana chain features Japanese décor and a 'Teppanyaki' table at which a chef prepares and serves food directly to the customers, next to whose table the apparatus is located.

Operant Class

At the first level of analysis, that of the operant behaviour class, the experience of dining in this context is apparently reinforced by high levels of utilitarian reinforcement and a low but not insignificant level of informational reinforcement. Evidence of the former is provided, first, by the behaviour of the chef (who, like the waitress who is the other person who delivers the service, is responsible for two tables): the chef prepares, cooks and serves the food with flourish and panache, the restaurant is generally acknowledged to be in show business as well as the food delivery industry and the gas fired Teppanyaki table, containing the grill and a ledge for the various implements used in cooking, lie at the heart of the showbiz. The native Japanese chefs are highly trained in a formal three-year apprenticeship: Benihana cooking is 'mostly showmanship' and requires such detailed training; chefs behaviour is controlled by competition among the chefs and through a travelling inspector. The product itself is highly visual.

The second, interrelated, aspect of utilitarian reinforcement is the food itself: highly palatable (to US customers) 'wholesome, familiar food, with unusual, unique and delicious preparation, served in a fun atmosphere'. The Benihana marketing philosophy continues, 'We want to intrigue the people celebrating an anniversary or taking Aunt Sally out to dinner. A Japanese restaurant would normally never cross their minds. We are saying we are a fun place to try, and there is no slithery fishy stuff' (Sasser *et al.* 1978: 54). The menu comprises a limited range of typically *American* foods – steak, shrimp, chicken – all of which are 'middle American entrées'. The limited accompaniments – bean sprouts, zucchini, fresh mushrooms, onion and rice – are similarly standardised and invariable. Exotically titled but familiar beverages are highly priced but served in cheap paper mugs.

Informational reinforcement consists predominantly in the social status gained from taking guests to this unusual and novel restaurant, a useful additional reward for whoever is treating 'Aunt Sally', or taking business colleagues for a short but unusual lunch or dinner prior to a business meeting perhaps.

Contingency Category

At the second level of analysis, that of the contingency category, there appears to be strong justification for designating this consumer activity as

inescapable entertainment, since the form of the showbiz is entirely beyond the control of the customer and there are numerous constraints on
behaviour that would lead to the view that the setting is closed.

Consumers would not go to Benihana if the food were not intrinsically
good to eat (and research shows that a high proportion of current consumers are returners). Therefore, the panache with which they are entertained
while eating and drinking is an inescapable extra, albeit pleasant and rewarding in itself. For all that the customer is free to walk out or try to ignore such entertainment, the setting is very different from, say, watching
television or listening to CDs or the radio in one's own home, where it is
possible to switch channels or tracks at will and to escape entertainment
altogether with ease. By comparison, eating at home or at a fast-food restaurant provides more choice and control; other forms of entertainment are
within the control of the consumer at each stage and at every moment: listening to music at home, watching television, walking the dog, for instance.

The Consumer Situation

The third level of analysis, that of the consumer situation, confirms this by
identifying the specific physical, social, temporal and regulatory discriminative stimuli by which the behaviour of consumers is shaped and constrained. Even before they get to the dining area guests are assembled
informally in the bar into groups of eight; each eight consists of groups and
individuals who are strangers to one another. Each of these groups of eight
is shepherded by a waitress to the table: the bench-style seats do not encourage lingering beyond about three-quarters of a hour; the limited menu
makes for speedy ordering; the food is grilled, which also encourages
speed of service; the chef 'force-feeds' customers by throwing them
pieces of food during the cooking; meat is cut up to assist faster eating; the
sole dessert, sherbet, is also quickly consumed and will begin to melt if it is
left too long.

The end of the 'show' is signalled by the chef's bow: this puts the clientele under some pressure to leave, but if it does not have the desired effect
then he can start to clean the grill in anticipation of the arrival of the next
group of diners. In any case, the surrounding showbiz does not encourage
extended discussions: 'normally a customer can come in, be seated, and be
on his way out in forty-five minutes, if need be. The average turnover was
an hour, up to an hour and a half in slower periods' (Sasser *et al.* 1978: 48).
The pace is set by the chef, who controls the proceedings, if only because
his take-home pay depends on tips.

The rules, all plys, which maintain this behaviour programme include the following: you should take a seat in the bar as directed and order a drink or drinks; you should move to the table when directed; you should order and eat relatively speedily; you should watch the 'show' rather than get involved in lengthy conversation; you should not converse at length with strangers; you should leave when the meal ends; you should not keep other customers waiting. Once one person leaves, follow them out. These rule-governed behaviours are encouraged and reinforced by the discriminative stimuli at the disposal of the waitress and the chef, and reinforce positively and negatively by the smiles, greetings, gestures and the appropriateness of the behaviour of these personnel.

ACCUMULATION: FREQUENT-FLYER PROGRAMMES

Introduction

The frequent-flyer programmes of major airlines provide an example of accumulation – a class of consumer behaviours in which informational reinforcement is particularly to the fore while utilitarian reinforcement is *relatively* unimportant. This case is based on the academic literature on frequent-flyer programmes (Gilbert 1996) and information relating to the Qantas Frequent Flyer Programme (Qantas n.d.) which appears typical of many other schemes offered. Members of such schemes acquire a standard number of points for every kilometre or mile travelled with the airline (and associated carriers) for which they have paid a full fare.

Business-class passengers accumulate points at a higher rate and first-class flyers at a higher rate still. Members who purchase or consume other services – such as selected car hire, credit card use, and hotel accommodation, or who use less-attractive (e.g. night) flights or new routes – may add further 'bonus' points to their total. Feedback is provided by statements frequently mailed to members of the scheme, which detail distances flown, bonuses and points accrued.

Operant Class

This case provides insight into the relationship between utilitarian and informational reinforcement. The feedback provided by the accumulation of points is, as just noted, dependent upon the consumption of services that provide mainly utilitarian rewards – air travel, car rental, etc. – though some informational reinforcement may be forthcoming directly from the

conspicuous consumption of some of these services that provide social
prestige. Additional points may be earned by using the American Express card issued in conjunction with the Qantas programme under the
American Express 'Membership Miles' scheme. Moreover, the ultimate
source of reinforcement is undoubtedly utilitarian – free air travel and
other benefits.

These 'other benefits' combine utilitarian and informational reinforcement in an interesting way. They include priority check-in at airports, an
additional baggage allowance, priority baggage handling facilities, and
a booking service for concerts and plays in London, Australia and the
United States. These additional benefits are available to holders of a 'silver' card, an item of performance feedback conferred when 70 000 points
have been earned on international flights or 17 500 on domestic routes or a
combination, within a twelve-month period. They are available only when
the cardholder is paying full fare for a journey.

When an even higher total of points is accumulated within a year
(250 000 for international flights, 62 500 for domestic, or a combination)
the member of the scheme may receive a 'gold' card, which confers further
privileges – e.g., access to 'Captain's Club' lounges at airports irrespective
of the class of travel selected as long as the trip is international. Points must
be redeemed within two years. Just joining attracts an informational reward
– a 'white' membership card that enables miles travelled to be tracked automatically as long as the card number is quoted when a reservation is made.

The operant class to which the behaviour under review belongs is accumulation. Informational reinforcement in the form of frequent/regular feedback on the number of miles travelled or points accumulated is the most
important means of maintaining the behaviour. That behaviour is travelling with the designated airline on a future trip. This does not imply that utilitarian reinforcement is either absent or unimportant: indeed, we have
noted the interaction of the two sources of reinforcement and the way in
which the informational is ultimately sustained by the utilitarian.

Contingency Category

At the second level of analysis, the behaviour of the scheme member
takes place within a relatively closed consumer behaviour-setting. Having entered the scheme, it is more attractive to continue flying with the
designated airline in order to realise both the informational reinforcement immediately available and the ultimate utilitarian reward contingent upon accumulation. To some degree the frequent flyer becomes
locked into being loyal to that airline. The opportunity to purchase other

services such as car rental further reduces the probability that the consumer will fly with another carrier, because those services are contingent upon his or her having travelled with the airline that operates the scheme.

By comparison, accumulation in the form of regular saving into a bank account or collecting part-works that build into a reference book or encyclopaedia takes place in a relatively open setting. The consumer is not locked in to the same degree: it is possible to transfer a savings account to another bank whose interest rates have been increased; missing a magazine is not punished by irretrievable loss, because it may be available by mail or when the part work is republished. (Recall that in the frequent-flyer scheme points must be used within a specific time frame.) The reinforcer obtained each week or month is an end in itself as well as being part of a growing whole. Thus continued accumulation is not compelled.

The Consumer Situation

At the third level of analysis, the consumer situation is marked especially by rules that determine whether behaviour will be followed by contingent reinforcement. Rules determine who is a member, how membership is defined, how points and bonuses will be added, how points (tokens) will be converted into back-up reinforcers, and so on. These rules are plys: compliance on the part of the traveller is at the heart of the entire enterprise. We can only assume that the traveller has a history of delayed utilitarian reinforcement supported by the apportionment of tokens that act as discriminative stimuli for further responding.

MAINTENANCE: THE DESIGN OF AIRPORT WAITING

Introduction

In 'maintenance', consumer behaviour of a particular topography is all but compelled by the contingencies: the consumer has no escape from the performance of the behaviour in question because so much depends upon it – usually a very significant utilitarian and/or informational reinforcer. In order to take an aeroplane to a necessary business trip or to an exotic holiday destination, it is necessary to reach the airport and to remain there for some considerable time prior to takeoff. The direct positive consequences of this airport waiting are minimal and the aversive consequences substantial.

Operant Class

The classification of airport waiting as 'maintenance' (level 1) follows from the above brief description: neither utilitarian nor informational reinforcement is other than fundamental – there is sufficient comfort to keep customers there without complaint; sufficient progress reports (e.g., in the form of announcements about the time remaining to wait until the flight is called) and other discriminative stimuli detailing the availability of the principle utilitarian and informational reinforcer – the flight – to maintain further waiting.

Contingency Category

The physical, social, temporal and regulatory environment is sufficiently prescribed as to enable this situation to be classified unambiguously as mandatory consumption. Sommers (1970: 2) describes 'hard' architecture as designed by those who know what is best for others. It cannot be destroyed since it is 'strong and resistant to human imprint'; to those who use it, it seems impervious, impersonal and inorganic; and it is characterised by 'a lack of permeability between inside and out'. Of all the forms of architecture he considers, Sommers describes airport terminals as 'among the hardest buildings in the land' (p. 70). By comparison, consumer behaviour for food products, which also qualifies as maintenance, usually takes place in a relatively open setting: the consumer is not compelled to shop at any particular store or to select specific brands or products on all occasions (Ehrenberg 1972; Foxall 1992a).

The Consumer Situation

Moving on to the third level of analysis, that of the consumer situation, it is clear that the scope of these consumer behaviour-settings is severely limited: by the physical surroundings that comprise the terminal, by the implications of the physical context of social behaviour, by time constraints, and by rules that influence where consumers can go and what they can do there. People have to spend considerable periods of time in airports – longer now that security checks often mean arriving two or three hours prior to departure. Sommers points out (p. 70) that 'no agency or organisation feels a responsibility for insuring that waiting time is pleasant or productive'. Such waiting time is especially long on trans- and intercontinental flights, which are often delayed, overbooked, consolidated or cancelled. The time is spent in a 'cold, sterile and unfriendly building'. The social and physical layout is fine for passengers who want to be alone, but there is nothing for those who would prefer 'a reassuring and comfortable environment' (p. 71).

Hence the passenger suffers first of all an arduous trip to the airport, treatment as a non-person by uniformed personnel and left to his own devices to find the right check-in desks, queues, seating areas and pathways. The seating is such that all the chairs are identical and are bolted together; the consumer is again ignored. It seems that officials only become aware of the existence of the customer and his needs when he or she is in the plane and is highly cosseted, though even here the consumer is socially isolated.

The seating in the waiting area, consonant with the entire building, is sociofugal rather than sociopetal (Osmond 1957); whereas the latter encourages social contact, the former isolates the individual – where there is crowding things are even worse, because the psychological apartness (Sommers 1970: 73) is emphasised. As a result people occupy small spaces, reading books and magazines, and thus avoiding interaction with others who are nearby.

The layout of the airport is such that both children and adults are 'restricted to a few role responses such as playing the insurance machine, walking up the down escalator, turning on the water fountain, riding the conveyor belt in the baggage section when the attendant is not present, inspecting the candy machine, checking out the waste baskets and pulling the levers on the cigarette machines' (Sommers 1970: 74). If children are to see the planes, they must often be lifted by an adult because of the high windows (this is not so true nowadays).

Older people are also very isolated, and their sense of separation is enforced by the institutional row of chairs. According to Sommers, airports seem deliberately designed to eliminate conversation among the passengers. The evidence for this is that the seats are fastened together with armrests that demarcate each individual's permitted space; rows are back to back or arranged in classroom style facing the counter, chairs are identical, because it is assumed that everyone is the same size and shape, there is nowhere to leave coats, there is a need to put parcels, cabin luggage, coats etc. on a lap or on the floor nearby and to police them so that they are not trodden on and that no one trips over them. The most important thing is that the chairs are unmovable; nobody is allowed to form them into a circle to enable social interaction within a group. Sommers sees in this sociofugal waiting area 'a conspiracy to drive passengers out to the concessions where they will spend money'.

He suggests that the seating in airport lounges is deliberately arranged to minimise social interaction and to encourage passengers to visit the profitable concessions such as shops and restaurants provided by airline operators. Airport operators derive a considerable proportion of their income from this source, and some airport retailers achieve far higher revenues than is the norm (Newman *et al.* 1994a, b and c; see also Chesterton 1993; Doganis 1992; Gilchrist 1994; Market Assessment 1992; Mayer 1993). UK airport authorities are, moreover, legally restricted in raising revenue from more traditional sources; retail sales at airports rose by 45 per cent between 1989 and 1993, while revenues of specialist retailers in airports increased by 22 per cent over this period (Baron and Wass 1996).

A major reason is 'large numbers of (relatively) high income consumers passing through, with little other than shopping available as a diversion' (Newman *et al.* 1994a: 1; Butler and Jernigan 1993). Some consumer behaviour at airports is also directly related to consumption requirements before and during the journey (Baron and Wass 1996). Airport retailers have deliberately 'taken retailing to the people' (Davies 1995: 22; see also Wileman 1993; Baron and Wass 1996; Baker *et al.* 1994).

However, airport retailers increasingly design and create prestige shopping environments and offer levels of service comparable with those made available in luxurious outlets in non-airport settings that are known to elicit positive emotions in prospective consumers that are related to propensity to purchase in general and to buy on impulse in particular (Bateson 1985; Donovan and Rossiter 1982; Hornik 1982; Gardner 1985; Snodgrass and Russell 1988). The use of shopping-mall-style or pavilion-type retailing environments is becoming the norm, especially for international airports (Newman *et al.* 1994c; see also Proctor 1992).

The probable result is that consumers are 'psychologically embroiled in a profound, captivating, and possible anxious experience and, as a result, are highly likely to be emotionally *aroused* by a diverse range of affluent stores, aesthetic designs, and high priced goods' (Newman *et al.* 1994c: 8). The expectant mood with which both business and vacation travellers enter the airport and which they maintain while there (in behaviourist terms, the effects of their learning histories in similar situations previously encountered) also makes purchase more probable; the particular setting is composed of discriminative stimuli intended to instigate consumer behaviours such as search, browsing, comparison, evaluation, purchasing and consumption (Newman, Davies and Dixon 1994b, 1994c).

Sommers's (1974: 70–80) view is that 'any effort to humanise or provide amenities in the waiting area is a threat to the restaurant, cocktail lounge, news stand, and gift shop. No one, including the airlines, has a financial stake in the comfort of passengers in the waiting areas'. Therefore 'passengers have no organisational representation to look after their interests' (p. 79). 'They are regarded by the airlines as merchandise to be shipped elsewhere and by the concessionaries as sheep to be sheared (ibid.).' Those with the greatest power and influence are bought off by being taken to their own luxurious lounges which are subsidised by economy passengers.

Conclusion

Overall the impersonal institutional atmosphere of the airport waiting area means that there is extremely limited social interaction even with the family group that one has arrived with. Bomb scares mean that passengers are routed through sanitised areas while family and friends are denied access to boarding areas. Moreover much of the architecture is identical from airport to airport (e.g. the restaurant). All of this is reinforced by a series of rules which make pliance the most obvious characteristic of consumer behaviour in this setting.

SUMMING UP

Marketing management emerges as a component of the consumer's behavioural environment that attempts to influence choice in ways reminiscent of the control of operant behaviour in the laboratory, the chief difference lying in the relatively open settings in which consumer behaviour occurs, the competition among marketing organisations for consumers' attention, and the reality of alternative, non-marketing control of consumer behaviour such as the influence of fellow consumers (Foxall 1995b).

In summary, *marketing management* is a function of the firm that involves managing the marketing relationships between the firm and its customers and suppliers (through behaviour-setting scope modification and the use of reinforcers). As will be shown, marketing management is but one activity of the marketing firm, which is additionally concerned with managing intra-firm (quasi-) marketing relationships (e.g. with employees) and extra-firm mutuality relationships (e.g. with stakeholders). We can also define *consumer–orientated management* as the activity of the firm that involves the creation and implementation of marketing mixes that reinforce consumers for purchasing the marketing organisation's brand (i.e. ensures that they are sufficiently satisfied to show some degree of loyalty for the firm's brand), as a result of which the firm is reinforced (i.e. keeps developing and offering marketing mixes of this kind which maintain consumer behaviour). In short, it requires the creation of conditions most conducive to consumers' buying the brand of the marketing organisation – using not only price but promotion, place/time and product utilities.

8 Marketing Relationships

THE NATURE OF THE MARKETING FIRM

Origins and Functions

This analysis of the marketing function leads naturally to consideration of the nature of the organisation responsible for marketing management. In this final chapter we return to the concerns of Chapter 6. Why do such business organisations exist within a market framework that presumably could undertake these functions in the absence of firms? This is of course related to the question raised by Coase (1937): why do firms come into being? Our questions are more complex, however: why do *marketing* firms exist? And what do they *do*?

Answering this question requires a more detailed examination of the nature of the marketing relationships that bind the firm to its publics. At the heart of the definition of economic behaviour is the idea of the transaction, a term that requires precise delineation in order to be analytically useful. It is not sufficient to point out that economic behaviour is that in which revenues and costs play a part, yielding a profit or loss, because all operant behaviour can be loosely cast in these terms. Economic behaviour is simultaneously reinforced and punished and its probability in any specific instance can be represented as a vector quantity derived from the strength of the individual's history of reinforcement for similar behaviour in the past *and* that of his or her history of punishment stemming from the same source. Alhadeff (1982) notes that consumer behaviour, for example, is determined at the intersection of two response strengths – that for approach (a function of the benefit likely to result from purchase and/or consumption) and that for avoidance (a function of the costs of that purchase/consumption). Each of these response strengths is the product of the reinforcement schedule on which it was acquired, the quality and quantity of reinforcement, and reinforcer delay. However, despite the centrality of this phenomenon to the analysis of economic behaviour, these 'contingencies of reinforcement' and even the presence of approach vs. avoidance response strengths are not definitive thereof.

Social relationships entail mutually reinforced actions. The behaviour of A (or its effects) reinforces that of B, while B's behaviour reinforces that of A. These behaviours are mutually contingent: each occurs only if the other is present to act as a discriminative stimulus for its enactment. Although social behaviours of this sort (say, two people waving to each other) are said to constitute exchanges, this usage is entirely metaphorical and does not apply to the economic behaviour of the marketing firm.

An essential characteristic of an *economic* transaction is exchange. A bilateral economic exchange is marked by mutual reinforcement, achieved through swapping or trading entities; for analytic purposes, its essence lies in its constituting genuine exchange, i.e. the literal swapping of things rather than the symbolic or metaphorical interaction that occurs when people are said to 'exchange glances'. (Note that literal exchange need not imply a market clearing price, nor that supply and demand are equated in some way by the transaction. The mutual reinforcement inherent in exchange signifies that the seller's opportunity costs of relinquishing the commodity are lower than the reinforcement he receives via the price he obtains. Similarly, the buyer's costs of surrendering that price are outweighed for him by the reinforcing consequences of owning and using the commodity.) In operant terms, an exchange transaction is marked by mutual reinforcement, though in each case what is received is as reinforcing as or more reinforcing than the retention of what is given up. (Strictly speaking, what is initially received must be more *rewarding* for the individual: only if a series of transactions occurs can we speak accurately of *reinforcement*; see Foxall 1990: chapter 2.) Some part of an economic exchange must be actual barter or pecuniary interchange.

The reason for insisting on literal exchange as integral to the definition of economic and marketing behaviour is that the marketing firm cannot function in its absence. In *economic* behaviour, the actions of A (or B) provide both utilitarian and informational reinforcement for those of B (or A). Supplier A provides goods for customer B; in return B provides A with money and market intelligence. The goods are utilitarian in that they provide legal entitlement to benefits, and informational in that they provide economic capital (if the customer is a firm) or social status (if a final consumer). The money is utilitarian for the supplier (who extracts profits from it) and informational as well (as it is recorded in the supplier's accounts). Market intelligence is an informational reinforcer, since it provides data on what consumers have bought, what they have paid, etc., which allows the supplier to behave rationally with respect to future production decisions (what to make, what to charge, etc.) The reduction of transaction costs requires that marketing intelligence of this kind be available to the firm. But such information is available only if transactions include literal exchange. (Note that the insistence on literalness of exchange may exclude from *economic* analysis some of the themes adopted by certain economics of law schools. See Duxbury 1995, chapter 5.)

However, the question of what is exchanged needs further clarification, else the insistence on simple, literal exchange as integral to the definition of economic behaviour will become problematic on occasion, e.g. where services, which are intangible, are concerned. What is exchanged is legal title to the outcome of a service performed – the benefits of, say, a haircut or insurance policy. As Coase (1988a: 11) puts it,

> Lawyers . . . habitually think of what is bought and sold as consisting of a bundle of rights. It is easy to see why I was led to adopt the same approach in dealing with the radio frequency spectrum, since it is difficult to treat the use of the right to emit electrical radiations solely in physical terms.

Economic exchange usually involves the parties' entering into an implicit or explicit contract to obtain or be recompensed for giving up goods under specified terms; the contract is enforceable either by process of law or by coercion. (See, in this context, the literature on hostages, e.g. Williamson 1985.) A transaction involves the exchange of two bundles of property rights (Demsetz 1967; Dnes 1996; Posner 1992).

Legal entitlement and contractual provisions are part of the contingencies of reinforcement and punishment by which behaviour is shaped and maintained. Another source of such contingencies (and the environmental control of behaviour which they signify) is the market. A market is in essence a set of contingent relationships among discriminative stimuli (e.g. contracts of employment), responses (e.g. working practices) and reinforcing/punishing consequences (e.g. wages, being fired). Market transactions denote competitive pressures on both buyer and seller: the former may purchase elsewhere the latter sell to someone else. As has been noted, such exchange does not imply maximisation, equilibration, or clearing. Maximisation is in any case a metaphysical concept, because its occurrence can never be empirically detected (and is inferred only by way of tendentious reasoning). Simply desiring more rather than less does not signify maximisation. Behavioural experimentation with the matching law implies melioration as well as maximisation (Herrnstein 1990); and matching may not occur consistently or at all in humans (Horne and Lowe 1996).

The definition of economic exchange also has an institutional component, because the behaviour it entails is reinforced and punished by deliberately established and maintained institutions in society: social, economic, political, legal, etc. The structural requirement of marketing-orientated management that there should be numerous consumers with the discretionary income to allow them choice and competition among a multiplicity of suppliers (Foxall 1981) means that the entities exchanged (legal rights) must be generally transferable through market transactions. The marketing firm is not engaged in a single bilateral relationship between itself and *a* buyer or supplier: if the property rights involved in a transaction are not for any reason exchanged, the structure of the market is such that another buyer or seller can be readily found. Market transactions are, therefore, *general*, though the marketing relationships that the firm engages in are specific to a given diadic association.

These considerations permit a clearer picture to be drawn of the marketing firm and its contrasts with certain notions of economic behaviour prevalent in marketing and economics. First, exchange theory (e.g. Homans 1974) does not capture economic exchange understood in this way. By assuming mutual reinforcement of the parties, it goes some way towards recognising mutuality; but it shows no appreciation of the necessity for economic exchange to be literal. Second, the market firm operates within markets which via the price mechanism signal what is to be produced, the amount to be produced, and its exchange value. Marketing as understood here necessarily involves economic exchanges. Third, the full complement of marketing mix elements is necessary in order to function as such a firm: hence, much 'social marketing' – the transmission of ideas, such as that of contraception in Third World countries threatened by over-population, rather than goods – which relies on moral obligation and symbolic exchange, is excluded on these criteria. Neither marketing relationships nor the economic behaviour of suppliers and customers can be understood if this is not grasped. Marketing requires the reciprocally reinforcing literal exchanges identified here as the *sine qua non* of economic behaviour. Marketing exchanges of this kind are usually accompanied by additional, social relationships, i.e. relationships characterised by reciprocally contingent reinforcement but not involving literal exchange. Although such mutuality relationships are a frequent accompaniment of marketing relationships, however, they do not of themselves constitute economic behaviour or marketing exchanges.

Hence, although the phenomena labelled social marketing undoubtedly exist, they are not marketing in the sense developed in this chapter. Social marketing is not marketing for three reasons. First, it does not involve literal exchange, nor any transfer of property rights; it depends upon no price mechanism, nor therefore any idea of how much to produce, etc. In the absence of these it could be a waste of corporate resources if conceived as marketing. Second, it does not use all of the marketing mix: it is fundamentally communication; the idea is a metaphor: no product, price, distribution. Third, it therefore consists of mutuality rather than exchange relationships. This is not to say these things are not useful and legitimate, only that it is inapt to apply the term marketing – as we have defined it here – to them. In practice, social marketing consists primarily of communication activities, which are then rationalised as 'marketing' by saying that the message is the 'product'; the audience has to be somewhere or read the message somewhere, so this is said to represent 'place'; the recipient of the message has to attend to it (rather than to something else), process the information it contains, act upon it, all of which are said to exact 'costs' and therefore to represent a 'price'.

However, when nothing is literally exchanged, this is nonsense: lacking any logic of price and value, it gives no indication of what should be produced (Why product A which results in 3 smiles from 'consumers' rather than B which results in only 2? How are smiles to be equated?), or how much, or for whom. So a figurative notion of exchange is substituted. In doing this, authors go entirely beyond the conceptualisation of marketing with which they began. This is fine as far as it goes: non-economic aspects of life cannot be measured with the accuracy that money or barter provides. But it should be conceptualised in terms of mutuality rather than exchange: i.e. reciprocal reinforcement that does not involve literal exchange.

In summary, *marketing*, the intersecting behaviours of consumers/ suppliers and marketers, requires mutual reinforcement, some or all of which involves a literal exchange of economic property rights. It therefore involves price (whether pecuniary or value expressed in whatever is exchanged for goods), which acts as a signal to firms with respect to what they should produce and in what quantity, and to consumers with respect to what and how much to buy. In a consumer-orientated economy, the exchange relationships that are the essence of this definition are usually accompanied by non-exchange relationships, which consist in mutual reinforcement without literal exchange. Literal economic exchange relationships are necessary and sufficient to marketing; mutuality relationships are neither necessary nor sufficient to marketing. Similar marketing relationships also exist between the firm and its suppliers. Other relationships, this time within the marketing firm, also involve literal, economic exchange, e.g. entrepreneur–employee interactions; other stakeholders in the marketing firm are linked to it only by mutuality relationships.

Bilateral Contingency

Economic transactions are represented in an operant account as a pattern of bilateral contingency. The behaviour of the consumer, say his or her making a purchase, is preceded by the discriminative stimulus (say a store logo) provided as a consequence of the marketer's behaviour. The behaviour of the consumer has consequences (e.g. repeat purchase rate, market research opinions) which are proximal causes of further action by the marketer. In general terms, marketer behaviour provides discriminative stimuli for consumer behaviour. The marketing firm also behaves in such a way as to provide and/or control discriminative stimuli in the consumer behaviour-setting that is likely to increase the probability of specific consumer responses.

This is done in two ways. The first is by altering those setting elements under whose direct control consumer behaviour falls, i.e. generalisation of stimulus control. The second is by ensuring that those discriminative stimuli that signal reinforcement contingent on consumer behaviour are primed to do so effectively. Both of these are concerned with consumer behaviour-setting scope management: they are designed to influence/ shape momentary behaviour, i.e. consumer behaviour in this setting. Note that we have extended operant analysis to the behaviour of an organisation – the firm – which involves an abstraction from the usual methodological individualism of operant behaviourism. This is an inevitable consequence of using the operant paradigm to deal with economic behaviour, but it is implicit in any case in the incorporation of firm-generated discriminative and consequence stimuli into the analysis. All sciences abstract in order to explain, though a micro-micro analysis of intra-firm behaviour would of course concentrate on individual-to-individual relationships.

Firms also attempt to shape streams of consumer behaviour over time by managing reinforcement over a period, thereby shifting from a concentration on transactions to one on relationships. The bilateral contingency can be depicted at a more complex level in which the behaviours of each party rather than the consequences of those behaviours act as discriminative stimuli. Consumer behaviour is a discriminative stimulus for firm behaviour. It informs market research, for instance. Consumer behaviour also determines reinforcing and punishing consequences (profit or loss) for the firm. In this case, firms are actively and deliberately involved in the manipulation of consumer behaviour-setting scope and in reinforcement manipulation. Consumers also, collectively, control the behaviour of the firm and the reinforcement/punishment it receives its profit or loss, and thus its future marketing offerings. But consumers rarely do this 'deliberately'; exceptions are organised consumer boycotts. Competitors deliberately influence another firm's setting scope and the consequences of its actions – just by competing in the normal way for consumers' attention, but also by fixing test markets, sabotage, espionage, etc.

A similar pattern of contingencies exists when two firms, a customer and a supplier, are involved. This time, both organisations are actively and deliberately involved in setting management and reinforcer management. ('Deliberately' means that this is an explicit goal, perhaps acting as a discriminative stimulus, not that it is causative in any ultimate sense.)

Mutual Qualification of Behaviour-Setting Scope

The concept of behaviour-setting scope, applied earlier to the circumstances that immediately determine consumer choice, can be extended to the understanding of marketer behaviour. The closedness of a behaviour-setting again refers to the extent to which the determinants of behaviour are under the control of the individual who performs it. Consumers have a central role in reducing the behaviour-setting scope of marketers by requiring quality control, value in exchange, etc. So does the action of rival firms in an economic system characterised by high levels of discretionary income and minimal governmental control lead to the closure of the behaviour-settings of those with whom they compete. The marketer behaviour-setting comprises physical constraints (need for extensive distribution), social constraints (other competitors and publics/stakeholders), regulatory constraints (social norms, state laws) and temporal considerations (again largely affecting distribution). Many of these basic requirements are beyond the control of the marketer; some but not all of them are under the control of consumers, not necessarily individually, not necessarily in an organised manner, but in the aggregate. The concept of managerial behaviour-setting scope underlies the analysis of organisational slack or X-inefficiency (Leibenstein 1966).

Similarly, the pattern of reinforcement (defined by relative utilitarian and relative informational reinforcement) is a concept applicable to the understanding of marketer behaviour. Utilitarian reinforcement again consists in the utilitarian consequences of behaviour, which in the consumer example refers to the basic requirements of maintaining the self as a biological and social entity: it is exemplified most obviously in the corporate sphere by revenue and profit; informational reinforcement consists again in performance feedback: data on return on investment, comparative performance in new product development.

Coase (1988a: 8) emphasises the need to analyse market structure in terms of 'the influence of the social institutions which facilitate exchange', i.e. the contingencies of reinforcement and punishment, the environmental factors that make exchange behaviours more or less probable. This is precisely what marketing institutions are. Within the operant purview, these contingencies consist in the scope of the setting in which behaviour takes place and the pattern of utilitarian and informational reinforcement that maintains such behaviour. Marketer behaviour is constrained by the scope of its settings, just as consumer behaviour is. This is true not only of markets known to be severely circumscribed say by government regulations; speaking of stock exchanges and commodity exchanges as markets often used to exemplify perfect competition, Coase (1988a: 8–9) points out that

> All [commodity and stock] exchanges regulate in great detail the activities of those who trade in these markets (the times at which transactions can be made, what can be traded, the responsibilities of the parties, the terms of settlement, etc.), and they all provide machinery for the settlement of disputes and impose sanctions against those who infringe the rules of exchange. It is not without significance that these exchanges, often used by economists as examples of a perfect market and perfect competition, are markets in which transactions are highly regulated . . .
> It suggests, I think correctly, that for anything approaching perfect competition to exist, an intricate system of rules and regulations would normally be needed.

In other words, transacting takes place within a framework of physical, social, temporal and regulatory discriminative stimuli, and is simultaneously reinforced by the benefits it brings and punished by the costs it imposes. Quoting Adam Smith, Coase notes that regulations may either 'widen the market' or 'narrow the competition', i.e. modify the scope of the marketer behaviour-setting.

The basis of bilateral contingency is the mutual (partial) closure of the parties' behaviour-settings, i.e. the restriction of their room for manoeuvre. In a market economy characterised by minimal state intervention, transactions occur when two parties (consumer and marketer; industrial supplier and industrial buyer; employee and employer; marketing department and production department) simultaneously effect a degree of closure of one another's behaviour-setting. Consider the case of marketer and consumer. Alpha, a marketer, attempts to reduce consumer discretion by making its marketing mix more attractive or less escapable than those of competing marketers.

This reduction in choice is acceptable to Beta, the consumer, because (given his learning history) it reduces his or her transactions costs, i.e. it becomes easier for the consumer to obtain the benefits of the product class by selecting the brand provided by Alpha. The consumer is willing to have the scope of his or her behaviour-setting reduced in order to minimise such marketing costs as search and evaluation. In turn, consumers act to reduce the scope of the marketer's behaviour-setting by demanding high levels of quality control, lower prices, etc. This is accepted by the marketer, because it allows it to reduce transactions costs: Alpha's brand can be economically tailored to the buying propensities of known and reliable market segment. The relationships so formed are 'by consent', but only because the consequences of behaving in this way are positively reinforced by the acquisition of benefits of trade (obtaining the product or the money) and negatively reinforced by avoidance of costs.

Bilateral contingency of this kind can occur only in a marketing-orientated economic system, i.e. one that allows consumer choice based on competition among marketers, and buyers' discretionary income. The result of these structural factors is consumer-orientated marketing management; the bilateral contingency discussed earlier makes clear that it is equally marketer-orientated consumption on the part of the buyer.

The array of marketing and non-marketing relationships in which the firm is embedded are topographically of two kinds. First are those that extend between the marketing firm and external organisations/groups, which give rise to consideration of 'relationship marketing'; second are those internal to the marketing firm, which relate to 'internal marketing'. The content and function of these external and internal relationships define the nature of the marketing firm.

Marketing Relationships

As has been argued, the firm is engaged in marketing relationships with its customers and suppliers. *Marketing relationships* consist of literal exchange relations, and are often but not essentially accompanied by mutuality, i.e. bonds consisting in reciprocated qualification of behaviour-setting scope and/or reciprocated reinforcement. Marketing relationships plus accompanying mutuality are essential components of *relationship marketing*, a term that requires careful consideration in view of its uncritical proliferation.

Several marketing authors have in recent years advocated the substitution of a relationship marketing paradigm for the traditional view of marketing mix management in which a relatively passive consumer is the target of product, price, promotion and distribution strategies and tactics launched by a relatively active marketer (Gronroos 1994). Within the relationship marketing framework of analysis, *transactions* – one-off deals – are contrasted with *relationships* – long-term, mutually satisfying associations involving considerations of customer service, quality, trust and commitment (Payne 1995; Payne *et al.* 1995; Webster 1992). The aim is to retain customers by developing alliances that transcend commercial exchanges rather than simply dealing with them afresh every time a transaction looms. The counterpart work of economists on relational contracting includes Macaulay (1963) and Macneil (1978).

To the extent that this is a descriptive account of relationships in marketing, it has engendered research conducted in a genuine spirit of enquiry with no axe to grind by way of proposing preordained guidelines for practical management. Much of the 'markets as networks' literature certainly falls into this camp. However, some writing on relationship marketing is more closely concerned with prescription. Barnes (1994), for instance, emphasises that relationship marketing is about 'caring for consumers'. Barnes thus rules out the erection of exit barriers such as the imposition of product switching costs from genuine relationship marketing. Such prescription militates against the positive investigation of the nature of the relationships that bind the marketing firm to its stakeholders.

Until we have an idea of the actual content and effects of marketing relationships, know what sustains them and the ways in which pressures to dissolve them are overcome, we will have no grounds for judging how far such prescriptions are realistic or naive. Exit barriers exist and need to be studied in the overall context of the marketing relationship to which they belong; they may make the sort of sense in that framework as does the retention of 'dogs' in a portfolio of interactive products: no dogs, no cash cows or stars. Relationships depend upon mutual contingency – and contingencies involve aversive consequences (or discriminative stimuli that threaten them) as well as positive reinforcers. Until the effects of the potential and real aversive consequences of a relationship can be ascertained, the notion of bond strength is meaningless. The reciprocity of marketing relationships cannot be ignored. It is a truism that firms come into existence to make full vertical integration a reality; relationship marketing is a means of achieving quasi-vertical integration.

Other external relationships, those between the firm and those of its stakeholders other than customers and suppliers (unions, shareholders, owners, government, and competitors), are non-marketing relationships because they do not (usually) involve literal exchange; they are, however, long-term relationships that are maintained over time by reciprocated behaviour-setting qualification and reciprocated reinforcement. In order to distinguish them from marketing relationships, we refer to them as *mutuality relationships*. Note that relationship marketing consists of both types of relationship, though what has here been termed the mutuality component has attracted most of the recent attention of those who have written on this theme (e.g. Gronroos 1994; Morgan and Hunt 1994; Perrien and Ricard 1995). The argument can be summarised thus. *Market transactions* are literal exchanges. They take place in the market before firms come into existence (whether or not one accepts the historicity of this Coasian sequence, it remains a useful analytical device; see Medema 1994). *Marketing relationships* consist of literal exchanges plus mutuality (i.e. reciprocal qualification of behaviour-setting scope and/or reciprocal reinforcement). Firms come into existence to add mutuality to market relationships, i.e. to make relationship more stable and predictable through contracts, etc. Marketing relationships are market relationships plus. They are bonds between the firm and its customers or suppliers. Relationship marketing is genuine marketing as defined in this chapter as long as it includes the literal exchange identified as the essential component of marketing relationships. It cannot consist solely in mutuality relationships, and will usually be part of a business strategy that employs the full marketing mix in response to the conditions requiring marketing-oriented management.

Quasi-marketing Relationships

It is just as legitimate to speak of market transactions in the analysis of intra-firm behaviour as to do so in exploring the nature of transactions in external markets. Moreover, market transactions can be conceptualised and analysed in terms identical to those used in the examination of consumer markets: i.e. conceptualised as literal exchange subject to mutual reinforcement, and analysed as bilateral contingency. This is so despite the apparent contention of transaction cost economists that the firm exists only as a means to circumvent the market and thereby replace market transactions with administrative decision-making (Williamson 1985).

There is no argument with Coase's (1937) insight that firms come into being in order to economise transaction costs (he calls them, revealingly, 'marketing costs'). These are the costs of finding out with whom one wishes or is able to deal, informing prospective co-transactors that one is available to deal and on what terms, negotiating a bargain, drawing up a contract and policing it, and so on (Coase 1960: 15). But two caveats are in order. First, firms appear when the transaction costs of both parties who would otherwise trade in the market are thereby reduced; and second, integration does not supersede or circumvent the market: it circumscribes the market by placing additional, usually contractual, contingencies alongside those that constitute the market; market relationships are thereby limited by contractual considerations but not removed (Alchian and Demsetz 1972; Hart 1989; Jensen and Meckling 1976). Compare a married couple who (a) have an exclusive relationship, (b) are devoted to each other's welfare, and (c) agree that if one of them is unfaithful the other has the right to leave the relationship. (This corresponds to the 'market'.) After a while, they may, in order to avoid disputes, decide mutually that A will spend £x a month on books, B £y a month on audio tapes. Drawing up these ground rules in no way invalidates the marriage, though it modifies their behaviour within the marriage framework. (This is what firms do.) They may co-operate more as a result of the additional rules: A does not mind B reading the books, B does not debar A from listening to the music. Each remains free to exit the relationship under certain circumstances if he or she wishes. The additional contract only strengthens the marriage.

As Coase (1988a, 7–8) puts it, 'Markets are institutions that exist to facilitate exchange, that is, they exist in order to reduce the cost of carrying out exchange transactions . . . The provision of markets is an entrepreneurial activity.' Hence the identification of entrepreneurship with functional marketing and/or marketing-oriented management (Foxall and Minkes 1996). Firms involve organisation, rules, customs, etc., which are brought into being to reduce transaction costs beyond what the market can accomplish. He goes on to say that the identifying character of the firm is its 'supersession of the price mechanism' (p. 36). But this surely can not imply that the firm is not subject to the market, nor that the relationships it contains are free from ultimate market control (Alchian and Demsetz 1972; Hart 1989; Jensen and Meckling 1976; Medema 1994).

Indeed, Coase acknowledges that the firm will continue to grow only until its marginal transaction can be more economically undertaken by the market. This stage will inevitably come: it is unlikely that the firm's long-term cost curve will decline indefinitely; only if this is so and if there is a single global firm could its expansion continue unremittingly. Firms are a mechanism for closing the setting – a means of co-ordinating/managing parts of the economics system in a less costly way than would be achieved without firms. The market is still there and remains the ultimate supplier of resources and arbiter of commercial success. Hence the firm is just a means of trying to control part of the price mechanism by closing the setting (e.g. through contracts of employment) for both parties. That is how firms reduce transaction costs. If this supersedes the price mechanism at all then it does so temporarily and provisionally.

Suppose Alpha is a widget entrepreneur who, instead of continuing to buy in widgets from Epsilon, a widget craftsman, employs Epsilon to produce widgets as a hired member of Alpha Enterprises. (The term 'entrepreneur' denotes the cadre of managers concerned with the strategic scope of the organisation [Foxall and Minkes 1996], especially in its relationships to other members of the firm.) The contractual arrangement thereby created economises the transactions costs of both Alpha and Epsilon. Alpha no longer has to search the market daily for the cheapest widgets; Epsilon no longer has to find a buyer for each day's production. But the market is still there as surely as before: if Epsilon cannot produce widgets of the required quality or quantity, he can be replaced (perhaps only at the expiration of his contract, rather than immediately: that is an extra contingency brought about by *circumscribing* the market). If Epsilon is a superb widgeter, his prowess is likely to come to the attention of Beta Enterprises, Alpha's rival, which will offer Epsilon higher remuneration than Alpha provides. Epsilon can move (again at the expiry of his contract). Moreover, our analysis is not confined to any particular world: Epsilon can leave Alpha and set up as a widget entrepreneur in his own right.

In the terminology of an operant approach to economic behaviour, firms economise on transaction costs by restricting the scope of behaviour-settings. That is, the firm is a mechanism for closing the behaviour-settings of the parties in mutually acceptable ways, for circumscribing the more costly effects of the market in order that both parties may prosper: in fact, not only by economising transaction costs but also by increasing the surplus of their revenues over all costs including those of open-market transacting (or, in Coase's terms, *marketing costs*). The firm is subject nevertheless to the reinforcing and punishing consequences of behaviour in the marketplace. Competitors cannot be ignored whether they are alternative sources of supply to Alpha or rivalrous sellers to Alpha's customers.

A major cost of using the market is discovering the rules under which it is operating (e.g. price–quantity relationships offered by a number of suppliers). Some of this cost is removed if transactions are carried out within the firm on the basis of rules worked out between entrepreneur and producer. Closing the setting is a means of predicting and controlling the behaviour of others. Each party enters this relationship only because it reduces his transaction costs and will remain in it for only as long as it reduces his transaction costs (the control is 'by consent', meaning that it brings economic benefits to both parties).

A special kind of internal relationship is that between the entrepreneur and the other members of the organisation. This is a marketing relationship in the sense that it involves genuine exchange (work done for wages), but it is severely modified by its incorporation within the firm. The firm exists in order to protect the relationship between entrepreneur and firm members from the day-to-day ravages of the market, and thereby to economise transaction costs by facilitating planning and prediction. The market is always there, of course, and will ultimately exert its influence on, for instance, how work is valued in wage terms. But because of the intervention of the firm it does not exercise this control on a continual basis: contracts of employment restrict it by providing that Alpha can only fire Epsilon by giving a period of notice, Epsilon can only take up another offer of employment at the end of such a period, and wages may be adjustable in line with competitive conditions at a specific time of the year.

Employment contracts vary of course, and Epsilon may have more or less favourable terms than those of Beta, Gamma and Delta. A highly rated employee may force an immediate payrise if he threatens to leave the firm in order to work for a competitor, and this capacity to use the external market severely modifies Alpha's authority over him. It seems clear that what distinguishes the quasi-marketing relationships of the intra-firm arrangement from the marketing relationships discussed above is that the former is based upon the authority of the entrepreneur, which is not absolute but which circumscribes the market (cf. Alchian and Demsetz 1972; Foxall 1988; Hart 1989; Jensen and Meckling 1976). Marketing relationships between suppliers and firms may also rest upon a degree of authority when there is quasi-vertical integration (Blois 1972; cf. Monteverde and Teece 1982).

This kind of modified market/contractual agreement is the essence of the marketing firm. Indeed, the firm comes into being for the purpose of circumscribing the competitive vicissitudes of the market in order that production can take place in a framework of stable and predictable relationships. The function of the marketing firm is to introduce mutuality into the relationships between entrepreneur and employer/supplier/customer, to modify market relationships by turning them into market*ing* relationships.

The marketing firm economises transaction costs that would otherwise be incurred by individuals transacting in the marketplace in the absence of firms. But, by engaging in marketing relationships, the firm incurs new transaction costs: those of keeping in touch with suppliers and customers, as well as firm members and other stakeholders, ensuring that the long-term relationship endures, and so on. These are the costs of mutuality relationships, essential as we have seen to relationship marketing. Thus, as

Coase points out, the marketing firm does not eliminate transaction costs; nor does it simply reduce those costs that are contingent upon trading in the open market. Rather, it changes the composition of the transaction cost structure that the firm encounters in order to receive the additional revenue and profit benefits of extending its marketing relationships. Intra-firm marketing of this kind is far from coterminous with so-called 'internal marketing', however.

Internal marketing refers to at least three essential functions of management: (i) ensuring that the entire organisation is focused on the marketing-orientated goal of ensuring that consumers receive the levels of service and quality necessary to retain their goodwill and patronage; (ii) internal communication of the aims and methods of the marketing function to other members of the organisation, especially those with responsibility for carrying out the marketing programme; and (iii) 'marketing' marketing within the firm, i.e. promoting the marketing philosophy and function as components of the organisation deserving of further resource allocation (Payne 1995). All of these things need to be done, but it is a misnomer to refer to them as 'marketing' because, like so much 'social marketing', they lack the definitive component of marketing, which is literal exchange. At most, therefore, they consist of mutuality relationships.

We may sum up the argument as follows. An entrepreneur and the members of the firm are linked by *quasi-marketing relationships*: they depend upon modified market relationships plus mutuality. They are the reason for the firm's existence, and their establishment and maintenance constitute its essential function. *Mutuality relationships* may consist of reciprocity alone (i.e. unaccompanied by market relationships); as such they characterise relationships between the firm and other organisations (especially the firm's stakeholders) where there is no (literal) exchange. Often, treatments of social, internal and relationship marketing deal only in mutuality relationships; thus defined, they are not genuine marketing relationships as understood here. True *relationship marketing* and *internal marketing* consist of marketing relationships, though the tendency has been to concentrate on the mutuality component and to embrace some non-market relationships under these terminologies.

Thus, in summary, *marketing-orientated management* is the management of marketing relationships with suppliers, customers and employees in order to produce mutual reinforcement; it is an activity of the marketing firm involving both marketing and mutuality relationships. It is enjoined upon the firm by external conditions of competitiveness and consumer choice: the environmental contingencies that determine 'marketing-orientated management' on the part of the firm are discretionary income and competitiveness of supply/purchase, giving rise to 'consumer choice' and 'managerial scope for entrepreneurship'. Marketing-orientated management does not belong where there is monopoly: e.g. nationalised industries. It is these external contingencies that bring the (marketing) firm into being and sustain its operations.

SUMMING UP

Part III has had two themes: marketing as behaviour and marketing management as behaviourism.

The development of a general operant theory of the firm requires the extension of consumer psychology into marketing psychology. While consumer psychologists are capable of extending the operant analysis of purchase and consumption, and other behavioural scientists in marketing can enlarge upon the account of organisational response given here, there remains a need for an intra-firm analysis of managerial behaviour directed towards the market place that tests the capacity of operant theory to explain what Leibenstein (1979) calls the micro-micro level of organisational analysis. Current applications of operant psychology to industrial behaviour are far too narrow and instrumental to accomplish this explicatory task (Guerin 1994b). The creation of an operant theory of the firm that interprets the behaviour of managers generally, marketing managers particularly, and the consumers who make up the key component of the firm's environment deserves priority.

This discussion has no more than sketched such a theory of the firm. Nevertheless, it suggests an alternative interpretation of how marketing organisations influence consumer behaviour to that found in marketing and economics textbooks. They act upon the scope of consumer behaviour-settings and the quality, quantity and scheduling of reinforcements. The scope of consumer behaviour-settings is manipulated directly by the arrangement of physical and temporal setting elements and indirectly by the provision of rules. In addition, consumer behaviour is influenced by the direct manipulation of reinforcers. However, consumer behaviour is actually determined by the individual's learning history, which determines the meaning of the setting elements (what they portend) and by his or her self-rules, which may or may not be consistent with the setting arranged by the marketing organisation and the contingencies inherent in the marketing mix.

Recognition that marketing management is *de facto* a behaviouristic pursuit has far-reaching implications for academic research and policy.

(There are parallels here with the view of the functioning of the criminal law system advanced by Posner (1990), who construes the working of the legal system as essentially behaviouristic despite much of the law's being cast in the language of intentionality.) The marketing firm acts as though consumer behaviour is environmentally controlled. Manipulating the scope of consumer behaviour-settings and managing reinforcer effectiveness attest to this. There are implications here for the ethics of marketing and for policy: as long as the principal concern of the operant analysis of economic behaviour was to propose an alternative (operant) explanation of consumer choice, ethical considerations did not arise. Marketers' behaviour might raise ethical considerations, but the operant interpretation of itself did not.

However, the extension of the model's sphere of applicability to marketer behaviour, plus the conclusion that marketers act as if consumer behaviour were environmentally controlled, has ethical and policy implications. But marketing is not the only influence on consumers (so other groups than marketers are under ethical scrutiny, too). The fact that marketing takes place within a competitive context – at least in affluent societies that ensure high levels of discretionary income, an excess of marketing capacity over demand, and thus consumer choice – means that closure strategies are limited by firms' resources and the actions of their rivals. Furthermore, the analysis suggests that the control is mutual and by consent – at least in economic systems whose structures require consumer-orientated management. Realising the significance of this finding for competition, competitiveness, profitableness and consumer satisfaction requires further detailed exploration of the interactive relationships of marketers and customers within the framework of analysis that has been presented. While we have arrived at a vision of how marketing management works, we have yet to ascertain its effectiveness. Though they lie beyond the scope of the present book, this interpretation of marketing management has intriguing implications for managerial and public policy recommendations.

References

Abelson, R. P. (1981) 'Psychological status of the script concept', *American Psychologist*, **36**, 715–29.

Ajzen, I. (1985) 'From intentions to actions: a theory of planned behavior'. In: Kuhl, J. and Beckman, J. (eds) *Action Control: From Cognition to Behavior*. Springer-Verlag, Berlin, pp. 11–39.

Ajzen, I. (1987) 'Attitudes, traits, and actions: dispositional prediction of behavior in personality and social psychology'. In: Berkovitz, L. (ed.) *Advances in Experimental Social Psychology*, **20**, Academic Press, San Diego, CA, 1–63.

Ajzen, I. (1988) *Attitudes, Personality and Behavior*. Open University Press, Milton Keynes.

Ajzen, I. (1991) 'The theory of planned behavior', *Organizational Behavior and Human Decision Processes*, **50**, 179–211.

Ajzen, I. and Driver, B. E. (1991) 'Prediction of leisure participation from behavioral, normative, and control beliefs', *Leisure Sciences*, **13**, 185–204.

Ajzen, I. and Driver, B. E. (1992) 'Application of the theory of planned behavior to leisure choice', *Journal of Leisure Research*, **24**, 207–24.

Ajzen, I. and Fishbein, M. (1977) 'Attitude–behavior relations: a theoretical analysis and review of empirical research', *Psychological Bulletin*, **84**, 888–918.

Ajzen, I. and Fishbein, M. (1980) *Understanding Attitudes and Predicting Social Behavior*. Prentice-Hall, Englewood Cliffs, NJ.

Ajzen, I. and Madden, T. J. (1986) 'Prediction of goal-directed behavior: attitudes, intentions, and perceived behavioral control', *Journal of Experimental Social Psychology*, **22**, 453–74.

Alba, J. W., Hutchinson, J. W. and Lynch, J. G. (1991) 'Memory and decision making'. In: Robertson, T. S. and Kassarjian, H. H. (eds) *Handbook of Consumer Behavior*. Prentice-Hall, Englewood Cliffs, NJ, pp. 1–49.

Alchian, A. A. and Demsetz, H. (1972) 'Production, information costs, and economic organization', *American Economic Review*, **62**, 777–95.

Alessi, G. (1992) 'Models of proximate and ultimate causation in psychology', *American Psychologist*, **47**, 1359–70.

Alhadeff, D. A. (1982) *Microeconomics and Human Behaviour: Toward a New Synthesis of Economics and Psychology*. University of California Press, Berkeley.

Allen, C. T., Machleit, K. A. and Kleine, S. S. (1992) 'A comparison of attitudes and emotions as predictors of behavior at diverse levels of behavioral experience', *Journal of Consumer Research*, **18**, 493–504.

Allport, G. W. (1935) 'Attitudes'. In: Murchison, C. (ed.) *Handbook of Social Psychology*. Clark University Press, Worcester, MA, pp. 798–844.

Anderson, A. S., Campbell, D. M. and Shepherd, R. (1995) 'The influence of dietary advice on nutrient intake during pregnancy', *British Journal of Nutrition*, **73**, 163–77.

Andreasen, A. (1965) 'Attitudes and customer behavior: a decision model'. In: Preston, L. E. (ed.) *New Research in Marketing*. University of California Press, Berkeley.

Assael, H. (1995) *Consumer Behavior and Marketing Action*. South-Western, New York.

Baars, B. (1986) *The Cognitive Revolution in Psychology*. The Guilford Press, New York.

Baer, D. M. and Stolz, S. B. (1978) 'A description of the Erhard Seminars Training (*est*) in the terms of behavior analysis,' *Behaviorism*, 6, 45–70.

Bagozzi, R. P. (1981) 'Attitudes, intentions, and behavior: a test of some key hypotheses', *Journal of Personality and Social Psychology*, 41, 607–27.

Bagozzi, R. P. (1984) 'Expectancy-value attitude models: an analysis of critical measurement issues', *International Journal of Research in Marketing*, 1, 295–310.

Bagozzi, R. P. (1985) 'Expectancy-value attitude models: an analysis of critical theoretical issues', *International Journal of Research in Marketing*, 2, 43–60.

Bagozzi, R. P. (1986) 'Attitude formation under the theory of reasoned action and a purposeful behaviour reformulation', *British Journal of Social Psychology*, 25, 95–107.

Bagozzi, R. P. (1988) 'The rebirth of attitude research in marketing', *Journal of the Market Research Society*, 30, 163–95.

Bagozzi, R. P. (1991) 'Enactment processes in the theory of reasoned action'. Unpublished manuscript, University of Michigan.

Bagozzi, R. P. (1992) 'The self-regulation of attitudes, intentions, and behavior', *Social Psychology Quarterly*, 55, 178–204.

Bagozzi, R. P. (1993) 'On the neglect of volition in consumer research: a critique and proposal', *Psychology and Marketing*, 10, 215–37.

Bagozzi, R. P. (1994) 'Effects of arousal on organization of positive and negative affect and cognitions: application to attitude theory', *Structural Equation Modeling*, 1, 222–52.

Bagozzi, R. P. (in press) 'The role of arousal in the creation and control of the halo effect in attitude models', *Psychology and Marketing*.

Bagozzi, R. P. and Foxall, G. R. (1996) 'Construct validation of a measure of adaptive-innovative cognitive styles in consumption', *International Journal of Research in Marketing*, 13, 201–13.

Bagozzi, R. P. and Kimmel, S. K. (1995) 'A comparison of leading theories for the prediction of goal-directed behaviours', *British Journal of Social Psychology*, 34, 472–61.

Bagozzi, R. P. and Kimmel, S. K. (1996) 'The role of self-schemas and action control in the regulation of goal-directed behaviors: making attitude theory more social.' Unpublished paper, University of Michigan.

Bagozzi, R. P. and Moore, D. J. (1994) 'Public service advertisements: emotion and empathy guide prosocial behavior', *Journal of Marketing*, 58, 56–70.

Bagozzi, R. P. and Van Loo, M. F. (1991) 'Motivational and reasoned processes in the theory of consumer choice'. In: Frantz, R., Singh, H. and Gerber, J. (eds) *Handbook of Behavioral Economics, vol. 2B: Behavioral Decision-Making*. JAI, Greenwich, CT, pp. 401–37.

Bagozzi, R. P. and Warshaw, P. R. (1990) 'Trying to consume', *Journal of Consumer Research*, 17, 127–40.

Bagozzi, R. P. and Warshaw, P. R. (1992) 'An examination of the etiology of the attitude–behavior relation for goal-directed behaviors', *Multivariate Behavioral Research*, 27, 601–34.

Bagozzi, R. P., Baumgartner, H. and Pieters, R. (1996) 'Goal-directed emotions.' Unpublished paper, University of Michigan.

Bagozzi, R. P., Baumgartner, H. and Yi, Y. (1992a) 'Appraisal processes in the enactment of intentions to use coupons', *Psychology and Marketing*, **9**, 469–86.

Bagozzi, R. P., Baumgartner, H. and Yi, Y. (1992b) 'State versus action orientation and the theory of reasoned action: an application to coupon usage', *Journal of Consumer Research*, **18**, 505–18.

Bagozzi, R. P. and Yi, Y. (1989) 'The degree of intention formation as a moderator of the attitude–behavior relationship', *Social Psychology Quarterly*, **52**, 266–79.

Bagozzi, R. P., Yi. Y. and Baumgartner, H. (1990) 'The level of effort required for behavior as a moderator of the attitude-behavior relation', *European Journal of Social Psychology*, **20**, 45–59.

Baker, J., Parasuraman, D. and Grewal, A. (1994) 'The influence of store environment on quality inferences and store image', *Journal of the Academy of Marketing Science*, **22**, 328–39.

Ball, D., Lamb, C. and Brodie, R. (1992) 'Segmentation and market structure when both consumer and situational characteristics are explanatory', *Psychology and Marketing*, **9**, 395–408.

Bandura, A. (1977) *Social Learning Theory*. Prentice-Hall, Englewood Cliffs, NJ.

Bandura, A. (1986) *Social Foundations of Thought and Action: A Social Cognitive Theory*. Prentice-Hall, Englewood Cliffs, NJ.

Bargh, J. A. (1994) 'The four horsemen of automaticity: awareness, intention, efficiency, and control in social cognition'. In: Wyer, R. S. and Srull, T. K. (eds) *Handbook of Social Cognition, vol. 1: Basic Processes*, 2nd edn. Erlbaum, Hillsdale, NJ, pp. 1–40.

Bargh, J. A., Chaiken, S., Govender, R. and Pratto, F. (1992) 'The generality of the automatic attitude activation effect', *Journal of Personality and Social Psychology*, **62**, 893–912.

Barker, R. G.(1968) *Ecological Psychology: Concepts and Methods for Studying the Environment of Human Behavior*. Stanford University Press, Stanford, CA.

Barker, R. G. (1987) 'Prospecting in environmental psychology: Oskaloosa revisited' in Stokols, D. and Altmann, I. (eds), *Handbook of Environmental Psychology*. John Wiley & Sons, New York, pp. 1413–32.

Barnes, J. G. (1994) 'Close to the customer: but is it really a relationship?' *Journal of Marketing Management*, **10**, 561–70.

Baron, S. and Wass, K. (1996) 'Towards an understanding of airport shopping behaviour', *International Review of Retail, Distribution and Consumer Research*, **6**, 301–22.

Bateson, J. (1985) 'Self service consumer: an exploratory study', *Journal of Retailing*, **61**, 49–75.

Battalio, R. C., Kagel, J. H., Winkler, R. C., Fisher, E. B., Basmann, R. L. and Krasner, L. (1974) 'An experimental investigation of consumer behavior in a controlled environment', *Journal of Consumer Research*, **1**, 52–60.

Baum, W. M. (1994) *Understanding Behaviorism: Science, Behavior and Culture*. HarperCollins, New York.

Bayés, R. (1992) 'The contribution of behavioural medicine to the research and prevention of AIDS', in Blackman D. E. and Lejeune, H. (eds) *Behaviour Analysis in Theory and Practice: Contributions and Controversies*. Lawrence Erlbaum Associates, Hove and London, pp. 243–58.

Beale, D. A. and Manstead, A. S. R. (1991) 'Predicting mothers' intentions to limit frequency of infants' sugar intake: testing the theory of planned behavior', *Journal of Applied Social Psychology*, **21**, 409–31.

Beck, L. and Ajzen, I. (1991) 'Predicting dishonest actions using the theory of planned behavior', *Journal of Research in Personality*, **25**, 285–301.

Belk, R. W. (1975) 'Situational variables and consumer behavior', *Journal of Consumer Research*, **2**, 157–64.

Belk, R. W. (ed.) (1991) *Highways and Buyways: Naturalistic Research from the Consumer Behavior Odyssey*. Association for Consumer Research, Provo, UT.

Bem, D. (1972). 'Self-perception theory'. In: Berkovitz, L. (ed.) *Advances in Experimental Social Psychology*, **6**, Academic Press, San Diego, CA, pp. 1–62.

Bentler, P. M. and Speckart, G. (1979) 'Models of attitude–behavior relations', *Psychological Review*, **86**, 452–64.

Bentler, P. M. and Speckart, G. (1981) 'Attitudes "cause" behaviors: a structural equation analysis', *Journal of Personality and Social Psychology*, **40**, 226–38.

Berger, I. E. (1992) 'The nature of attitude accessibility and attitude confidence: a triangulated experiment', *Journal of Consumer Psychology*, **1**, 103–24.

Berger, I. E., Ratchford, B. T. and Haines, G. T. (1994) 'Subjective product knowledge as a mediator of the relationship between attitudes and purchase intentions for a durable product', *Journal of Economic Psychology*, **15**, 301–14.

Bettman, J. R. (1979) *An Information Processing Theory of Consumer Choice*. Addison-Wesley, Reading, MA.

Bettman, J. R. (1986) 'Consumer psychology', *Annual Review of Psychology*, **37**, 257–89.

Bettman, J. R., Johnson, E. J. and Payne, J. W. (1991) 'Consumer decision-making'. In: Robertson, T. S. and Kassarjian, H. H. (eds) *Handbook of Consumer Behavior*. Prentice-Hall, Englewood Cliffs, NJ, pp. 50–84.

Bitner, M. J. (1990) 'Evaluating service encounters: the effects of physical surroundings and employee responses', *Journal of Marketing*, **54**, 69–82.

Bitner, M. J. (1992) 'Servicescapes: the impact of physical surroundings on customers and employees', *Journal of Marketing*, **56**, 57–71.

Blackman D. E. and Lejeune, H. (eds) (1990) *Behaviour Analysis in Theory and Practice: Contributions and Controversies*. Lawrence Erlbaum Associates. Hove and London.

Blascovich, J., Ernst, J. M., Tomaka, J., Kelsey, R. M., Salomon, K. L. and Fazio, R. H. (1993) 'Attitude accessibility as a moderator of automatic reactivity during decision-making', *Journal of Personality and Social Psychology*, **64**, 165–76.

Blois, K. (1972) 'Vertical quasi-integration,' *Journal of Industrial Economics*, **20**, 253–72.

Bogardus, E. S. (1925) 'Measuring social distances', *Journal of Applied Sociology*, **9**, 299–308.

Bohner, G., Moskowitz, G. B. and Chaiken, S. (1995) 'The interplay of heuristic and systematic processing of social information'. In: Stroebe, W. and Hewstone, M. (eds) *European Review of Social Psychology*, **6**. Wiley, Chichester, pp. 33–68.

Boldero, J. (1995) 'The prediction of household recycling of newspapers – the role of attitudes, intentions and situational factors', *Journal of Applied Social Psychology*, **25**, 440–62.

Boldero, J., Moore, S. and Rosenthal, D. (1992) 'Intentions, context and safe sex', *Journal of Applied Social Psychology*, **22**, 1374–96.

Borgida, E., Conner, C. and Manteufel, L. (1992) 'Understanding living kidney donation: a behavioural decision making perspective'. In: Spacapan, S. and Oskamp, S. (eds) *Helping and Being Helped: Naturalistic Studies.* Sage, Newbury Park, CA, pp. 183–212.

Boyd, B. and Wandersman, A. (1991) 'Predicting undergraduate condom use with the Fishbein and Ajzen and the Triandis attitude–behavior models: implications for public health interventions', *Journal of Applied Social Psychology,* **21**, 1810–30.

Bradshaw, C. M., H. V. Ruddle and E. Szabadi (1981) 'Studies of concurrent performances in humans,' in C. M. Bradshaw, E. Szabadi and C. Fergus Lowe (eds) *Quantification of Steady State Operant Behaviour.* Amsterdam: North Holland, 225–59.

Bradshaw, C. M., E. Szabadi and P. Bevan (1976) 'Behavior of humans in variable-interval schedules of reinforcement,' *Journal of the Experimental Analysis of Behavior,* **26**, 135–41.

Bradshaw, C. M., E. Szabadi and P. Bevan (1977) 'Effect of punishment on human variable interval performance,' *Journal of the Experimental Analysis of Behavior,* **27**, 275–79.

Bradshaw, C. M., E. Szabadi and P. Bevan (1979) 'The effect of punishment on free operant choice behavior in humans,' *Journal of the Experimental Analysis of Behavior,* **31**, 71–81.

Bradshaw, C. M., E. Szabadi, P. Bevan and H. V. Ruddle (1979) 'The effect of signalled reinforcement availability on concurrent performance in humans,' *Journal of the Experimental Analysis of Behavior,* **32**, 65–74.

Brown, S. P. and Stayman, D. M. (1992) 'Antecedents and consequences of attitude toward the ad: a meta-analysis', *Journal of Consumer Research,* **19**, 34–51.

Budd, R. J., North, D. and Spencer, C. (1984) 'Understanding seat-belt use: a test of Bentler and Speckart's extension of the "theory of reasoned action"', *European Journal of Social Psychology,* **14**, 69–78.

Butler, D. Y. and Jernigan, M. H. (1993) 'Air passengers' satisfaction with merchandise offered in airport shops', *Proceedings of the International Conference on Research in the Distributive Trades,* Stirling, 164–71.

Castleberry, S. B., Barnard, N. R., Barwise, T. P., Ehrenberg, A. S. C. and Dall'Olmo Riley, F. (1994) 'Individual attitude variations over time', *Journal of Marketing Management,* **10**, 153–162.

Catania, A. C. (1992a) *Learning,* 3rd edn. Prentice-Hall, Englewood Cliffs, NJ.

Catania, A. C. (1992b) 'B. F. Skinner, organism', *American Psychologist,* **47**, 1521–30.

Catania, A. C. and Harnad, S. (eds) (1988) *The Selection of Behavior. The Operant Behaviorism of B. F. Skinner: Comments and Consequences.* New York, Cambridge University Press.

Catania, A. C., Matthews, B. A. and Shimoff, E. (1982) 'Instructed versus Shaped Human Verbal Behavior: Interactions with Nonverbal Responding', *Journal of the Experimental Analysis of Behavior,* **38**, 233–48.

Catania, A. C., Matthews, B. A. and Shimoff, E. H. (1990) 'Properties of rule-governed behaviour and their implications'. In: Blackman, D. E. and Lejeune, H. (eds) *Behaviour Analysis in Theory and Practice: Contributions and Controversies.* Erlbaum, London. pp. 215–30.

Catania, A. C., Shimoff, E. and Matthews, B. A. (1989) 'An experimental analysis of rule-governed behavior'. In: Hayes, S. C. (ed.) *Rule-Governed Behavior: Cognition, Contingencies, and Instructional Control*. Plenum, New York, pp. 119–50.

Chaiken, S. (1980) 'Heuristic versus systematic information processing and the use of source versus message cues in persuasion', *Journal of Personality and Social Psychology*, **39**, 752–66.

Chan, D. K. S. and Fishbein, M. (1993) 'Determinants of college women's intentions to tell their partners to use condoms', *Journal of Applied Social Psychology*, **23**, 1455–70.

Charng, H., Piliavin, J. A. and Callero, P. L. (1988) 'Role identity and reasoned action in the prediction of repeated behavior', *Social Psychology Quarterly*, **51**, 133–51.

Chase, P. N. and Danforth, J. S. (1991) 'The role of rules in concept formation'. In: Hayes, L. J. and Chase, P. N. (eds) *Dialogues on Verbal Behavior*. Context Press, Reno, NV, pp. 205–25.

Chase, P. N. and Bjamadottir, G. S. (1992) 'Instructing variability: some features of a problem-solving repertoire'. In: Hayes, S. C. and Hayes, L. J. (eds) *Understanding Verbal Relations*. Context Press, Reno, NV, pp. 181–96.

Chase, P. N. and Parrott, L. J. (eds) (1986) *Psychological Aspects of Language: The West Virginia Lectures*. Charles C. Thomas Springfield, IL.

Chesanow, N., (1985), 'Prize flights: all about frequent flier programs', *Savvy* (June), 67–9.

Chesterton Research (1993) *Airport Retailing: The Growth of a New 'High Street'*, London.

Chiesa, M. (1995) *Radical Behaviorism: The Philosophy and the Science*. Authors Cooperative Inc, Boston, MA.

Chomsky, N. (1959) 'Review of B. F. Skinner's *Verbal Behavior*'. *Language*, **35**, 26–58.

Christopher, M., Payne, A. and Ballantyne, D. (1991) *Relationship Marketing*. London: Butterworth-Heinemann.

Coase, R. H. (1937) 'The nature of the firm', *Economica*, n.s. **4**, 386–405.

Coase, R. H. (1960) 'The problem of social cost', *Journal of Law and Economics*, **3**, 1–44.

Coase, R. H. (1988a) *The Firm, the Market, and the Law*. University of Chicago Press, Chicago and London.

Coase, R. H. (1988b) 'The nature of the firm: origin, meaning, influence', *Journal of Law, Economics and Organisation*, **4**, 3–47.

Cohen, A. (1964) *Attitude Change and Social Influence*. Basic Books, New York.

Cohen, J. B. and Chakravarti, D. (1990) 'Consumer psychology', *Annual Review of Psychology*, **41**, 243–88.

Commons, J. R. (1924/1974) *The Legal Foundations of Capitalism*. Augustus M. Kelley, Clifton, NJ.

Cone, J. D. and Hayes, S. C. (1980) *Environmental Problems/Behavioral Solutions*. Brooks Cole, Monterey, CA.

Courneya, K. S. (1995) 'Understanding readiness for regular physical activity in older individuals: an application of the theory of planned behavior', *Health Psychology*, **14**, 80–7.

Dabholkar, P. A. (1994) 'Incorporating choice into an attitudinal framework: analyzing models of mental comparison processes', *Journal of Consumer Research*, **21**, 100–18.

Davey, G. C. L. and Cullen, C. (eds) (1988) *Human Operant Conditioning and Behaviour Modification.* Chichester, Wiley.

Davies, G. (1995) 'Bringing stores to shoppers – not shoppers to stores', *International Journal of Retail and Distribution Management*, **23**, 18–23.

Davies, M. A. P. and Wright, L. T. (1994) 'The importance of labelling examined in food marketing', *European Journal of Marketing*, **28**(2), 57–67.

Dawkins, R. (1982) *The Extended Phenotype: The Long Reach of the Gene.* Oxford University Press, Oxford.

Dawkins, R. (1988) 'Replicators, consequences, and displacement activities', in Catania, A. C. and Harnad, S. (eds) (1988) *The Selection of Behavior. The Operant Behaviorism of B. F. Skinner: Comments and Consequences* New York, Cambridge University Press, pp. 33–5.

Delprato, D. J. and Midgley, B. D. (1992) 'Some fundamentals of B. F. Skinner's behaviorism', *American Psychologist*, **47**, 1507–20.

Demsetz, H. (1967) 'Toward a Theory of Property Rights,' *American Economic Review*, **57**, 347–59.

Demsetz, H. (1995) *The Economics of the Business Firm: Seven Critical Commentaries*, Cambridge University Press, Cambridge.

Dennison, C. M. and Shepherd, R. (1995) 'Adolescent food choice: an application of the theory of planned behaviour', *Journal of Human Nutrition and Dietetics*, **8**, 9–23.

Desroches, J. J. Y. and Chebat, J. C. (1995) 'Why Quebec businesses go public: attitudes and the decision-making process', *Revue Canadienne des Sciences de l'Administration*, **12**, 27–37.

DeVellis, B. M., Blalock, S. J. and Sandler, R. S. (1990) 'Predicting participation in cancer screening: the role of perceived behavioural control', *Journal of Applied Social Psychology*, **20**, 639–60.

Dewey, J. (1966) *Democracy and Education*, Free Press, New York.

Dewit, J. B. F. and Teunis, G. J. P. (1994) 'Behavioral risk reduction strategies to prevent HIV-infection among homosexual men', *Aids Education and Prevention*, **6**, 493–505.

Dnes, A. W. (1996) *The Economics of Law*, International Thompson Business Press, London.

Doganis, R. (1992) *The Airport Business*, Routledge, London.

Doll, J. and Ajzen, I. (1992) 'Accessibility and stability of predictors in the theory of planned behavior', *Journal of Personality and Social Psychology*, **63**, 754–65.

Donovan, R. J. and Rossiter, J. R. (1982) 'Store atmosphere: an experimental psychology approach,' *Journal of Retailing*, **58**, 34–57.

Doob L. W. (1947) 'The behavior of attitudes', *Psychological Review*, **54**, 135–56.

Dosi, G. and Orsenigo, L. (1988) 'Coordination and transformation: an overview of structures, behaviours and change in evolutionary environments'. In Dosi, G., Freeman, C., Nelson, R. Silverberg, G. and Soete, L. (eds) *Technical Change and Economic Theory.* Pinter, London, pp. 13–37.

Downing, J. W., Judd, C. M. and Brauer, M. (1992) 'Effects of repeated expressions on attitude extremity', *Journal of Personality and Social Psychology*, **62**, 17–29.

Dugdale, N. and Lowe, C. F. (1990) Naming and Stimulus Equivalence. In: Blackman, D. E. and Lejeune, H. H. (eds) *Behavior Analysis in Theory and Practice.* Erlbaum, London, pp. 115–38.

Duxbury, N. (1995), *Patterns of American Jurisprudence*, Clarendon, Oxford.

Eagly, A. H. and Chaiken, S. (1993) *The Psychology of Attitudes*. Harcourt Brace Jovanovich, Fort Worth, TX.

Earl, P. E. (ed.) (1988a). *Behavioural Economics*, vols I and II. Edward Elgar, Aldershot.

Earl, P. E. (ed.) (1988b). *Psychological Economics*. Kluwer, Boston, MA.

Earl, P. E. (1990) 'Economics and psychology: a survey', *Economic Journal*, **100**, 718–55.

East, R. (1990) *Changing Consumer Behaviour*. Cassell, London.

East, R. (1992) 'The effect of experience on the decision-making of expert and novice buyers', *Journal of Marketing Management*, **8**, 167–76.

East, R. (1993) 'Investment decisions and the theory of planned behaviour', *Journal of Economic Psychology*, **14**, 337–75.

East, R. (1997) *Consumer Behaviour: Advances and Applications in Marketing*. Prentice-Hall, London.

East, R. (1996) 'Redress seeking as planned behavior', *Journal of Consumer Satisfaction, Dissatisfaction and Complaining Behavior*, **9**, 27–34.

Easterbrook, F. H. and Fischel, D. R. (1991) *The Economic Structure of Corporate Law*, Harvard University Press, Cambridge, MA.

Echabe, A. E., Rovira, D. P. and Garate, J. F. V. (1988) 'Testing Ajzen and Fishbein's attitude model: the prediction of voting', *European Journal of Social Psychology*, **18**, 181–9.

Ehrenberg, A. S. C. (1972, 1988) *Repeat Buying*: 1st edn, North Holland, Amsterdam; 2nd edn, Griffin, London.

Ehrenberg, A. S. C. (1992) 'Theory or well-based results: which comes first?' Paper, EIASM Conference on Research Traditions in Marketing, Brussels, January.

Ehrenberg, A. S. C. and Scriven, J. (1996) 'Brand loyalty under the microscope'. Working paper, South Bank Business School, London.

Ehrenberg, A. S. C. and Uncles, M. D. (1995) 'Dirichlet-type markets: a review'. Unpublished manuscript, South Bank Business School, London.

Eiser, J. R. (1980) *Cognitive Social Psychology: A Guide to Theory and Research*. McGraw-Hill, London.

Eiser, J. F. (1986) *Social Psychology: Attitudes, Cognition and Social Behaviour*. Cambridge University Press.

Eiser, J. R. (1987) *The Expression of Attitude*. Springer-Verlag, New York.

Eiser, J. R. and van der Pligt, J. (1988) *Attitudes and Decisions*. Routledge, London.

Engel, J. F., Blackwell, R. D. and Miniard, P. W. (1995) *Consumer Behavior*, 8th edn. Dryden, Fort Worth, TX.

Engel, J. F., Kollat, D. T. and Blackwell, R. D. (1968) *Consumer Behavior*. Holt, Rinehart and Winston, New York.

Epling, W. F. and W. D. Pierce (1983) 'Applied behavior analysis: new directions from the laboratory,' *Behavior Analyst*, **6**, 27–37.

Epling, W. F. and Pierce, W. D. (1988) 'Applied behavior analysis: new directions from the laboratory'. In Davey, G. C. L. and Cullen, C. (eds) *Human Operant Conditioning and Behaviour Modification*. Wiley, Chichester, pp. 43–58.

Ericsson, K. A. and Simon, H. A. (1993) *Protocol Analysis: Verbal Reports as Data*. MIT Press, Cambridge, MA.

Fallon, D. (1992) 'An existential look at B. F. Skinner', *American Psychologist*, **47**, 1441–53.

Fazio, R. H. (1986) 'How do attitudes guide behavior?' In: Sorrentino, R. M. and Higgins, E. T. (eds) *Handbook of Motivation and Cognition: Foundations of Social Behavior*. Wiley, Chichester, pp. 204–43.

Fazio, R. H. (1989) 'On the power and functionality of attitudes: the role of attitude accessibility'. In Pratkanis, A. R., Breckler, A. J. and Greenwald, A. G. (eds) *Attitude Structure and Function*. Erlbaum, Hillsdale, NJ, pp. 153–80.

Fazio, R. H. (1990) 'Multiple processes by which attitudes guide behavior: the MODE model as an integrative framework'. In: Zanna, M. P. (ed.) *Advances in Experimental Social Psychology*, **23**, Academic Press, San Diego, CA, pp. 75–109.

Fazio, R. H. (1994) 'Attitudes as object-evaluation associations: determinants, consequences, and correlates of attitude accessibility'. In: Petty, R. E. and Krosnick, J. A. (eds) *Attitude Strength: Antecedents and Consequences*, Erlbaum, Hillsdale, NJ.

Fazio, R. H. and Zanna, M. P. (1978a) 'Attitudinal qualities relating to the strength of the attitude–behavior relationship', *Journal of Experimental Social Psychology*, **14**, 398–408.

Fazio, R. H. and Zanna, M. P. (1978b) 'On the predictive validity of attitudes: the roles of direct experience and confidence', *Journal of Personality*, **46**, 228–43.

Fazio, R. H. and Zanna, M. P. (1981) 'Direct experience and attitude–behavior consistency', *Advances in Experimental Social Psychology*, **14**, 161–202.

Fazio, R. H., Powell, M. C. and Williams, C. J. (1989) 'The role of attitude accessibility in the attitude-to-behavior process', *Journal of Consumer Research*, **16**, 280–8.

Fazio, R. H., Chen, J., McDonel, E. C. and Sherman, S. J. (1982) 'Attitude accessibility, attitude–behavior consistency, and the strength of the object-evaluation association', *Journal of Experimental Social Psychology*, **18**, 339–57.

Feyerabend, P. (1970) 'Consolations for the specialist'. In: Lakatos, I. and Musgrave, A. (eds) *Criticism and the Growth of Knowledge*. Cambridge University Press, Cambridge, pp. 197–230.

Feyerabend, P. (1975) *Against Method*. NLB, London.

Finkelstein, P., Wenegrat, B., Yalom, I. (1982) 'Large group awareness training', *Annual Review of Psychology*, **33**, 515–39.

Fishbein, M. (ed.) (1967). *Readings in Attitude Theory and Measurement*. Wiley, New York.

Fishbein, M. (1972) 'The search for attitudinal-behavioral consistency'. In: Cohen, J. S. (ed.) *Behavorial Science Foundations of Consumer Behavior*. Free Press, New York.

Fishbein, M. and Ajzen, I. (1975) *Belief, Attitude, Intention and Behavior*. Addison-Wesley, Reading, MA.

Fishbein, M. and Stasson, M. (1990) 'The role of desires, self-predictions, and perceived control in the prediction of training session attendance', *Journal of Applied Social Psychology*, **20**, 173–98.

Fisher, J. D., Silver, R. C., Chinsky, J. M., Goff, B. and Klar, Y. (1990). *Evaluating a Large Group Awareness Training: A Longitudinal Study of Psychosocial Effects*. Springer-Verlag, New York.

Fiske, S. T. (1993) 'Social cognition and social perception', *Annual Review of Psychology*, **44**, 155–94.

References 177

Flanagan, O. J. (1991). *The Science of the Mind*, 2nd edn. MIT Press, Cambridge, MA.

Folkes, V. S. and Kiesler, T. (1991) 'Social cognition: consumers' inferences about the self and others'. In: Robertson, T. S. and Kassarjian, H. H. (eds) *Handbook of Consumer Behaviour*. Prentice-Hall, Englewood Cliffs, NJ, pp. 281–315.

Foxall, G. R. (1981) *Strategic Marketing Management*. Routledge, London and New York.

Foxall, G. R. (1983) *Consumer Choice*. Macmillan, London, and St Martin's Press, New York.

Foxall, G. R. (1984) 'Consumers' intentions and behaviour', *Journal of the Market Research Society*, **26**, 231–41.

Foxall, G. R. (1987) 'Radical behaviourism and consumer research: theoretical promise and empirical problems', *International Journal of Research in Marketing*, **4**, 111–29.

Foxall, G. R. (1988) 'Markets, Hierarchies and User-initiated Innovation', *Managerial and Decision Economics*, **9**, 237–52.

Foxall, G. R. (1990) *Consumer Psychology in Behavioural Perspective*. Routledge, London.

Foxall, G. R. (1992a) 'The consumer situation: an integrative model for research in marketing', *Journal of Marketing Management*, **8**, 392–404.

Foxall, G. R. (1992b) The Behavioral Perspective Model of Purchase and Consumption: From Consumer Theory to Marketing Management. *Journal of the Academy of Marketing Science*, **20**, 189–98.

Foxall, G. R. (1993a) 'Consumer behaviour as an evolutionary process', *European Journal of Marketing*, **27**(8), 46–57.

Foxall, G. R. (1993b) 'Situated consumer behavior: a behavioural interpretation of purchase and consumption'. In: Costa, J. A. and Belk, R. W. (eds) *Research in Consumer Behavior*, **6**, JAI, Greenwich, CT, pp. 113–52.

Foxall, G. R. (1993c) 'Variety seeking and cognitive style', *British Food Journal*, **95**(7), 32–36.

Foxall, G. R. (1994a) 'Behaviour analysis and consumer psychology', *Journal of Economic Psychology*, **15**, 5–91.

Foxall, G. R. (1994b) 'Consumer choice as an evolutionary process: an operant interpretation of adopter behavior', *Advances in Consumer Research*, **21**, 312–17.

Foxall, G. R. (1994c) 'Environment-impacting consumer behaviour: a framework for social marketing and demarketing'. In Baker, M. J. (ed.) *Perspectives on Marketing Management*, **4**, Wiley, Chichester, pp. 27–53.

Foxall, G. R. (1994d) 'Consumer initiators: adaptors and innovators', *British Journal of Management*, **5**, S3–S12.

Foxall, G. R. (1994e) 'Consumer decision-making'. In: Baker, M. J. (ed.) *The Marketing Book*, Butterworth-Heinemann, London, pp. 193–215.

Foxall, G. R. (1995a) 'Science and interpretation in consumer research: a radical behaviourist perspective', *European Journal of Marketing*, **29**(9), 3–99.

Foxall, G. R. (1995b) 'The psychological basis of marketing'. In Baker, M. J. (ed.) *The Companion Encyclopedia of Marketing*. Routledge, London.

Foxall, G. R. (1995c) 'Environment-impacting consumer behavior: an operant analysis', *Advances in Consumer Research*, **22**, 262–8.

Foxall, G. R. (1996a) *Consumers in Context: The BPM Research Program*, London and New York: ITP.

Foxall, G. R. (1996b) 'Consensual availability and predictive validity of the BPM interpretation of consumer behaviour'. Working paper, Research Centre for Consumer Behaviour, University of Birmingham.

Foxall, G. R. (1997a) 'The explanation of consumer behaviour: from social cognition to environmental control'. In: Cooper, C. L. and Robertson, I. (eds) *International Review of Industrial and Organizational Psychology*. Wiley, Chichester, pp. 229–87.

Foxall, G. R. (1997b) 'The emotional texture of consumer environments: a systematic approach to atmospherics', *Journal of Economic Psychology*, 18, in press.

Foxall, G. R. (1997c) 'Situational influence on consumers' affective response: theory and research'. Working paper, Research Centre for Consumer Behaviour, University of Birmingham.

Foxall, G. R. and Goldsmith, R. E. (1994) *Consumer Psychology for Marketing*. Routledge, London and New York.

Foxall, G. R. and Hackett, P. (1992) 'Consumers' perceptions of micro-retail location: wayfinding and cognitive mapping in planned and organic shopping environments', *International Review of Retail, Distributive and Consumer Research*, 2, 309–27.

Foxall, G. R. and Hackett, P. (1994) 'Consumer satisfaction with Birmingham's International Convention Centre', *Service Industries Journal*, 14, 369–80.

Foxall, G. R. and Minkes, A. L. (1996) 'Beyond marketing: the locus of entrepreneurship in the modern corporation,' *Journal of Strategic Marketing*, 4, 71–94.

Fredericks, A. J. and Dossett, D. L. (1983) 'Attitude–behavior relations: a comparison of the Fishbein–Ajzen and Bentler–Speckart models', *Journal of Personality and Social Psychology*, 45, 501–12.

Gardner, M. P. (1985) 'Mood states and consumer behavior: a critical review', *Journal of Consumer Research*, 12, 281–300.

Gilbert, D. (1996) 'Airlines', in Buttle, F. (ed.) *Relationship Marketing: Theory and Practice*, Paul Chapman, London, pp. 131–44.

Gilchrist, S. (1994) 'Retailers aim to cash in on relieving terminal boredom', *The Times*, 12 January.

Giles, M. and Cairns, E. (1995) 'Blood donation and Ajzen's theory of planned behaviour: an examination of perceived behavioural control', *British Journal of Social Psychology*, 34, 173–88.

Godin, G., Valois, P. and LePage, L. (1993) 'The pattern of influence of perceived behavioral control upon exercising behavior – an application of Ajzen's theory of planned behavior', *Journal of Behavioral Medicine*, 16, 81–102.

Godin, G., Valois, P., LePage, L. and Desharnais, M. (1992) 'Predictors of smoking behaviour: an application of Ajzen's theory of planned behaviour', *British Journal of Addiction*, 87, 1335–43.

Goldsmith, T. H. (1991) *The Biological Roots of Human Nature: Forging Links between Evolution and Behavior*. Oxford University Press, New York.

Gould, J. and Kolb, W. L. (eds) (1964) *A Dictionary of the Social Sciences*. Tavistock, London.

Granberg, D. and Holmberg, S. (1990) 'The intention–behavior relationship among U.S. and Swedish voters', *Social Psychology Quarterly*, 53, 44–54.

Greenwald, A. G. and Banaji, M. R. (1995). 'Implicit social cognition: attitudes, self-esteem, and stereotypes', *Psychological Review*, **102**, 4–27.

Griffin, J. and Parfitt, D. (1987) 'Hedonism'. In: Eatwell, J., Milgate, M. and Newman, P. (eds) *The New Palgrave: A Dictionary of Economics*. Macmillan, London.

Gronroos, C. (1994) 'Quo vadis, marketing? Towards a relationship marketing paradigm', *Journal of Marketing Management*, **10**, 347–60.

Guerin, B. (1992) 'Behavior analysis and the social construction of knowledge', *American Psychologist*, **47**, 1423–32.

Guerin, B. (1994a) *Analyzing Social Behavior: Behavior Analysis and the Social Sciences*. Context Press, Reno, NV.

Guerin, B. (1994b) 'Attitudes and beliefs as verbal behavior', *The Behavior Analyst*, **17**, 155–63.

Hackenberg,, T. D. and Joker, V. R. (1994) 'Instructional versus schedule control of humans' choices in situations of diminishing returns', *Journal of the Experimental Analysis of Behavior*, **62**, 367–83.

Hackett, P., Foxall, G. R. and van Raaij, W. F. (1993) 'Consumers in retail environments'. In: Garling, T. and Golledge, R. G. (eds) *Behavior and Environment: Psychological and Geographical Approaches*, Amsterdam: North-Holland, pp. 378–99.

Hamblin, R. L. (1979) 'Behavioral choice and social reinforcement,' *Social Forces*, **57**, 1141–1156.

Harrison, D. A. and Liska, L. Z. (1994) 'Promoting regular exercise in organizational fitness programs: health related differences in motivational buildingblocks', *Personnel Psychology*, **47**, 47–71.

Hart, O. (1989) 'An economist's perspective on the theory of the firm', *Columbia Law Review*, 1757–74.

Hart, O. (1995) *Firms, Contracts and Financial Structure*, Clarendon, Oxford.

Haugtvedt, C. P. and Petty, R. E. (1992) 'Personality and persuasion: need for cognition moderates the persistence and resistance of attitudes', *Journal of Personality and Social Psychology*, **62**, 308–19.

Haugtvedt, C. P. and Wegener, D. T. (1994) 'Message order effects in persuasion: an attitude strength perspective', *Journal of Consumer Research*, **21**, 205–18.

Haugtvedt, C. P., Schumann, D. W., Schneier, W. L. and Warren, W. L. (1994) 'Advertising repetition and variation strategies: implications for understanding attitude strength', *Journal of Consumer Research*, **21**, 176–89.

Hawkins, S. A. and Hoch, S. J. (1992) 'Low-involvement learning: memory without evaluation', *Journal of Consumer Research*, **19**, 212–25.

Hayes, L. J. (1991) 'Substitution and reference'. In: Hayes, L. J. and Chase, P. N. (eds) *Dialogues on Verbal Behavior*. Context Press, Reno, NV, pp. 3–18.

Hayes, L. J. (1994) 'Thinking'. In: Hayes, S. C., Hayes, L. J., Sato, M. and Ono, K. (eds) *Behavior Analysis of Language and Cognition*. Context Press, Reno, NV, pp. 149–64.

Hayes, L. J. and Chase, P. N. (1991) (eds) *Dialogues on Verbal Behavior*. Context Press, Reno, NV.

Hayes, S. C. (1986) 'The case of the silent dog – verbal reports and the analysis of rules', *Journal of the Experimental Analysis of Behavior*, **45**, 351–63.

Hayes, S. C. (1989) (ed.) *Rule-Governed Behavior: Cognition, Contingencies, and Instructional Control*. Plenum, New York.

Hayes, S. C. (1994) 'Relational frame theory: a functional approach to verbal events'. In: Hayes, S. C., Hayes, L. J., Sato, M. and Ono, K. (1994) (eds) *Behavior Analysis of Language and Cognition*. Context Press, Reno, NV, pp. 9–30.

Hayes, S. C. and Hayes. L. J. (1989) 'The verbal action of the listener as a basis for rule-governance'. In: Hayes, S. C. (ed.) *Rule-Governed Behavior: Cognition, Contingencies, and Instructional Control*. Plenum, New York. pp. 153–90.

Hayes, S. C. and Hayes, L. J. (1992a) 'Verbal relations and the evolution of behavior analysis', *American Psychologist*, **47**, 1383–95.

Hayes, S. C. and Hayes, L. J. (1992b) (eds) *Understanding Verbal Relations*. Context Press, Reno, NV.

Hayes, S. C., Hayes, L. J., Reese, H. W. and Sarbin, T. R. (eds) (1993) *Varieties of Scientific Contextualism*. Context Press, Reno, NV.

Hayes, S. C., Brownstein, A. J., Haas, J. R. and Greenway, D. E. (1986) 'Instructions, multiple schedules, and extinction: distinguishing rule-governed from schedule-controlled behavior', *Journal of the Experimental Analysis of Behavior*, **46**, 137–47.

Hayes, S. C., Hayes, L. J., Sato, M. and Ono, K. (eds) (1994) *Behavior Analysis of Language and Cognition*. Context Press, Reno, NV.

Herrnstein, R. J. (1961) 'Relative and absolute strength of response as a function of frequency of reinforcement', *Journal of the Experimental Analysis of Behavior*, **4**, 267–72.

Herrnstein, R. J. (1970) 'On the law of effect', *Journal of the Experimental Analysis of Behavior*, **13**, 243–66.

Herrnstein, R. (1990) 'Rational choice theory: necessary but not sufficient', *American Psychologist*, **45**, 356–67.

Hillner, K. P. (1984) *History and Systems of Modern Psychology: A Conceptual Approach*, Gardner Press Inc. New York.

Hineline, P. (1990) 'The origins of environment-based psychological theory', *Journal of the Experimental Analysis of Behavior*, **53**, pp. 305–20.

Hineline, P. (1992) 'A self-interpretive behavior analysis', *American Psychologist*, **47**, 1274–86.

Homans, G. C. (1950) *The Human Group*. Harcourt Brace, New York.

Homans, C. G. (1974) *Social Behavior*. Harcourt, Brace, Jovanovich, New York.

Horne, P. J. and Lowe, C. F. (1993) 'Determinants of human performance on concurrent schedules', *Journal of the Experimental Analysis of Behavior*, **59**, 29–60.

Horne, P. J. and Lowe, C. F. (1996) 'On the origins of naming and other symbolic behavior', *Journal of the Experimental Analysis of Behavior*, **65**, 185–241.

Hornik, J. (1982) 'Situational effects on the consumption of time', *Journal of Marketing*, **46**, 44–55.

Howard, J. A. (1989) *Consumer Behavior in Marketing Strategy*. Prentice-Hall, Englewood Cliffs, NJ.

Howard, J. A. and Sheth, J. N. (1969) *The Theory of Buyer Behavior*. Wiley, New York.

Hyten, C. M. and Burns, R. (1986) 'Social relations and social behavior'. In: Reese, H. W. and Parrott, L. J. (eds) *Behavior Science: Philosophical, Methodological, and Empirical Advances*. Erlbaum, Hillsdale, NJ, pp. 163–83.

Hyten, C. M. and Chase, P. N. (1991) 'An analysis of self-editing: method and preliminary findings'. In: Hayes, L. J. and Chase, P. N. (eds) *Dialogues on Verbal Behavior*. Context Press, Reno, NV, pp. 67–81.

Ito, Y. (1994) 'Models and problem solving: effects and use of the "views of probability"'. In: Hayes, S. C., Hayes, L. J., Sato, M. and Ono, K. (eds) *Behavior Analysis of Language and Cognition.* Context Press, Reno, NV, pp. 259–80.

Iversen, I. H. (1992) 'Skinner's early research: from reflexology to operant conditioning', *American Psychologist*, **47**, 1318–28.

Janiszewski, C. (1988) 'Preconscious processing effects: the independence of attitude formation and conscious thought', *Journal of Consumer Research*, **15**, 199–209.

Jensen, M. C. and Meckling, W. H. (1976) 'Theory of the Firm: Managerial Behavior, Agency Costs and Ownership Structure,' *Journal of Financial Economics*, **3**, 305–60.

Journal of Consumer Research (1994) 'Summaries and Index, Volumes 1–20. June 1974 through March 1994', *Journal of Consumer Research*, **21**, Supplement, 1–117.

Kagel, J. H. (1988) 'Economics according to the rats (and pigeons too): what have we learned and what can we hope to learn?' In: Roth, A. E. (ed.) *Laboratory Experiments in Economics*, Cambridge, Cambridge University Press.

Kardes, F. R. (1988) 'Spontaneous inference processes in advertising: the effects of conclusion omission and involvement on persuasion', *Journal of Consumer Research*, **15**, 225–33.

Kardes, F. R. (1994) 'Consumer judgment and decision processes'. In: Wyer, R. S. and Srull, T. K. (1994) (eds) *Handbook of Social Cognition, vol. 2: Application*, 2nd edn. Erlbaum, Hillsdale, NJ, pp. 399–466.

Kashima, Y., Gallois, C. and McCamish, M. (1993) 'The theory of reasoned action and cooperative behaviour: it takes two to use a condom', *British Journal of Social Psychology*, **32**, 227–39.

Kassarjian, H. H. (1982) 'Consumer psychology', *Annual Review of Psychology*, **33**, 619–49.

Katona, G. (1951) *Psychological Analysis of Economic Behavior.* McGraw-Hill, New York.

Katona, G. (1975) *Psychological Economics.* Elsevier, New York.

Keehn, J. D. (1996) *Master Builders of Modern Psychology: From Freud to Skinner.* Duckworth, London.

Kelly, C. and Breinlinger, S. (1995) 'Attitudes, intentions and behavior: a study of women's participation in collective action', *Journal of Applied Social Psychology*, **25**, 1430–45.

Keng, A. K. and Ehrenberg, A. S. C. (1985) 'Patterns of store choice', *Journal of Marketing Research*, **21**, 399–409.

Kimble, G. A. (1994) 'A new formula for behaviorism', *Psychological Review*, **101**, 254–8.

Kimble, G. A. (1996) *Psychology: The Hope of a Science.* MIT Press, Cambridge, MA.

Kimiecik, J. (1992) 'Predicting vigorous activity of corporate employees: comparing the theories of reasoned action and planned behavior', *Journal of Sport and Exercise Psychology*, **14**, 192–206.

Klobas, J. E. (1995) 'Beyond information quality: fitness for purpose and electronic information resource use', *Journal of Information Science*, **21**, 95–114.

Knox, S. and de Chernatony, L. (1994) 'Attitude, personal norms and intentions'. In: Jenkins, M. and Knox, S. (eds) *Advances in Consumer Marketing.* Kogan Page, London, pp. 85–98.

Kuhn, T. S. (1962/1970) *The Structure of Scientific Revolutions*, 1st and 2nd edns. Chicago University Press, IL.

Kuhn, T. S. (1963) 'The function of dogma in scientific research', in A. C. Crombie (ed.) *Scientific Change*. Heinemann, London, pp. 347–69.

Lalljee, M., Brown, L. B. and Ginsburg, G. P. (1984) 'Attitudes: disposition, behaviour or evaluation?', *British Journal of Social Psychology*, **23**, 233–44.

Langer, E. J. (1989a) *Mindfulness*. Addison-Wesley, Reading, MA.

Langer, E. J. (1989b) 'Minding matters: the consequences of mindlessness-mindfulness'. In: Berkowitz, L. (ed.) *Advances in Experimental Social Psychology*, **22**, Academic Press, San Diego, CA, pp. 137–73.

Laudan, L. (1984) *Science and Values: The Aims of Science and their Role in Scientific Debate*. University of California Press, Berkeley, CA.

Lea, S. E. G. (1992) 'On parent and daughter disciplines: economic psychology, occupational psychology, and consumer science', *Journal of Economic Psychology*, **13**, 1–3.

Lea, S. E. G., Tarpy, R. M. and Webley, P. (1987) *The Individual in the Economy*. Cambridge University Press, Cambridge.

Leahey, T. H. (1987) *A History of Psychology: Main Currents in Psychological Thought*. Prentice-Hall, Englewood Cliffs, NJ.

Lee, V. L. (1988) *Beyond Behaviorism*, Erlbaum, London.

Lee, V. L. (1992) 'Transdermal interpretation of the subject matter of behavior analysis', *American Psychologist*, **47**, 1337–43.

Leibenstein, H. (1979) 'A branch of economics is missing: micro-micro theory', *Journal of Economic Literature*, **17**, 477–502.

Leibenstein, H. (1966) 'Allocative Efficiency v. X-Efficiency', *American Economic Review*, **56**, 392–415.

Lewis, A., Webley, P. and Furnham, A. (1995) *The New Economic Mind*. Harvester Wheatsheaf, Hemel Hempstead.

Lieberman, D. A. (1993) *Learning*. Pacific Grove, CA: Brooks/Cole.

Likert, R. (1932) 'A technique for the measurement of attitudes', *Archives of Psychology*, **140**, 5–53.

Liska, A. E. (1984) 'A critical examination of the causal structure of the Fishbein/Ajzen attitude–behavior model', *Social Psychology Quarterly*, **47**, 621–74.

Lowe, C. F. (1979) 'Determinants of human operant behavior', in Zeiler, D. M. and Harzem, P. (eds) *Advances in Analysis of Behavior: Vol. 1. Reinforcement and the Organization of Behavior*. Wiley Chichester, pp. 159–92.

Lowe, C. F. (1983) 'Radical behaviorism and human psychology', in Davey, G. C. L. (ed.) *Animal Models of Human Behavior: Conceptual, Evolutionary, and Neurobiological Perspectives*. Wiley Chichester, pp. 71–93.

Lowe, C. F. (1989) *From Conditioning to Consciousness: The Cultural Origins of Mind*. University College of North Wales, Bangor.

Lowe, C. F. and Horne, P. J. (1985) 'On the generality of behavioural principles: human choice and the matching law', in Lowe, C. F., Richelle, M., Blackman, D. E. and Bradshaw, C. M. (eds) *Behaviour Analysis and Contemporary Psychology*. Lawrence Erlbaum Associates, London, 97–116.

Lowe, C. F., Richelle, M., Blackman, D. E. and Bradshaw, C. M. (eds) (1985) *Behaviour Analysis and Contemporary Psychology*. Lawrence Erlbaum Associates, London.

Macaulay, S. (1963), 'Non-contractual Relations in Business,' *American Sociological Review*, **28**, 55–70.

MacCorquodale, K. (1969) 'B. F. Skinner's *Verbal Behavior*: a retrospective appreciation', *Journal of the Experimental Analysis of Behavior*, **12**, 831–41.

MacCorquodale, K. (1970) 'On Chomsky's review of Skinner's *Verbal Behavior*', *Journal of the Experimental Analysis of Behavior*, **13**, 85–99.

MacFadyen, A. J. and MacFadyen, H. (eds) (1986) *Economic Psychology: Intersections in Theory and Application*. Amsterdam: North Holland.

Mackenzie, B. (1988) 'The challenge to Skinner's theory of behavior'. In Catania, A. C. and Harnad, S. (eds) *The Selection of Behavior. The Operant Behaviorism of B. F. Skinner: Comments and Consequences*. Cambridge University Press, New York, pp. 111–13.

MacKenzie, S. B. and Spreng, R. A. (1992) 'How does motivation moderate the impact of central and peripheral processing on brand attitudes and intentions?' *Journal of Consumer Research*, **18**, 519–29.

Macneil, I. R. (1978) 'Contracts: adjustment of long-term economic relations under classical, neoclassical and relational contract law,' *Northwestern Law Review*, **72**, 854–905.

Madden, T. J., Ellen, P. S. and Ajzen, I. (1992) 'A comparison of the theory of planned behavior and the theory of reasoned action', *Personality and Social Psychology Bulletin*, **18**, 3–9.

Madden, T. J. and Sprott, D. E. (1995) 'A comparison of theoretical extensions to the theory of reasoned action', *Proceedings of the Society of Consumer Psychology*, 1995 Annual Convention, La Jolla, CA, pp. 1–9.

Maio, G. R. and Olson, J. M. (1994) 'Value-attitude-behaviour relations: the moderating role of attitude functions', *British Journal of Social Psychology*, **33**, 301–12.

Malott, R. (1986) 'Self-management, rule-governed behavior and everyday life'. In: Reese, H. W. and Parrott, L. J. (eds) *Behavior Science: Philosophical, Methodological, and Empirical Advances*. Erlbaum, Hillsdale, NJ, pp. 207–28.

Malott R. W. (1989) 'The achievement of evasive goals: control by rules describing contingencies that are not direct acting'. In: Hayes, S. C. (ed.) *Rule-Governed Behavior: Cognition, Contingencies, and Instructional Control*. Plenum, New York, pp. 269–324.

Malott, R. W. and Garcia, M. E. (1991) 'Role of private events in rule-governed behavior'. In: Hayes, L. J. and Chase, P. N. (eds) *Dialogues on Verbal Behavior*. Context Press, Reno, NV, pp. 237–54.

Mandler, G. (1985) *Cognitive Psychology: An Essay in Cognitive Science*. Lawrence Erlbaum Associates, Hillsdale, NJ.

Manstead, A. S. R. and Parker, D. (1995) 'Evaluating and extending the theory of planned behaviour'. In: Stroebe, W. and Hewstone, M. (eds) *European Review of Social Psychology*, **6**, Wiley, Chichester, pp. 69–95.

Market Assessment (1992) *Market Sector Report: Travel,* Market Assessment Ltd, London.

Marsh, A. and Matheson, J. (1983) *Smoking Attitudes and Behaviour*. HMSO, London.

Marx, M. H. and Hillix, W. A. (1979) *Systems and Theories in Psychology*, 3rd edn. McGraw-Hill, New York.

Mason, R. (1988) 'The psychological economics of conspicuous consumption'. Earl, P. ed. *Psychological Economics*. Boston, MA, v Kluwer. pp. 147–162.

184   *References*

Matthews, B. A., Catania, C. A. and Shimoff, E. (1985) 'Effects of uninstructed verbal behavior on nonverbal responding: contingency descriptions versus performance descriptions, *Journal of the Experimental Analysis of Behavior*, **43**, 155–64.
Mayer, C. (1993) 'UK airports see retailing as profitable way ahead', *Property*, 16 August, p. 16.
Maynard Smith, J. (1986) *The Problems of Biology*. Oxford University Press, Oxford.
McCaul, K. D., Sandgren, A. K., O'Neill, H. K. and Hinsz, V. B. (1993) 'The value of the theory of planned behavior, perceived control and self-efficacy expectations for predicting health-protective behaviors', *Basic and Applied Social Psychology*, **14**, 231–52.
McDowell, J. J (1981) 'On the validity and utility of Herrnstein's hyperbola in applied behavior analysis', in Bradshaw, C. M., Szabadi, E. and Lowe, C. F. (eds) *Quantification of Steady-State Operant Behaviour*, Amsterdam: Elsevier/North Holland, pp. 311–24.
McDowell, J. J. (1982) 'The importance of Herrnstein's mathematical statement of the law of effect for behavior therapy,' *American Psychologist*, **37**, 771–9.
Medema, S. G. (1994) *Ronald H. Coase*. Macmillan, London.
Menger, C. (1956) *Gruendste der Volkswirtschaftslehre*, trans. Dingwall, J. and Hoselitz, B. F. Free Press, Glencoe, IL.
Mick, D. G. (1992) 'Levels of subjective comprehension in advertising processing and their relations to ad perceptions, attitudes, and memory', *Journal of Consumer Research*, **18**, 411–24.
Mill, J. S. (1859) 'On Liberty' in J. S. Mill, *Utilitarianism, Liberty and Representative Government*. Dent, London, 1910, p. 97. First published 1859.
Miniard, P. W., Sirdeshmukh, D. and Innis, D. E. (1992) 'Peripheral persuasion and brand choice', *Journal of Consumer Research*, **19**, 226–39.
Mittal, B. (1988) 'Achieving higher seat belt usage: the role of habit in bridging the attitude–behavior gap', *Journal of Applied Social Psychology*, **18**, 993–1016.
Modgil, S. and Modgil, C. (eds) (1987) *B. F. Skinner: Consensus and Controversy*. Falmer Press, Brighton.
Monteverde, K. and Teece, D. (1982) 'Supplier switching costs and vertical integration in the automobile industry', *Bell Journal of Economics*, **13**, 206–13.
Moore, J. (1985) 'Some historical and conceptual relations among logical positivism, operationism, and behaviorism', *The Behavior Analyst*, **8**, 53–63.
Moore, J. (1994) 'On introspection and verbal reports'. In: Hayes, S. C., Hayes, L. J., Sato, M. and Ono K. (eds) *Behavior Analysis of Language and Cognition*. Context Press, Reno, NV, pp. 281–99.
Morgan, R. M. and Hunt, S. D. (1994) 'The commitment–trust theory of relationship marketing', *Journal of Marketing*, **58**, 20–38.
Morojele, N. K. and Stephenson, G. M. (1992) 'The Minnesota model in the treatment of addiction: a social psychological assessment of changes in beliefs and attributions', *Journal of Community and Applied Social Psychology*, **2**, 25–41.
Morris, E. K. (1991) 'The contextualism that is behaviour analysis: an alternative to cognitive psychology'. In: Still, A. and Costall, A. (eds) *Against Cognitivism: Alternative Foundations for Cognitive Psychology*. Harvester Wheatsheaf, Hemel Hempstead, pp. 123–49.
Morris, E. K. (1993a) 'Behavior analysis and mechanism: one is not the other', *The Behavior Analyst*, **16**, 25–43.

Morris, E. K. (1993b) 'Mechanism and contextualism in behavior analysis: just some observations', *The Behavior Analyst*, **16**, 255–68.

Morris, E. K. and Midgley, B. D. (1990) 'Some historical and conceptual foundations of ecobehavioral analysis'. In: Schroeder, S. R. (ed.) *Ecobehavioral Analysis and Developmental Disabilities*. Springer-Verlag, New York, pp. 1–32.

Morris, E. K., Todd, J. T., Midgley, B. D., Schneider, S. M. and Johnson, L. M. (1990) 'The history of behavior analysis: some historiography and a bibliography', *The Behavior Analyst*, **13**, 131–58.

Morrison, D. M., Gillmore, M. R. and Baker, S. A. (1995) 'Determinants of condom use among high-risk heterosexual adults: a test of the theory of reasoned action', *Journal of Applied Social Psychology*, **25**, 651–76.

Morwitz, V. G., Johnson, E. and Schmittlein, D. (1993) 'Does measuring intent change behavior?' *Journal of Consumer Research*, **20**, 46–61.

Mostyn, B. (1978) *The Attitude–Behaviour Relationship*. MCB, University Press, Bradford.

Myers-Levy, J. (1991) 'Elaborating on elaboration: the distinction between relational and item-specific elaboration', *Journal of Consumer Research*, **18**, 358–67.

Nataraajan, R. (1993) 'Prediction of choice in a technically complex, essentially intangible, highly experiential and rapidly evolving consumer product', *Psychology and Marketing*, **10**, 367–79.

Navarick, D. J. and Chellsen, J. (1983) 'Matching versus undermatching in the choice behavior of humans', *Behavior Analysis Letters*, **3**, 325–35.

Netemeyer, R. G. and Burton, S. (1990) 'Examining the relationships between voting behavior, intention, perceived behavioral control, and expectations', *Journal of Applied Social Psychology*, **20**, 661–80.

Netemeyer, R. G., Andrews, J. C. and Durvasala, S. (1993) 'A comparison of three behavioral intentions models: the case of Valentine's Day gift-giving', *Advances in Consumer Research*, **20**, 135–41.

Netemeyer, R. G., Burton, S. and Johnston, M. (1991) 'A comparison of two models for the prediction of volitional and goal-directed behaviors: a confirmatory analysis approach', *Social Psychology Quarterly*, **54**, 87–100.

Newman, A., Davies, B. J. and Dixon, G. (1994a) 'Identifying the social and physical environs affecting persons in UK airports: an archetypal model of consumption advanced', *Proceedings of the MEG Annual Conference*, University of Salford.

Newman, A., Davies, B. J. and Dixon, G. (1994b) 'Evaluating consumers' moods in airport retailing', *Proceedings of the Annual Conference of the British Academy of Management*, 310.

Newman, A., Davies, B. J. and Dixon, G. (1994c) 'The marketing psychology of store image research,' *Proceedings of the MEG Annual Conference*, 729.

Nicosia, F. M. (1966) *Consumer Decision Processes*, Prentice-Hall, Englewood Cliffs, NJ.

Norman, P. and Smith, L. (1995) 'The theory of planned behavior and exercise: an investigation into the role of prior behavior, behavioral intentions, and attitude variability', *European Journal of Social Psychology*, **25**, 403–15.

Olson, J. M. and Zanna, M. P. (1993) 'Attitudes and attitude change', *Annual Review of Psychology*, **44**, 117–54.

Ono, K. (1994) 'Verbal control of superstitious behavior: superstitions as false rules'. In: Hayes, S. C., Hayes, L. J., Sato, M. and Ono, K. (eds) *Behavior Analysis of Language and Cognition*. Context Press, Reno, NV, pp. 181–96.

Oscar-Berman, M., G. M. Heyman, R. T. Bonner and J. Ryder (1980) 'Human neuropsychology: some differences between Korsakoff and normal operant performance,' *Psychological Research*, **41**, 235–47.

O'Shaughnessy, J. (1992) *Explaining Buyer Behavior: Central Concepts and Philosophy of Science Issues*. Oxford University Press, New York.

Osmond, H. (1957) 'Function as the basis of psychiatric ward design', *Mental Hospitals*, **8** (April), 23–9.

Ostrom, T. M. (1994) 'Foreword'. In: Wyer, R. S. and Srull, T. K. (eds) *Handbook of Social Cognition, vol. 1: Basic Processes*. Erlbaum, Hillsdale, NJ, pp. vii–xii.

Ostrom, T. M., Prior, J. B. and Simpson, D. D. (1981) 'The organization of social information'. In: Higgins, E. T., Herman, C. P. and Zanna, M. P. (eds) *Social Cognition: The Ontario Symposium*. Erlbaum, Hillsdale, NJ, pp. 3–38.

Overskeid, G. (1995) 'Cognitive or behaviourist – who can tell the difference? The case of implicit and explicit knowledge', *British Journal of Psychology*, **46**, 312–19.

Owen, N., Borland, R. and Hill, D. (1991) 'Regulatory influences on health-related behaviors: the case of workplace smoking bans', *Australian Psychologist*, **26**, 188–91.

Parker, D., Manstead, A. S. R. and Stradling, S. G. (1995) 'Extending the theory of planned behaviour: the role of the personal norm', *British Journal of Social Psychology*, **34**, 127–38.

Parker, D., Manstead, A. S. R., Stradling, S. G., Reason, J. T. and Baxter, J. S. (1992) 'Intentions to commit driving violations: an application of the theory of planned behavior', *Journal of Applied Psychology*, **77**, 94–101.

Parker, D., Reason, J. T., Manstead, A. S. R. and Stradling, S. G. (in press) 'Driving errors, driving violations, and accident involvement'. *Ergonomics*.

Parrott, L. J. (1986) 'The role of postulation in the analysis of inapparent events'. In: Reese, H. W. and Parrott, L. J. (eds) *Behavior Science: Philosophical, Methodological, and Empirical Advances*. Erlbaum, Hillsdale, NJ, pp. 35–60.

Parsons, H. M. (1974) 'What happened at Hawthorne?' *Science*, **183** (8 March), 922–32.

Payne, A. (1995) (ed.) *Advances in Relationship Marketing*. Kogan Page, London.

Payne, A., Christopher, M. Clark, M. and Peck, H. (1995) *Relationship Marketing for Competitive Advantage: Winning and Keeping Customers*. Butterworth-Heinemann, London.

Perrien, J. and Ricard, L. (1995) 'The Meaning of a Marketing Relationship', *Industrial Marketing Management*, **24**, 37–43.

Percy, L. and Rossiter, J. R. (1992) 'A model of brand awareness and brand attitude advertising strategies', *Psychology and Marketing*, **9**, 262–74.

Petty R. E. and Cacioppo, J. T. (1984a) 'The effects of involvement on responses to argument quantity and quality: central and peripheral routes to persuasion', *Journal of Personality and Social Psychology*, **46**, 69–81.

Petty, R. E. and Cacioppo, J. T. (1984b) 'Source factors and the elaboration likelihood model of persuasion', *Advances in Consumer Research*, **11**, 668–72.

Petty, R. E. and Cacioppo, J. T. (1986a) *Communication and Persuasion: Central and Peripheral Routes to Attitude Change*. Springer-Verlag, New York.

Petty, R. E. and Cacioppo, J. T. (1986b) 'The elaboration likelihood model of persuasion'. In: Berkowitz, L. (ed.) *Advances in Experimental Social Psychology*, **19**, 123–205.

Petty, R. E., Unnava, R. and Strathman, A. J. (1991) 'Theories of attitude change'. In: Robertson, T. S. and Kassarjian, H. H. (eds) *Handbook of Consumer Behavior*. Prentice-Hall, Englewood Cliffs, NJ, pp. 241–80.

Petty, R. E., Priester, J. R. and Wegener, D. T. (1994) 'Cognitive processes in attitude change'. In: Wyer, R. S. and Srull, T. K. (eds) *Handbook of Social Cognition, vol. 2: Application*, 2nd edn. Erlbaum, Hillsdale, NJ.

Phillips, D. C. (1992) *The Social Scientist's Bestiary: A Guide to Fabled Threats to, and Defences of, Naturalistic Social Science*. Pergamon, Oxford.

Phillips, H. and Bradshaw, R. (1993) 'How customers actually shop: customer interaction with the point of sale', *Journal of the Market Research Society*, **35**, 51–62.

Pierce, W. D. and W. F. Epling (1980) 'What happened to analysis in applied behavior analysis?' *Behavior Analyst*, **3**, 1–9.

Pierce, W. D. and W. F. Epling (1983) 'Choice, matching, and human behavior', *Behavior Analyst*, 6, 57–76.

Pierce, W. D., Epling, W. F. and Greer, S. M. (1981) 'Human communication and the matching law', in C. M. Bradshaw, E. Szabadi and C. F. Lowe (eds), *Quantification of Steady State Operant Behavior*, Amsterdam: North-Holland, 345–8.

Pieters, R. G. M. (1988) 'Attitude–behavior relationships'. In: Van Raaij, W. F., Van Veldhoven, G. M. and Warneryd, K.-E. (1998) (eds) *Handbook of Economic Psychology*. Kluwer, Dordrecht, pp. 144–204.

Pieters, R. G. M. and Van Raaij, W. F. (1988) 'The role of affect in economic behavior'. In: Van Raaij, W. F., Van Veldhoven, G. M. and Warneryd, K.-E. (1998) (eds) *Handbook of Economic Psychology*. Kluwer, Dordrecht, pp. 108–42.

Pieters, R. G. M. and Verplanken, B. (1995) 'Intention–behaviour consistency: effects of consideration set size, involvement and need for cognition', *European Journal of Social Psychology*, **25**, 531–43.

Poppen, R. L. (1989) 'Some clinical implications of rule-governed behavior'. In: Hayes, S. C. (ed.) *Rule-governed Behavior*. Plenum, New York, pp. 325–57.

Posner, R. A. (1990) *The Problems of Jurisprudence*. Harvard University Press, Cambridge, MA.

Posner, R. A. (1992) *The Economic Analysis of Law*. Little, Brown, New York.

Proctor, P. (1992) 'New $250 million Karachi terminal will be flagship for airport upgrades', *Aviation Week and Space Technology*, **137**, 44–5.

Qantas (n.d.) *Qantas Frequent Flyer. The Program for People Going Places*. ACN: Qantas Airways Limited.

Raats, M. N., Shepherd, R. and Sparks, P. (1995) 'Including moral dimensions of choice within the structure of the theory of planned behavior', *Journal of Applied Social Psychology*, **25**, 484–94.

Rachlin, H. (1980) "Economics and behavioral psychology," in John E. R. Staddon (ed.), *Limits to Action: The Allocation of Individual Behavior*, Academic Press, New York, 205–36.

Rachlin, H. (1992) 'Teleological behaviorism', *American Psychologist*, **47**, 1371–82.

188 *References*

Rachlin, H. (1995) *Behavior and Mind: The Roots of Modern Psychology*. Oxford University Press, New York.

Rajecki, D. W. (1982) *Attitudes: Themes and Advances*. Sinauer, Sunderland, MA.

Ramsey, S. L., Lord, C. G., Wallace, D. S. and Pugh, M. A. (1994) 'The role of subtypes in attitudes towards superordinate social categories', *British Journal of Social Psychology*, **33**, 387–403.

Randall, D. M. and Wolff, J. A. (1994) 'The time interval in the intention-behaviour relationship', *British Journal of Social Psychology*, **33**, 405–18.

Rao, A. R. and Monroe, K. B. (1988) 'The moderating effect of prior knowledge on cue utilization in product evaluations', *Journal of Consumer Research*, **15**, 253–63.

Rao, A. R. and Sieben, W. A. (1992) 'The effects of prior knowledge on price acceptability and the type of information examined', *Journal of Consumer Research*, **19**, 256–70.

Reese, H. W. (1992a) 'Rules as nonverbal entities'. In: Hayes, S. C. and Hayes, L. J. (eds) *Understanding Verbal Relations*. Context Press, Reno, NV, pp. 121–34.

Reese, H. W. (1992b) 'Problem solving by algorithms and heuristics'. In: Hayes, S. C. and Hayes, L. J. (eds) *Understanding Verbal Relations*. Context Press, Reno, NV, pp. 153–80.

Reese. H. W. (1994) 'Cognitive and behavioral approaches to problem-solving'. In: Hayes, S. C., Hayes, L. J., Sato, M. and Ono, K. (eds) *Behavior Analysis of Language and Cognition*. Context Press, Reno, NV, pp. 197–258.

Reese, H. W. and Parrott, L. J. (eds) (1986) *Behavior Science: Philosophical, Methodological, and Empirical Advances*. Lawrence Erlbaum Associates, Hillsdale, NJ.

Rhinehart, L. (1976) *The Book of est*. Sphere, London.

Ribes, E. (1991) 'Language as contingency-substitution behavior'. In: Hayes, L. J. and Chase, P. N. (eds) *Dialogues on Verbal Behavior*. Context Press, Reno, NV, pp. 47–58.

Ribes, E. (1992) 'An analysis of thinking'. In: Hayes, S. C. and Hayes, L. J. (eds) *Understanding Verbal Relations*. Context Press, Reno, NV, pp. 209–24.

Richard, L., Dedobbeleer, N., Champagne, F. and Potvin, L. (1994) 'Predicting child restraint device use: a comparison of two models', *Journal of Applied Social Psychology*, **24**, 1837–47.

Richard, R. (1994) 'Regret is what you get: the impact of anticipated feelings and emotions on human behaviour'. Unpublished doctoral dissertation, University of Amsterdam.

Richard, R., van der Pligt, J. and de Vries, N. (1995) 'Anticipated affective reactions and prevention of AIDS', *British Journal of Social Psychology*, **34**, 9–21.

Richardson, N. J., Shepherd, R. and Elliman, N. A. (1993) 'Current attitudes and future influences on meat consumption in the U.K.', *Appetite*, **21**, 41–51.

Richelle, M. (1987) 'Variation and selection: the evolutionary analogy in Skinner's theory' in Modgil, S. and Modgil, C. (eds) *B. F. Skinner: Consensus and Controversy*. Falmer Press, Brighton pp. 127–138.

Richelle, M. N. (1993) *B. F. Skinner: A Reappraisal*. Erlbaum, London.

Ronis, D. L., Yates, J. F. and Kirscht, J. P. (1989) 'Attitudes, decisions and habits as determinants of repeated behavior'. In: Pratkanis, A. R., Breckler, S. J. and Greenwald, A. G. (eds) *Attitude Structure and Function*. Erlbaum, Hillsdale, NJ, pp. 213–40.

Ruddle, H., C. M. Bradshaw, E. Szabadi and P. Bevan (1979) 'Behavior of humans in concurrent schedules programmed on spatially separated operanda', *Quarterly Journal of Experimental Psychology*, **31**, 509–17.

Russell, J. A. and Mehrabian, A. (1976) 'Environmental variables in consumer research', *Journal of Consumer Research*, **3**, 62–3.

Sahni, A. (1994) 'Incorporating perceptions of financial control in purchase prediction: an empirical examination of the theory of planned behavior', *Advances in Consumer Research*, **21**, 442–8.

Sarver, V. T. (1983) 'Ajzen and Fishbein's "theory of reasoned action": a critical assessment', *Journal for the Theory of Social Behaviour*, **13**, 155–63.

Sasser, W. E., Olsen, R. P., and Wyckoff, D. D. (1978). *The Management of Service Operations: Text, Cases, and Readings.* Allyn and Bacon, Boston, MA.

Sato, M. and Sugiyama, N. (1994) 'Lying'. In: Hayes, S. C., Hayes, L. J., Sato, M. and Ono, K. (eds) *Behavior Analysis of Language and Cognition.* Context Press, Reno, NV, pp. 165–80.

Schlegel, R. P., Davernas, J. R. and Zanna, M. P. (1992) 'Problem drinking: a problem for the theory of reasoned action', *Journal of Applied Social Psychology*, **22**, 358–85.

Schmitt, D. R. (1974) 'Effects of reinforcement rate and reinforcer magnitude on choice behavior of humans', *Journal of the Experimental Analysis of Behavior*, **21**, 409–19.

Schroeder, S. R. (1975) 'Perseveration in concurrent performances by the developmentally retarded', *Psychological Record*, **25**, 51–64.

Schroeder, S. R. and J. G. Holland (1969) 'Reinforcement of the eye movement with concurrent schedules', *Journal of the Experimental Analysis of Behavior*, **12**, 897–903.

Schumann, D. W., Petty, R. E. and Clemons, D. S. (1990) 'Predicting the effectiveness of different strategies of advertising variation: a test of the repetition-variation hypotheses', *Journal of Consumer Research*, **17**, 192–202.

Schwartz, S. H. (1978) 'Temporal instability as a moderator of the attitude–behavior relationship', *Journal of Personality and Social Psychology*, **36**, 715–24.

Schwartz, B. and Reisberg, D. (1991) *Learning and Memory* W. W. Norton, New York.

Scitovsky, T. (1986) *The Joyless Economy.* Oxford University Press, New York.

Sharp, B. and Sharp, A. (1996) 'Loyalty programs and their impact on repeat-purchase loyalty patterns'. Working paper, Marketing Science Centre, University of South Australia, Adelaide.

Shavitt, S. (1989) 'Operationalizing functional theories of attitude'. In: Pratkanis, A. R., Breckler, S. J. and Greenwald, A. G. (eds.) *Attitude Structure and Function.* Erlbaum, Hillsdale, NJ, pp. 311–37.

Shepherd, R. and Towler, G. (1992) 'Nutrition knowledge, attitudes and fat intake: application of the theory of reasoned action', *Journal of Human Nutrition and Dietetics*, **5**, 387–97.

Shepherd, R., Sparks, P., Bellier, S. and Raats, M. M. (1991/2) 'Attitudes and choice of flavoured milks: extension of Fishbein and Ajzen's theory of reasoned action', *Food Quality and Preference*, **3**, 157–64.

Sheppard, B. H., Hartwick, J. and Warshaw, P. R. (1988) 'The theory of reasoned action: a meta-analysis of past research with recommendations for modifications and future research', *Journal of Consumer Research*, **15**, 325–43.

Sidman, M. (1990) 'Equivalence Relations: Where do they Come From?' in Blackman, Derek E. and Lejeune, Helga H. (eds), *Behavior Analysis in Theory and Practice*' Erlbaum, London, pp. 93–114.

Sidman, M. (1992). Equivalence Relations: Some Basic Considerations, in Hayes, Stephen C. and Hayes, Linda J. (eds), *Understanding Verbal Relations*. Context Press, Reno, NV, pp. 15–28.

Silberberg, A., J. R. Thomas, and N. Berendzen (1991) 'Human Choice on Concurrent Variable-Interval Variable Ratio Schedules', *Journal of the Experimental Analysis of Behavior*, **56**, 575–84.

Skinner, B. F. (1938) *The Behavior of Organisms*. Century, New York.

Skinner, B. F. (1945) 'The operational analysis of psychological terms', *Psychological Review*, **52**, 270–7, 291–4.

Skinner, B. F. (1947) 'Experimental Psychology'. In: Denis, W. (ed.) *Current Trends in Psychology*. University of Pittsburgh Press, Pittisburgh, PA.

Skinner, B. F. (1950) 'Are theories of learning necessary?', *Psychological Review*, **57**, 193–216.

Skinner, B. F. (1953) *Science and Human Behavior*. Macmillan, New York.

Skinner, B. F. (1957) *Verbal Behavior*. Century, New York.

Skinner, B. F. (1963) 'Behaviorism at fifty', *Science*, **140**, 951–8.

Skinner, B. F. (1969) *Contingencies of Reinforcement: A Theoretical Analysis*. Prentice-Hall, Englewood Cliffs, NJ.

Skinner, B. F. (1971) *Beyond Freedom and Dignity*. Knopf, New York.

Skinner, B. F. (1974) *About Behaviorism*. Knopf, New York.

Skinner, B. F. (1977) 'Why I am not cognitive psychologist', *Behaviorism*, **5**, 1–10.

Skinner, B. F. (1981) 'Selection by consequences', *Science*, 213 (31 July), 501–4.

Skinner, B. F. (1988a) 'Reply to Schnaitter'. In Catania, A. C. and Harnad, S. (eds) *The Selection of Behavior. The Operant Behaviorism of B. F. Skinner: Comments and Consequences*. Cambridge University Press, New York, p. 354.

Skinner, B. F. (1988b) 'Reply to Mackenzie'. In: Catania, A. C. and Harnad, S. (eds) *The Selection of Behavior. The Operant Behaviorism of B. F. Skinner: Comments and Consequences*. Cambridge University Press, New York, pp. 113–14.

Skinner, B. F. (1989) 'The behavior of the listener'. In: Hayes, S. C. (ed.) *Rule-governed Behavior: Cognition, Contingencies, and Instructional Control*. Plenum, New York, pp. 85–96.

Skinner, B. F. (1990) 'Can psychology be a science of mind?', *American Psychologist*, **45**, 1206–10.

Smith, L. D. (1986) *Behaviorism and Logical Positivism: A Reassessment of the Alliance*. Stanford University Press, Stanford, CA.

Smith, S. M., Haugtvedt, C. P. and Petty, R. E. (1994) 'Need for cognition and the effects of repeated expression on attitude accessibility and extremity', *Advances in Consumer Research*, **21**, 234–7.

Snodgrass, J. and Russell, J. A. (1988) 'Planning, mood, and place-liking', *Journal of Environmental Psychology*, **8**, 209–22.

Sommers, R. (1974). *Tight Spaces: Hard Architecture and How to Harmonize It*. Prentice-Hall, Englewood Cliffs, NJ.

Sparks, P. and Shepherd, R. (1992) 'Self-identity and the theory of planned behavior: assessing the role of identification with "green consumerism"', *Social Psychology Quarterly*, **55**, 388–99.

Sparks, P., Hedderley, D. and Shepherd, R. (1991) 'Expectancy-value models of attitudes: a note on the relationship between theory and methodology', *European Journal of Social Psychology*, **21**, 261–71.

Sparks, P., Hedderley, D. and Shepherd, R. (1992) 'An investigation into the relationship between perceived control, attitude variability and the consumption of two common foods', *European Journal of Social Psychology*, **22**, 55–71.

Sparks, P., Shepherd, R. and Frewer, L. J. (1995) 'Assessing and structuring attitudes toward the use of gene technology in food production: the role of perceived ethical obligation', *Basic and Applied Social Psychology*, **16**, 267–85.

Staddon, J. E. R. (1993) *Behaviorism*. Duckworth, London.

Stayman, D. M. and Kardes, F. R. (1992) 'Spontaneous inference processes in advertising: effects of need for cognition and self-monitoring on inference generation and utilization', *Journal of Consumer Psychology*, **1**, 125–42.

Sutton, S. A. and Hallett, R. (1989) 'Understanding seat belt intentions and behavior: a decision making approach', *Journal of Applied Social Psychology*, **19**, 1310–25.

Sutton, S. A., Marsh, A. and Matheson, J. (1987) 'Explaining smokers' decisions to stop. Test of an expectancy-value model', *Social Behaviour*, **2**, 35–50.

Takahashi, M. and T. Iwamoto (1986) 'Human concurrent performances: the effects of experience, instructions, and schedule-correlated stimuli', *Journal of the Experimental Analysis of Behavior*, **45**, 257–67.

Taylor, R. B. (1991) *Human Territorial Functioning*. Cambridge University Press, Cambridge.

Taylor, S. and Todd, P. (1995) 'An integrated model of waste management behavior: a test of household recycling and composting intentions', *Environment and Behavior*, **27**, 603–30.

Terry, D. J. and O'Leary, J. E. (1995) 'The theory of planned behaviour: the effects of perceived behavioural control and self-efficacy', *British Journal of Social Psychology*, **34**, 199–220.

Tesser, A. and Shaffer, D. (1990) 'Attitudes and attitude change', *Annual Review of Psychology*, **41**, 479–524.

Tesser, A., Martin, L. L. and Mendolia, M. (1994) 'The role of thought in changing attitude strength'. In: Petty, R. E. and Krosnick, J. A. (eds) *Attitude Strength: Antecedents and Consequences*. Erlbaum, Hillsdale, NJ.

Thompson, K. E., Haziris, N. and Alekos, P. J. (1994) 'Attitudes and food choice behaviour', *British Food Journal*, **96**(11), 9–13.

Thompson, K. E., Thompson, N. J. and Hill, R. W. (1995) 'The role of attitude, normative and control beliefs in drink choice behaviour'. Unpublished paper, Cranfield University.

Thompson, R. F. (1994) 'Behaviorism and neuroscience', *Psychological Review*, **101**, 259–65.

Timmermans, H. (1993) 'Retail environments and spatial shopping behavior'. In: Garling, T. and Golledge, R. G. (eds) *Behavior and Environment: Psychological and Geographical Approaches*, Amsterdam: North-Holland. pp. 342–77.

Towler, G. and Shepherd, R. (1991/2) 'Modification of Fishbein and Ajzen's theory of reasoned action to predict chip consumption', *Food Quality and Preference*, **3**, 37–45.

Todd, J. T. and Morris, E. K. (1992) 'Case histories in the great power of steady misrepresentation', *American Psychologist*, **47**, 1441–53.

Towler, G. and Shepherd, R. (1992) 'Application of Fishbein and Ajzen's expectancy-value model of understanding fat intake', *Appetite*, **18**, 15–27.

Trafimow, D. and Fishbein, M. (1995) 'Do people really distinguish between behavioural and normative beliefs?' *British Journal of Social Psychology*, **34**, 257–66.

Triandis, H. C. (1977) *Interpersonal Behavior*. Brooks Cole, Monterey, CA.

Triandis, H. (1980) 'Values, attitudes and interpersonal behavior'. In: Howe, H. E. and Page, M. M. (eds) *Nebraska Symposium on Motivation 1979*, **27**, University of Nebraska Press, Lincoln. pp. 195–259.

Tripp, C., Jensen, T. D. and Carlson, L. (1994) 'The effects of multiple product endorsements by celebrities on consumers' attitudes and intentions', *Journal of Consumer Research*, **20**, 535–47.

Tversky, A. and Kahneman, D. (1974) 'Judgment under uncertainty: heuristics and biases', *Science*, **185**, 1124–31.

Tybout, A. M. and Artz, N. (1994) 'Consumer psychology', *Annual Review of Psychology*, **45**, 131–69.

Upmeyer, A. (ed.) (1989) *Attitudes and Behavioral Decisions*. Springer-Verlag, New York.

Valentine, E. R. (1992) *Conceptual Issues in Psychology*. 2nd edn. Routledge, London.

Van den Putte, B. (1993) 'On the theory of reasoned action'. Unpublished doctoral dissertation, University of Amsterdam.

van Knippenberg, D., Lossie, N. and Wilke, H. (1994) 'In-group prototypicality and persuasion: determinants of heuristic and systematic message processing', *British Journal of Social Psychology*, **33**, 289–300.

Van Parijs, P. (1981) *Evolutionary Explanation in the Social Sciences: An Emerging Paradigm* Rowman and Littlefield, Totowa, NJ.

van Raaij, W. F. (1988) 'Information processing and decision-making. Cognitive aspects of economic behavior'. In: Van Raaij, W. F., Van Veldhoven, G. M. and Warneryd, K.-E. (1998) (eds) *Handbook of Economic Psychology*. Kluwer, Dordrecht, pp. 74–106.

van Raaij, W. F. (1991) 'The formation and use of expectations in consumer decision-making'. In: Robertson, T. S. and Kassarjian, H. H. (eds.) *Handbook of Consumer Behaviour*. Prentice-Hall, Englewood Cliffs, NJ, pp. 401–18.

van Raaij, W. F., Van Veldhoven, G. M. and Warneryd, K.-E. (1998) (eds) *Handbook of Economic Psychology*. Kluwer, Dordrecht.

van Ryn, M. and Vinokur, A. D. (1990) 'The role of experimentally manipulated self-efficacy in determining job search behavior among the unemployed'. Unpublished manuscript, University of Michigan.

Vaughan, M. (1987) 'Rule-governed behavior and higher mental processes' in Modgil, S. and Modgil, C. (eds), *B. F. Skinner: Consensus and Controversy*. Falmer Press Brighton. pp. 257–64.

Vaughan, M. (1989) 'Rule-governed behavior in behavior analysis: a theoretical and experimental history'. In: Hayes, S. C. (ed.) *Rule-governed Behavior: Cognition, Contingencies, and Instructional Control*. New York: Plenum. pp. 97–118.

Vaughan, M. E. (1991) 'Toward a methodology for studying verbal behavior'. In: Hayes, L. J. and Chase, P. N. (eds) *Dialogues on Verbal Behavior*. Context Press, Reno, NV, pp. 82–4.

Viner, J. (1925) 'The utility concept in value theory and its critics', *Journal of Political Economy*, **33**, 369–87.

Ward, J. C., Bitner, M. J. and Barnes, J. (1992) 'Measuring the prototypicality and meaning of retailing environments', *Journal of Retailing*, **68**, 194–220.

Warshaw, P. R., Sheppard, B. H. and Hartwick, J. (1990) 'The intention and self-prediction of goals and behaviors'. In: Bagozzi, R. P. (ed.) *Advances in Marketing Communications Research*. JAI Press, Greenwich, CT.

Watters, A. E. (1989) 'Reasoned/intuitive action: an individual difference moderator of the attitude–behavior relationship in the 1988 U.S. presidential election'. Unpublished thesis, University of Michigan.

Wearden, J. (1988) 'Some neglected problems in the analysis of human operant behaviour'. In: Davey, G. C. L. and Cullen, C. (eds) *Human Operant Conditioning and Behaviour Modification*. Wiley, Chichester.

Webster, F. E. (1992) 'The changing role of marketing in the corporation', *Journal of Marketing*, **56**, 1–17.

Webster, R. (1995) *Why Freud Was Wrong: Sin, Science and Psychoanalysis*. HarperCollins, London.

Webster, R. 1996 *Why Freud was Wrong*. HarperCollins, London.

White, K. M., Terry, D. J. and Hogg, M. A. (1994) 'Safer sex behavior: the role of attitudes, norms and control factors', *Journal of Applied Social Psychology*, **24**, 2164–92.

Wicker, A. W. (1969) 'Attitude versus actions: the relationship of verbal and overt behavioural responses to attitude objects', *Social Issues*, **25**, 41–78.

Wicker, A. W. (1971) 'An examination of the "other variables" explanation of attitude–behavior inconsistency', *Journal of Personality and Social Psychology*, **19**, 18–30.

Wicker, A. W. (1979) *An Introduction to Ecological Psychology*. Cambrdige University Press, Cambridge.

Wicker, A. W. (1987) 'Behavior-settings reconsidered: temporal stages, resources, internal dynamics, context', in Stokols, D. and Altmann, I. (eds) *Handbook of Environmental Psychology* John Wiley & Sons, New York, pp. 613–53.

Wileman, A. (1993) 'Destination retailing', *International Journal of Retail and Distribution Management*, **21**, 3–9.

Williamson, O. E. (1975) *Markets and Hierarchies: Analysis and Antitrust Implications*. Free Press, New York.

Williamson, O. E. (1985) *The Economic Institutions of Capitalism*, Free Press, New York.

Winkler, R. C. (1980) 'Behavioral economics, token economies and applied behavior analysis,' in John E. R. Staddon (ed.) *Limits to Action: The Allocation of Individual Behavior*, Academic Press, New York, 269–97.

Wittenbraker, J., Gibbs, B. L. and Khale, L. R. (1983) 'Seat belt attitudes, habits, and behaviors: an adaptive amendment tot he Fishbein model', *Journal of Applied Social Psychology*, **13**, 406–21.

Wurster, R. M. and R. R. Griffiths (1979) 'Human concurrent performances: variation of reinforcer magnitude and rate of reinforcement', *Psychological Record*, 29, 341–54.

Wyer, R. S. and Srull, T. K. (1986) 'Human cognition in its social context', *Psychological Review*, **93**, 322–59.

Wyer, R. S. and Srull, T. K. (1989) *Memory and Cognition in Its Social Context*. Erlbaum, Hillsdale, NJ.

Wyer, R. S. and Srull, T. K. (eds) (1994a) *Handbook of Social Cognition, vol. 1: Basic Processes*, 2nd edn. Erlbaum, Hillsdale, NJ.

Wyer, R. S. and Srull, T. K. (eds) (1994b) *Handbook of Social Cognition, vol. 2: Application*, 2nd edn. Erlbaum, Hillsdale, NJ.

Yi, Y. (1990) 'The indirect effects of advertisements designed to change product attribute beliefs', *Psychology and Marketing*, **7**, 47–63.

Zaltman, G. and Bonoma, T. V. (1984) 'The lack of heresy in marketing, in Brown, S. W. and Fisk, Raymond P. (eds), *Marketing Theory: Distinguished Contributions*. John Wiley Sons, New York, pp. 329–35.

Zettle, R. D. and Hayes, S. C. (1982) 'Rule-governed behavior: a potential framework for cognitive-behavioral therapy'. In: Kendall, P. C. (ed.) *Advances in Cognitive-behavioral Research and Therapy*. Academic Press, New York, pp. 73–117.

Zimmer, M. R. and Golden, L. L. (1988) 'Impressions of retail stores: a content analysis of consumer images', *Journal of Retailing*, **64**, 265–93.

Zuriff, G. E. (1985) *Behaviorism: A Conceptual Reconstruction*. Columbia University Press, New York.

Index

Abelson, R. P., 39, 168
accomplishment
  in contingency matrix, 95, 96–7
  defined, 88–90
  and informational
    reinforcement, 83
  large group awareness training
    as, 136–40
  marketing management, 132, 134
  and saving and collecting, 94
accumulation
  in contingency matrix, 95, 97–8
  defined, 88–90
  frequent-flyer programmes, 143–5
  marketing management, 133
  and saving and collecting, 94
advertising 131–2
  in consumer behaviour setting, 90
  as other-rules, 109
airport waiting 145–9
Ajzen, I., 12, 21, 24, 25, 26, 27,
  29, 30, 31, 32, 36, 39, 45,
  48, 168, 171, 174, 176
Alba, J. W., 17, 168
Alchian, A. A., 162, 164, 168
Alessi, G., 55, 168
Alhadeff, D. A., 84, 120, 121,
  151, 168
Allen, C. T., 32, 168
Allport, G. W., 20, 168
Anderson, A. S., 32, 168
Andreasen, A., 17, 168
Artz, N., 9, 192
Assael, H., 18, 169
attitudes 4–5
  behavioural consistency, 19–22
  definitions, 19–20
  deliberative processing, 25–32
  direct experience, 24–5
  Eagly–Chaiken model, 42
  elaboration-likelihood, 42–3
  guidance of behaviour, 23–4
  heuristic-systematic model,
    41–2, 103–8

MODE model 40–1, 103–8
  as object-evaluations, 22–3
  spontaneous processing, 22–5,
    103–8
  theory of planned behaviour, 30–2
  theory of reasoned action, 26–30,
    73–6
  theory of trying, 35–40
attitude–behaviour relationships
  Chapter 2 *passim*
  behaviourist interpretation, 73–6
  models of, 40–43, 48–9
attitude functions 42, 92–3
aversive consequence 58, 121

Baars, B., 55, 169
Baer, D. M., 129, 139, 140, 169
Bagozzi, R. P., 17, 21, 25,
  28, 29, 30, 35, 36, 37,
  38, 39, 40, 48, 169–70
Baker, J., 148, 170
Ball, D., 28, 170
Bandura, A., 50, 170
Bargh, J. A., 23, 24, 170
Barker, R. G., 9, 170
Barnes, J. G., 160, 170
Baron, S., 148, 170
Bateson, J., 148, 170
Battalio, R. C., 129, 170
Baum, W. M., 71, 72, 170
Bayés, R., 16, 170
Beale, D. A., 31, 39, 171
Beck, L., 30, 171
behaviour
  and attitudes, Chapter 2 *passim*,
    48–9
  cognitive rationale, 44–6
  consequences, 80–89
  habit, 46–7
  meaning of, 77
  operant, defined 58; *see also*
    operant classification of
    consumer behaviour;
    operant conditioning

behaviour (*contd.*)
  prior, 33–4, 36–40, 43–7
  verbal, 67–76
behaviour analysis, 4
  see also radical behaviourism
behavioural perspective model
    (BPM), Chapter 5 *passim*
  behaviour of the firm, Chapter 6
    passim
  consumer decision-making,
    103–10
  consumer situation analysis,
    79, 100–3
  contingency category analysis,
    90–9
  contingency matrix, 93–6
  derivation, 78–80
  explanatory basis, 78–80
  interpretation, 80–103
  location of consumer behaviour,
    79–80
  operant classification, 80–9
  rule-governed behaviour, 103–10
behaviourism, *see* radical
    behaviourism
Belk, R. W., 9, 171
Bem, D., 24, 43, 171
Bentler, P. M., 30, 36, 171
Berger, I. E., 23, 28, 171
Bettman, J. R., 7, 9, 17, 171
bilateral contingency, 156–7, 158–9
Bitner, M. J., 126, 171
Blackman, D. E., 55, 171
Blascovich, J., 24, 171
Blois, K., 164, 171
Bogardus, E. S., 20, 171
Bohner, G., 22, 41, 171
Boldero, J., 31, 171
Bonoma, T., 5, 193
Borgida, E., 31, 172
Boyd, B., 30, 172
Bradshaw, C. M., 70, 172
Bradshaw, R., 126, 187
Breinlinger, S., 31, 181
Brown, S. P., 19, 29, 172
Budd, R. J., 36, 172
Burns, R., 90, 180–1, 184
Burton, R., 32, 185
Butler, D. Y., 148, 172

Cacioppo, J. T., 22, 42, 103, 186
Cairns, E., 30, 31, 178
Castleberry, S. B., 20, 172
Catania, A. C., 39, 63, 70, 71, 72,
    73, 74, 91, 108, 172, 173
Chaiken, S., 19, 22, 24, 25, 29,
    30, 32, 34, 35, 36, 40, 41,
    42, 44, 46, 47, 93, 103, 173
Chakravarti, D., 9, 173
Chan, D. K. S., 31, 173
Charng, H., 36, 173
Chase, P. N., 55, 71, 72,
    105, 173, 179, 181
Chebat, J. C., 31, 174
Chellsen, J., 70
Chesanow, N., 98, 129, 173
Chesterton Research, 148, 173
Chiesa, M., 57, 173
Chomsky, N., 68, 173
closure
  in competitive strategy, 157
  of consumer setting, 128–9
  of marketer setting, 157–9
  mutual qualification of, 157–9
  sales environment, 127–8
Coase, R. H., 117, 151, 153,
    158, 161, 162, 165, 173
cognitivism, Chapter 2 *passim*; *see
    also* consumer research,
    cognitive
Cohen, A., 9, 173
Cohen, J. B., 25, 173
Cone, J. D., 84, 173
consumers
  and the marketing firm, 117–19
  marketing response to, 18–19
  placelessness of, 9–10
  social cognitive, 17ff
consumer behaviour 17
  approach, 121
  BPM interpretation, Chapter 5
    passim, 121
  escape, 121
consumer behaviour setting (CBS),
    4–5, 90–9
  in BPM contingency matrix, 93–9
  in bilateral contingency, 156–7,
    158–9
  defined, 90–1, 101

and learning history, 92–3
mutual qualification, 157–9
scope, 4–5, 90–1, 100–3, 157–9;
management of, 124–9,
Chapter 7 *passim*
consumer choice, behaviourally
defined, 121
consumer decision-making, 4–5
behaviourist interpretation,
103–8
as rule formation, 108–10
consumer-orientated management,
149–50
consumer research, *passim*
BPM, 55–7, 77–111
cognitive, 43–7
progress, 5–7, 10–12
social cognitive, 7–9
consumer situation
analysis, 79, 100–3
airport waiting, 146–9
defined, 100–3
frequent-flyer programme, 145
large-group awareness training,
138
managed restaurant experience,
142–3
consumption
contingent, 131
status, 95, 96, 128, 132
contingencies of reinforcement,
58–9
contingency category
airport waiting, 146
in accomplishment, 96–7
in accumulation, 97–8
defined, 94
frequent-flyer programme,
144–5
in hedonism, 97
large-group awareness training,
137–8
in maintenance, 98–9
managed restaurant experience,
141–2
contingency matrix, BPM, 93–9
contractual relationships, 164
Courneya, K. S., 32, 173
Cullen, C., 55, 174

Dabholkar, P. A., 29, 174
Danforth, J. S., 71, 173
Davies, M., 22, 174
Davey, G. C. L., 55, 174
Dawkins, R., 62, 63, 174
de Chernatony, L., 33, 182
decision making, *see* consumer
decision making
deliberative processing, 25–32,
40–3, 103–8, 109–10
see also attitudes
Delprato, D. J., 59, 174
Demsetz, H., 118, 153, 162,
164, 168, 174
Dennison, C. M., 31, 174
Desroches, J. J. Y., 31, 174
DeVellis, B. M., 32, 174
Dewey, J., 60, 174
Dewit, J. B. F., 31, 174
direct experience, 24–5
discriminative stimulus, 58
in behaviour setting,
90–1
and transactions, 158
Dnes, A. W., 153, 174
Doganis, R., 148, 174
Doll, J., 24, 32, 174
Donovan, R. J., 126, 148, 174
Doob, L. W., 20, 174
Dosi, G., 64, 174
Dossett, D. L., 30, 36, 178
Downing, J. W., 24, 175
Dugdale, N., 73, 175
Duxbury, N., 153, 175
Driver, B. E., 32, 175
dual consequences of consumer
behaviour, 81–9

Eagly, A. H., 19, 22, 24, 25, 29, 30,
32, 34, 35, 36, 40, 41, 42, 44,
46, 47, 93, 103, 178
Eagly–Chaiken attitude model, 42
and BPM, 93
Earl, P. E., 18, 81, 175
East, R., 28, 30–3, 36, 175
Easterbrook, F. H., 118, 175
Echabe, A. E., 36, 175
economic behaviour, operant,
119–24

economic transactions, 117,
Chapter 8 *passim*
and exchange, 116–17
Ehrenberg, A. S. C., 7, 29, 47, 98, 106,
130, 146, 175, 181
Eiser, R. J., 17, 44, 175
elaboration-likelihood model (ELM),
42–3, 103–10
Engel, J. F., 17, 175
Epling, W. F., 70, 175, 187
Ericsson, K. A., 26, 176
exchange, Chapter 8 *passim*
economic, 152–5; bilateral
contingency, 156–7; and setting
scope, 157–9
literal, 152–166
marketing, 159–61; bilateral
contingency, 156–7;
quasi-, 161–6
social, 151–2
theory, 154

Fallon, D., 55, 176
Fazio, R. H., 20, 21, 22, 23, 24,
40, 41, 103, 106, 176
Feyerabend, P., 3, 5, 6, 11, 115, 176
Finkelstein, P., 136, 137, 176
Fischel, D. R., 118, 175
Fishbein, M., 12, 21, 25, 26, 27, 29,
30, 31, 45, 48, 173, 176, 191
Fisher, J. D., 137, 138, 139, 177
Fiske, S. T., 17, 177
Folkes, V. S., 18, 177
Foxall, G. R., xii, 11, 13, 14, 17, 18,
20, 28, 33, 45, 46, 55, 56, 61,
73, 75, 76, 78, 79, 82, 84, 88,
94, 100, 113, 114, 115, 119,
120, 121, 122, 124, 125, 126,
129, 136, 137, 146, 152, 154,
162, 163, 164, 177, 178
Fredericks, A. J., 30, 36, 178
frequent-flyer programme, 143–5
Freud, S., 6
fulfilment, 95, 96–7, 128

Garcia, M. E., 73, 183
Gardner, M. P., 148, 178
Gilbert, D., 143, 178
Gilchrist, S., 148, 178

Giles, M., 30, 31, 178
Godin, G., 31, 32, 178
Golden, L. L., 126, 194
Goldsmith, R. E., 18,
125, 126, 178
Goldsmith, T. H., 64–7, 110, 178
Gould, J., 82, 179
Granberg, D., 30, 179
Greenwald, A. G., 17, 179
Griffin, J., 82, 179
Griffiths, R. R., 70, 193
Gronroos, C., 161, 179
Guerin, B., 55, 60, 74–6, 82,
90, 107, 166, 179

habit, 46–7
Hackenberg, T. D., 108, 179
Hackett, P., 126, 179
Hallett, R., 36
Hamblin, R. L., 70, 179
Harnad, S., 63, 172
Harrison, D. A., 32, 179
Hart, O., 118, 162, 164, 179
Haugtvedt, C. P., 24, 28, 179
Hawkins, S. A., 17, 179
Hayes, L. J., 55, 68, 70, 71, 72, 108,
179, 180
Hayes, S. C., 55, 68, 70, 71, 72, 84,
104, 108, 180
hedonism
defined, 88–90
marketing management, 131–2,
133
managed restaurant experience as,
140–3
Herrnstein, R. J., 69, 153, 180
heuristic-systematic model (HSM),
41–2, 103–10
Hillner, K. P., 10, 180
Hillix, W. A., 10, 183
Hineline, P., 57–8, 180
Hoch, S. J., 17, 179
Holland, J. G., 70
Holmberg, S., 30, 179
Homans, G. C., xi, 50, 154, 180
Horne, P. J., 69, 70, 71,
108, 153, 180, 182
Hornik, J., 148, 180
Howard, J. A., 6, 7, 17, 18, 180

Hunt, S. D., 161, 184
Hyten, C. M., 90, 105, 180, 181

industrial psychology, xi–xiii
inescapable entertainment, 95, 97
internal marketing, defined, 165
Iversen, I. H., 57–8, 181
Iwamoto, I., 70

Janiszewski, C., 17, 181
Jensen, M. C., 162, 164, 181
Jernigan, M. H., 148, 172
Joker, V. R., 108, 179

Kagel, J. H., 119, 120, 181
Kahnemann, D., 39, 192
Kardes, F. R., 7, 18, 23, 24, 79, 181
Kashima, Y., 31, 181
Kassarjian, H. H., 6, 9, 181
Katona, G., 81, 181
Keehn, J. D., 55, 181
Kelly, C., 31ʹ, 181
Keng, A. K., 29, 181
Kiesler, T., 18, 177
Kimble, G. A., 55, 110, 181
Kimiecik, J., 32, 181
Kimmel, S. K., 30, 35, 37, 38, 169
Klobas, J. E., 32, 182
Knox, S., 33, 182
Kolb, W. L., 82, 179
Kuhn, T. S., 5, 11, 182

Lalljee, M., 75, 182
Langer, E. J., 39, 104, 182
large-group awareness training
    (LGAT), 136–40
Laudan, L., 11, 182
Lea, S. E. G., 13, 18, 116, 182
learning history, 4–5
    and consumer behaviour
        setting, 92–3
    and consumer decision
        making, 103–10
    defined, 58
Lee, V. L., 7, 12, 51, 53, 55,
    80, 89, 102, 119, 182
Leibenstein, H., 157, 166, 182
Lejeune, H., 55, 171
Lewis, A., 18, 182

Likert, R., 20, 182
Liska, A. E., 29, 30, 32, 179, 182
Lowe, C. F., 55, 67, 69, 70, 71, 73,
    108, 153, 175, 180, 182

Macaulay, S., 160, 184
MacCorquodale, K., 68, 183
MacFadyen, A. J., 18, 183
MacFadyen, H., 18, 183
Mackenzie, B., 61, 73, 183
MacKenzie, S. B., 22, 183
Macneil, I. R., 160, 184
Madden, T., 31, 36, 38, 39, 183
maintenance
    airport waiting as, 145–9
    defined, 88–90
    marketing management, 131
Maio, G. R., 30, 183
Malott, R., 57, 71, 73, 132, 183
managed restaurant experience, 140–3
mandatory purchasing, 95, 98–9, 131
Mandler, G., 55, 183
Manstead, A. S. R., 30, 31,
    32, 39, 171, 183
marketing
    functions, 115–116
    quasi-, 161–6
    relationships, Chapter 8 *passim*;
        and bilateral contingency,
        156–7; defined, 161; quasi-,
        161–6; and social relationships,
        151–2; and transaction costs,
        152–3, 161–5
    social, 151–2, 154–5, 165,
    transactions, 117–119, 161; and
        setting closure, 126–9
    see also marketing management,
        marketing behaviour
marketing behaviour, cases, 136–50
marketing firm 115–35 *passim*
    bilateral contingency, 156–7
    consumers in, 117–9
    functions, 115–6, 151–6
    origins, 151–6
    setting scope of, 157–9
marketing management
    behaviouristic, 166–7
    of consumer setting scope, 124–9
    defined, 121–2, 149

marketing management (*contd.*)
  operant, 121–4
  of reinforcement, 129–35
  and social cognitivism, 18–19
marketing mix, operant
  analysis, 122–4, 129–35
marketing-orientated management,
  117, 154, 159
  defined, 165–6
Marsh, A., 30, 36, 183
Marx, M. H., 10, 183
Mason, R., 81, 184
matching, 67–71
Matheson, J., 30, 36, 183
Matthews, B. A., 70, 183
Mayer, C., 148, 183
Maynard Smith, J., 63
McCaul, K. D., 32, 184
McDowell, J. J., 70, 194
Meckling, W. H., 162, 164, 181
Medema, S. G., 161, 162, 184
Mehrabian, A., 126
Menger, C., 82, 184
methodological pluralism, 3
Mick, D. G., 28, 184
micro–micro analysis, 156, 166
Midgley, B. D., 58, 59, 174, 185
Mill, J. S., 1, 184
Miniard, P. W., 22, 184
Minkes, A. L., 162, 163
Mittal, B., 36, 184
MODE (motivation and opportunity
  as determinants), 40–1,
  103–10
Modgil C., 55, 184
Modgil S., 55, 184
Monroe, K. B., 33, 188
Moore, D., 30, 169
Moore, J., 59, 64, 72, 105, 184
Monteverde, K., 164, 184
Morgan, R. M., 161, 184
Morojele, N. K., 31, 33, 184
Morris, E. K., 55, 58, 59,
  60, 184, 185, 191
Morrison, D. M., 31, 185
Morwitz, V. G., 23, 185
Mostyn, B., 8, 185
mutuality relationships, 118, 154–5,
  and bilateral contingency, 156–7

and consumer behaviour setting
  scope, 157–9
  defined, 165
  in marketing relationships, 159–61
  quasi-marketing relationships,
    161–6
Myers-Levy, J., 24, 185

Nataraajan, R., 28, 185
natural selection, 62–7
Navarick, D. J., 70, 185
Netemeyer, R. G., 32, 185
Newman, A., 148, 185
Nicosia, F. M., 7, 17, 185
non-marketing relationships, 119,
  151ff
Norman, P., 32, 185

Olson, J. M., 19, 21, 29, 30, 183, 185
O'Leary J. E., 30, 191
Ono, K., 74, 186
operant classification of consumer
  behaviour
  accomplishment, 89, 90, 95, 96–7
  accumulation, 89, 90, 95, 97–8
  airport waiting, 146
  definition, 88–9
  frequent-flyer programme,
    143–4
  hedonism, 89, 90, 95, 97
  large-group awareness training, 137
  maintenance, 89, 90, 95, 98–9
  managed restaurant experience, 141
operant conditioning, and natural
  selection, 62–7
operant response, defined, 58
Oscar-Berman, M. G., 70, 186
Orsenigo, L., 64, 174
O'Shaughnessy, J., 11, 186
Osmond, H., 147, 186
Ostrom, T. M., 5, 17, 186
Overskied, G., 73, 186
Owen, N., 99, 186

Parfitt, D., 82, 179
Parker, D., 30, 31, 32, 183, 186
Parrott, L. J., 55, 68, 173, 186, 188
Parsons, H. M., xi, 11, 186
Pavlov, I., 12

Payne, A. F. T., 160, 165, 186
Percy, L., 28, 186
Perrien, J., 161, 186
Petty, R. E., 18, 19, 22, 24,
    28, 42, 103, 179, 186, 187
Phillips, D. C., 60, 187
Phillips. H., 126, 187
Pierce, W. D., 70, 187
Pieters, R., 20, 30, 187
Poppen, R. L., 72, 187
popular entertainment, 95, 97, 133
Posner, R. A., 153, 187
private events, 57, 61, 72–3
Proctor, P., 148, 187

Raats, M. N., 31, 32, 187
Rachlin, H., 55, 70, 187
radical behaviourism, 6–7, 49–51
    current status, 55–7
    dual causation, 64–7, 81–8
    interpretation, 59–61
    science, 57–9
    selection by consequences, 62–4
    theory, 59, 61–2
    verbal behaviour, 67–71
Rajecki, D. W., 23, 187
Ramsey, S. L., 29, 188
Randall, D. M., 25, 188
Rao, A. R., 33, 188
Reese, H. W., 55, 188
reinforcement
    bifurcation, 82–5
    contingency-derived, 85–8
    defined, 58–9
    informational, 4–5, 82–8, 157;
        control of by marketer, 121–4,
        129–35, Chapter 7 *passim*;
        defined, 82–3; and marketer
        behaviour, 157–9; and operant
        classification, 88–9
    and operant classification, 88–8
    and reward, 152
    rule-derived, 85–8
    quality, 134–5
    quantity, 134–5
    scheduled, 131–5
    utilitarian, 4–5, 82–8, 157; control
        of by marketer, 121–4, 129–35,
        Chapter 7 *passim*; defined,

82–3; and marketer; behaviour,
        157–9; and operant classification,
        88–9
reinforcer
    contingency-derived, 85–8
    delay, 133–4
    effectiveness, 129–31
    primary, 85–8
    rule-derived, 85–9
    secondary, 85–8
Reisberg, D., 17, 189
relationship marketing, 116,
    119, 159–166
    defined, 165
retail design 126
Rhinehart, L., 137, 188
Ribes, E., 48, 188
Ricard, L., 161, 186
Richard, L., 31, 188
Richardson, N. J., 30, 188
Richelle, M., 55, 64, 68, 188
Ronis, D. L., 47, 188
Rossiter, J. R., 28, 126, 148
routine purchasing 95, 98–9, 126
Ruddle, H., 70, 188
rule-governed behaviour, and setting
    scope, 91
rules
    and decision-making, 103–8
    functional typology, 71–2
    other-, 103–110
    self-, 103–110
    tracks, 71–2
Russell, J., 126, 148, 184

Sahni, A., 32, 189
sales promotions, 130–1, 132
Sarver, V. T., 45, 189
Sasser, W. E., 140–3, 189
Sato, M., 75, 189
saving and collecting, 95,
    97–8, 120, 125, 129,
    130–1, 133–4
Schlegel, R. P., 31, 189
Schmitt D. R., 70, 189
Schroeder, S. R., 70, 189
Schumann, D. W., 22, 189
Schwartz, B., 17, 189
Schwartz, S. H., 23, 189

Scitovsky, T., 81, 189
Scriven, J., 130, 175
Shaffer, D., 19, 191
Sharp, A., 130, 189
Sharp, B., 130, 189
Shavitt, S., 42, 92, 93, 189
Shepherd, R., 29, 30, 32, 189, 191
Sheppard, B. H., 28, 29, 31, 32, 189
Sheth, J. N., 6, 7, 17, 180
Sidman, M., 73, 189, 190
Sieben, W. A., 33, 188
Silberberg, A., 70
Simon, H. A., 26, 176
Skinner, B. F., xi, 12, 48, 50,
    55, 56, 59, 60, 61, 62, 63,
    68, 72, 73, 77, 78, 83, 101,
    107, 108, 125, 190
Smith, L., 32, 185
Smith, L. D., 58, 190
Smith, S. M., 24, 190
Snodgrass, J., 148, 190
social relationships, 151–2
social marketing, 151–2,
    154–5, 165
Sommers, R., 146–9
Sparks, P., 28, 30, 31, 32, 190
Speckart, G., 30, 36, 171
spontaneous processing, 104–10
Spreng, R. A., 22, 183
Sprott, D. E., 38, 183
Srull, T. K., 17, 20, 193
Staddon, J. E. R., 55, 191
Stasson, M., 30, 176
status consumption, 95, 96, 128, 132
Stephenson, G. E., 31, 33, 183
Stern, B., 126
Stayman, D. M., 19, 24, 29, 172, 191
stimulus equivalence, 73
Stoltz, S. B., 129, 139, 140, 169
Sugiyama, N., 75, 189
Sutton, S. A., 36, 191

Takahashi, M., 70, 191
Taylor R. B., 31, 124, 191
Teece, D., 164, 184
Terry, D. J., 30, 191
Tesser, A., 19, 24, 191
Teunis, G. J. P., 31, 174
theories of the firm, 115–19

theory of planned behaviour (TPB)
    critique, 32
    derivation, 30–31
    and prior behaviour, 33–4, 39–40
    research, 31–2, 37–9
theory of reasoned action (TRA)
    behaviourist interpretation, 73–6
    critique, 28–30
    derivation, 26–8
    and prior behaviour, 39–40
    research 28, 37–9
theory of trying
    derivation, 35–6
    and prior behaviour, 36, 39–40
    research, 35–6, 37–9
Thompson, K. E., 33, 191
Thompson, R. F., 55, 191
Timmermans, H., 126, 191
Todd, J. T., 31, 60, 191
token buying, 95, 98
token economy, 90, 129–30, 133
Towler, G., 29, 30, 189, 191
Trafimow, D., 27, 191
transaction costs, 152–3, 161–5
Triandis, H. C., 46, 191
Tripp, C., 25, 192
Tversky, A., 39, 192
Tybout, A. M., 9, 192

Uncles, M., 29, 47, 106, 175
Upmeyer, A., 21, 192

Valentine, E. R., 10, 192
Van Den Putte, B., 28, 192
van Der Pligt, J., 44, 175
van Knippenberg, D., 41, 192
Van Loo, M. F., 29, 169
Van Parjis, P., 64, 192
van Raaij, W. F., 13, 18,
    20, 116, 187, 192
van Ryn, M., 32, 192
Vaughan, M., 105, 192
verbal behaviour, 4–5
    attitudes and intentions as, 74–6
    instructed, 71–3
    of listener, 67–71
    and matching, 69–71
    and non-verbal behaviour, 73–6
    as prior behaviour, 48–9

private events, 72–3
  of speaker, 67–71
Verplanken, B., 30, 187
Viner, J., 82, 192
Vinokur, A. D., 32, 192

Wandersman, A., 30, 172
Ward, J. C., 126, 192
Warshaw, P. R., 21, 25, 30,
  35, 36, 37, 38, 39, 40,
  48, 192
Wass, K., 148, 170
Watson, J. B., 12
Watters, A. E., 32, 192
Wearden, J., 84, 193
Webster, F. E., 160, 193
Webster, R., 6, 51, 193
Wegener, D. T., 28, 179
White, K. M., 31, 193

Wicker, A., 9, 20, 21,
  25, 124, 127, 193
Wileman, A., 148, 193
Williamson, O. E., 117, 118,
  153, 161, 193
Winkler, R. C., 70, 193
Wittenbraker, J., 36, 193
Wolff, J. A., 26, 188
Wright, L. T., 22
Wurster, R. M., 70, 193
Wyer, R. S., 17, 20, 193

Yi, Y., 28, 31, 193

Zaltman, G., 5, 193
Zanna, M. P., 19, 20, 21,
  22, 24, 29, 185
Zettle, R. D., 71, 72, 104, 194
Zimmer, M. R., 126, 194
Zuriff, G. E., 58, 194